Finding Chuck

In Memory of Charles Kemsley
1932 - 2015

SYLVIA COURT

Copyright © 2017 Sylvia Court

All rights reserved.

ISBN-13: **978-1973988618**

INTRODUCTION

This is a book in three parts – a tale of love, loss, and reconciliation.

It is the story of a mother's deep and undying love for her newborn son and her ultimate sacrifice to give him the best start in life.

It is the story of a tragic family secret; the discovery of a long-lost brother and a desperate search to find him before it was too late.

It is the story of a remarkable man who lived life on the edge, seeking danger and defying death; a man with a chip on his shoulder and a volatile temper who was driven to travel the world, fearless, tough and invincible; a man who eventually discovered an amazing rapport with animals and became one of the world's leading authorities in canine and equine behaviour.

It is a story that needs to be told in order to appreciate the changing attitudes and values in our modern world.

Please note:
This book was written, produced and edited in the UK where spellings, punctuation and word usage can vary from US English. It also contains colloquialisms, regional dialect, and other typically British expressions.
Names haven't been changed and any offence caused to persons either living or dead is purely unintentional.

CONTENTS

		Acknowledgments	i
Part 1		Our Story	1
Part 2		Mum's Story	9
Part 3		Chuck's Story	27
	1	Foster Care: 1932 – 1938	28
	2	My First Memory: 1937	30
	3	Schooldays: 1938 - 1948	32
	4	Apprenticeship: 1948 - 1954	47
	5	At Sea: Mid 1950s	71
	6	Thrills and Spills: Late 1950s	93
	7	Love at First Sight: Early 1960s	115
	8	London & Brixham Mid 1960s	123
	9	Gloucestershire: Late 1960s	127
	10	Sussex: Early - Mid 1970s	143
	11	Berkshire: Mid - Late 1970s	152
	12	Kent: 1980 - 2001	165
		In Conclusion	182
		About the Author	187

ACKNOWLEDGMENTS

We are very grateful to the Foundling Museum and the social workers at Coram (a charity committed to improving the lives of the UK's most vulnerable children and young people) who were able to provide all the missing pieces that helped us to solve a mysterious and challenging puzzle. Thanks to their extensive records, we now know the truth about those traumatic events that unfolded over nine decades ago. Without their help and cooperation, this book would not have been possible.

PART 1

OUR STORY

I hung up the phone with trembling hands; my sister Marilyn's words echoing in my ears: "I've found him…"

The strange thing was that, until just a short time before, we hadn't even been looking.

It all began with a trip to Stratford on Avon. My husband, David, and I were visiting the birthplace of the great British poet and playwright, William Shakespeare. The guide had shown us the room where Shakespeare was born in 1564, and then told us about the subsequent history of the house. She explained that at the time of Shakespeare's death in 1616, it was occupied by Joan Hart, his recently widowed sister. It had remained in the Hart family for almost two hundred years, being run as an inn known as the Swan and Maidenhead. In 1806 it was sold to a butcher, Thomas Court who continued living there with his family until 1847, when it was sold at Auction and bought by the Shakespeare Trust, who restored it back to the house it is today.

David and I looked at each other. Perhaps Thomas Court was one of David's ancestors! That seemed most unlikely but it occurred to us that we knew absolutely nothing about our respective family's history and perhaps it was about time that we did a bit of investigating.

Fascinated by how we could use websites to unravel genealogical mysteries, it didn't take me long to verify that the Thomas Court in question *was* related – in fact, he was actually David's great-great-great grandfather! Even more exciting was the discovery that his son, William, (David's great-great grandfather) and possibly William's son, Leonard (David's great grandfather) were probably all born in that very same bedroom where William Shakespeare began his illustrious life!

Because of this Shakespearean connection, and the help we were given from the archives of The Shakespeare Birthplace Trust; we were able to trace my husband's ancestry right back to the birth of William Court of Armscott in 1450, eighteen generations and almost six hundred years ago.

This was all very exciting and very addictive, so when we could go back no further with my husband's ancestors, I turned my attention to my side of the family.

My Dad was adopted, which I knew would cause complications, so I decided to start with Mum's history. Her maiden name was Mundon, which was quite unusual, so I didn't foresee any problems. How wrong I was! I soon realized that because the family was in service, most of the census forms would have been filled in by their employers. They invariably used an incorrect but more common version of the name (Munden), making records very difficult to trace.

I did, however, come across a birth entry dated 1932, which had the correct spelling of the name. David John Mundon was born on 19th August 1932. This was intriguing and worthy of further investigation as it didn't match up with any of the families I already knew about.

"It's strange," I said, ringing up Marilyn. "All I can locate is his date of birth. There's nothing about his parents.

I wondered if he might be a distant relative – and if so, whether he was still alive.

"I know how to find out," Marilyn replied. "I'll send off for a copy of his birth certificate.

A couple of weeks later, she phoned, sounding very excited.

"A copy of David John Mundon's birth certificate has just dropped through my letter box. And you'll never believe it – his mother must have been our Mum, Joyce Mundon!"

I was stunned. How could that be? Marilyn went on to say that the baby boy was born in Twyford Lodge, Acton which, when she looked it up, was a euphemism for the maternity section of the Willesden Workhouse although it was then known as Park Royal Hospital. There were no father's details listed on the certificate.

Not only was this a complete shock but it also presented us with quite a dilemma. We had unintentionally discovered a tragic secret that Mum had kept throughout her life and taken to the grave when she died, aged 89 in June 2000. Back in those days, in the 1930s, such a situation would have caused lasting shame and reproach, not just on the unmarried mother but on her entire family. It was no wonder that it would be hidden under the carpet and never openly discussed.

It was Marilyn who pointed out the obvious when she said: "We have a big brother!" But now it was no longer a secret, what should we do about it? Marilyn and Christine, my younger sister, were keen to find him, but I was wary. Would Mum have wanted us to investigate further? Even more importantly, would she have wanted her secret being revealed to others?

"We could be opening a can of worms," I warned. If he was still alive he would be in his 80s. Would he really want to see us? What sort of life had he experienced? Did he know about us and would he want us to find him? I wasn't sure about meeting a stranger - brother or not.

Marilyn, however, was determined to find out what she could. She trawled through phone books and searched all the available records, and at last, she thought she had struck gold.

She managed to come across just one person with the right name, and she couldn't wait to contact him. Her hopes soared when she learnt that this David Mundon had been adopted at birth, but then dropped again when she discovered he was the wrong age and therefore the wrong man.

There were no other traces of David Mundon anywhere; no records of him marrying, having children or passing away. It was as if he had never existed.

Maybe he had changed his name. If so, we had little chance of ever finding him. We were on the point of giving up when Christine had an idea. Mum had lived with her in Ramsgate before she died and there was a remote possibility that she might have kept something that would give us a clue.

"There's a little leather case in the attic where she kept important documents. If there *is* anything it probably would be in there."

We found the case, and without much expectation, opened it and sifted through the pile of papers. We had hoped that we might find David's original birth certificate or possibly even adoption documents – but there was nothing like that. There were plenty of out-of-date guarantee forms, instruction manuals for long gone appliances, insurance documents, envelopes containing various old letters and greeting cards and even some of our childhood school reports and drawings.

We did, however, find an envelope containing three and a half old photographs – the half was an extra bit, cut off from another photo.

One photo was of a small baby in a pram, another was of Marilyn and me, together with an older boy, taken when we were quite small, and the third, more recent photo, was a young couple with a dog.

I recognized the picture of us in the garden. It was similar to one in our family photo album – but there was an ominous difference. The photo in the album had been cut in half and it was just of Marilyn and me. I often wondered what had become of the cut-off portion – but now I knew. It was in the envelope together with a copy of the complete photograph. This was significant. Why had the boy been removed from the album? Could he be David - Mum's secret son?

I vaguely remembered that photo being taken when I was about seven, shortly after we moved to our new house at St. Paul's Cray in 1950. Mum had prepared a special tea for a visitor who I think had been introduced as one of Dad's friends. Interestingly, I don't think Dad was actually around at the time. I couldn't remember his name but I seemed to recall that the young man was nice and we talked about horses. Horses and ponies were a passion of mine when I was young and some of my toy horses are in the picture.

Marilyn and Christine remembered the later photograph, which was taken about 1966, soon after I was married. My husband and I were living in Kent at the time, but Mum and my two sisters had gone off on a nostalgic visit to Gloucestershire. They wanted to see the little house in Driffield where Mum and I had been evacuated during the war and also the quaint Cotswold stone cottage in Daglingworth, where Mum had spent some idyllic childhood holidays with her grandmother. For some reason, they had also called in to visit that couple in the photo, who lived in a caravan on Leckhampton Hill, near Cheltenham.

"The man's name definitely wasn't David," Marilyn said. "It was an unusual name – something like 'Chick' or 'Chuck', and I think his wife was called Yvonne.

Although I didn't go on that visit, I had a good reason to remember it. I had asked Mum to bring back a local newspaper so we could check out if house prices were cheaper in Gloucestershire than in Kent, and since they were, we managed to buy a little house in Stroud.

None of us recognized the third picture, a photo of a baby with blond hair in an old fashioned pram.

The three pictures were obviously important to Mum - and since she had kept them together, it seemed likely that they were linked in some way. Was this the all-important clue for which we had been searching? Assuming that all three photographs were of the same person, could this be our long lost brother?

If that *was* the case, we had two pieces of the jigsaw. His name could have been changed to 'Chuck' and he could have a wife named Yvonne.

It seemed that all our searches for 'David Mundon' had been in vain and now, with no idea of a potential surname we had come to the end of the road.

"I've just had a thought," Marilyn said. "Maybe the main reason we went to Gloucestershire that year was actually to visit *them* rather than looking for Granny's cottage. If that was the case Mum obviously knew where they lived and surely she would have known their name!"

"Mum's old address book!" Chris and I both exclaimed in unison.

We found the little red note book in the bureau, but try as we might, we couldn't find a single address in Cheltenham. However, there was one entry with the initials 'C & Y'. The surname was 'Kemsley', but the address was a boarding kennels, somewhere in Sussex.

Our hearts sank; we seemed to have drawn another blank.

"They could have moved," Chris said, trying to sound positive. "There were dogs around when we saw them; dogs would be in the kennels, so maybe dogs are the missing link!"

We tried the phone number for the kennels but, as expected, the Kemsleys had long gone - but if 'C & Y' did stand for Chuck and Yvonne, at least we had a possible surname to go on.

With nothing to lose, Marilyn typed 'Kemsley' and 'dogs' into a search engine and couldn't believe her eyes when up popped several references to Charles Kemsley, leading dog trainer and animal behaviour expert – complete with a phone number and address. Surely, after all the setbacks we had experienced, it couldn't be that easy!

"I'm sorry to be pessimistic," I said, "But Charles Kemsley could be a common name. How do we know we've got the right one?"

"Because," Marilyn observed thoughtfully, "People can change their name but they can't change the date on which they were born!"

Later, when Marilyn got home, she plucked up the courage to dial the number. The phone rang for what seemed like ages and she waited with both trepidation and anticipation. She almost put the phone down - but then a man answered.

"Charles Kemsley?" she asked. "This may seem strange but I think we may be related. Would you mind telling me your date of birth?"

The man who answered was indeed Charles Kemsley and he then confirmed that he was born on 19th August 1932.

"But not only that," Marilyn continued excitedly. "He actually wants to meet us!"

When Marilyn asked if he remembered meeting us all those years ago, he said he did, but he'd kept quiet about who he was, as Mum didn't want us to know.

Now aged 81, Chuck was bedbound by a neurological condition called Charcot-Marie-Tooth Disease (CMT) – the same condition from which our mother suffered during the final years of her life.

He was keen for a reunion, so with a barrage of questions to be answered, we set off for his home near Rochester in Kent.

~~~

We arrived at the address at Marina Park in Hoo, beside the River Medway, and were greeted by a neighbor who was looking at us rather dubiously.

"Chuck is expecting you. The door is open, just walk in," he said. "But I must warn you that I'm Bob – and I am Chuck's next of kin." It seemed a strange thing to say and we wondered what he meant, but later it dawned on us that we must have seemed rather suspicious – three total strangers turning up on an old man's doorstep, claiming to be his long lost sisters. No wonder he doubted our motives!

We walked in and saw a frail elderly man sitting up in bed, bright as a button and with a cheeky grin.

"Call me Chuck – everyone does!"

He seemed quite pleased to see us and was more than happy to talk about himself and his experiences.

He had certainly lived a very colourful and eventful life. He'd been a merchant sailor, a smuggler, a gun runner, a biker and even a stuntman before settling down with his wife, Yvonne, as a dog breeder and trainer.

There was so much we wanted to ask him but didn't want to tire him out.

"I could write a book about all my adventures," he declared, with a glint in his eye.

"Why don't you?" I suggested, "It sounds really interesting and we could learn all about your life."

"I might just do that," he laughed, "And if I do, I promise I will email you every chapter as I write it!" – And he really was true to his word!

I desperately wanted to ask him why his name had been changed. I eventually plucked up the courage to broach the subject but he seemed reluctant to talk about it. His demeanor changed and he suddenly looked very tired.

"I don't remember anything about it. I was told I had been abandoned on a doorstep in London when I was two months old. Apparently, nobody knew my name - so they decided to call me Charles Kemsley!"

I was horrified; I just couldn't believe what I was hearing. "Who told you that?" I gasped.

"I've been told a lot of horrible things about my past from some very cruel and vindictive people, but that came from somebody I could trust. In fact, they actually told me the address where I was found - and it's something I've never forgotten."

"So where was it?"

"Apparently, I was found on the doorstep of 40, Brunswick Square in London," he said softly.

This information and the sense of betrayal and rejection that it caused had obviously affected him deeply. He told us that it had left him feeling bitter and traumatised and he grew up with a chip on his shoulder and a volatile temper. When he was younger he had a death wish and lived from one dangerous experience to another, oblivious of the consequences.

We felt devastated. What he had told us just didn't make any sense and I couldn't believe that Mum, however desperate her circumstances, would ever abandon a baby on a doorstep. I needed to know the truth.

~~~

The first thing I did when I got home, was to get onto the Internet and look up '40, Brunswick Square'. To my surprise, I discovered that it is now the address of the Foundling Museum, formally the Foundling Hospital, in London. This was established in 1739 by a very kind philanthropist, Thomas Coram, to care for babies at risk of abandonment. Apparently, there was a time in the mid-eighteenth century when a basket was actually hung at the gates to enable babies to be left anonymously. But that was way back then; surely it didn't happen in our day and age.

The Foundling Hospital, which continues today as the children's charity Coram, has a comprehensive website, so I emailed them for more information. I explained that Chuck had told us that he had been abandoned on their doorstep and asked if that could actually be true.

Amazingly the Foundling Hospital, right from its inauguration, had kept meticulous records of every child who passed through the institution, so with their help and with Chuck's permission we were able to discover the remarkable truth about what really happened back then in 1932.

I was able to make contact with Val, a very helpful senior social worker within the organization. Even though it was so long ago, she was able to look up complete details of everything that had happened; the circumstances of his birth, the name of his father and even statements from my mother's family, friends, and employers.

As opposed to all the lies Chuck had been told, we found out that my mother had done her very best to try to keep him.

Finally all the pieces of the jigsaw had fallen into place and at last, we had the complete picture. For the first time in eighty years, Chuck would know the truth.

PART 2

MUM'S STORY

Our Mum, Joyce Mundon, was born on the 14th January 1911 at West End Cottage in Totteridge. Her parents, Annie and Edward, were in service at Barnes Park, the home of Sir William Barclay Peat and his wife Edith; Edward was the butler and Annie the cook. (They had met while working at Cragside, the wonderful home of Lord and Lady Armstrong in Northumberland,)

As well as their country estate in Totteridge, Lord and Lady Peat also kept a London residence in Eaton Square. In 1914, when Joyce was 3, the Mundon family moved to Chelsea, where they were to stay for the next 17 years.

Joyce & Dot in Gertrude Street.

They lived on the first floor of 26, Gertrude Street. Three families lived in this beautiful old house with its impressive entrance and leafy garden; all sharing the same toilet and tap. Mum had vivid recollections of the house.

The Stringers lived in the basement. They were a strange family who kept chickens and had a dog called Nigger. They always had a number of lodgers who seemed to be drunk most of the time.

Mrs. Long and her son 'Bubbles' lived on the ground floor. She had the best of everything; her front room was very modern for its day with an Indian carpet and 'Gay Nineties' pictures. She had a wooden bed (not the common cast iron type), a wash stand and the very best china in the kitchen.

Annie and Edward had four daughters. Gladys, who was always known as 'Ciss', was seven years older than Mum. Dorothy ('Dot') was four years older and Edna ('Eddie') was two years younger. They lived on the first floor in very cramped conditions, and the four girls had to share two single beds. There were two big windows in the front room and a cooking range sat in the marble fireplace. Rows of white canvas shoes were always lined up on the sunny kitchen windowsill. A grapevine thrived outside the window, and in the garden, beyond a flower covered archway, were two large sycamore trees. The toilet, which was shared by everyone, contained the only tap in the house and had a stained glass window depicting a knight in armour wielding a sword.

Mum and her sisters attended Park Walk School near the Kings Road, which is still in existence today. Joyce did well and won a number of prizes for good work. On Saturdays, if the weather was fine, the children would walk across the river to the nearby Battersea Park. On more inclement days they would visit the museums in South Kensington

In the summer, a special treat for the girls was their regular trip to the Cotswolds, to stay with Granny Simpson in Daglingworth. They travelled down from London by steam train and their Uncle Jim would be waiting on the platform at Swindon, where he worked, with refreshments for the journey.

Mum & Dot visiting Granny's Cottage in Daglingworth in 1919

In 1921, when Joyce was 10, Edward was working as a butler and chauffeur to Sir Robert Burnett in Eaton Square. He drove a state-of-the-art Minerva Limousine. His brother, Charles, was working as a London cabbie, and

Edward had spent long winter evenings studying 'the Knowledge'. He also was about to embark on a new career as a taxi driver.

One day, when attempting to start the engine of the limousine, the starting handle kicked back as it often did, and grazed his hand. Unfortunately, this small scratch became infected and, without the antibiotics we have today, he soon became fatally ill with septicemia (blood poisoning) and died just a few days later. Edward was young and healthy and had never had a day's illness in his life, so his tragic death came as a terrible shock. Mum was heartbroken as she was a real 'Daddy's girl'. Her mother was distraught and the whole family was devastated. As well as the emotional distress, there were also the financial implications caused by the death of the main bread winner. Her bereavement left Annie so traumatised that Joyce was sent away to live with her rich Aunt Alice in the North of England.

Alice was actually Mum's cousin, who was brought up in a humble farmworker's cottage in the Cotswolds. As a young girl she went into service, and at the age of 21, she worked as a barmaid in London. Alice, however, had greater aspirations, and just seven years later she had changed her name to Alys Maude and married into the aristocracy. Her husband was Francis Gage and they lived in a large country house at Rowlands Gill near Newcastle. (Apparently, the origin of the name of the 'greengage' fruit was from one of his ancestors, Sir William Gage who, in 1724, first imported it to England.).

Although the area around Rowlands Gill in the Derwent Valley was beautiful and the house was grand, Mum was not happy. Aunt Alice, despite her lowly origins, was a snob and very mean. She was embarrassed by Mum's shabby coat and decided she must have a smart new wardrobe. Despite her wealth, Alice insisted that Mum draw out every penny of her own meagre life savings to buy some new clothes.

After six months, Mum could stand it no longer and returned to London in January 1922. Her mother, however, was still experiencing a very difficult time. Not only did she have to support the family, but she also had to cope single-handedly with four young and attractive daughters.

Annie and Edward had instilled strict moral values into their daughters, insisting that were always chaperoned and returned home at a reasonable time in the evening. Dot, Mum, and Eddie were sensible and studious girls who were happy to respect her wishes, whereas Ciss was a bit of a wild child. She was popular and very good looking and determined to become part of the exclusive London social scene, which included such well known and controversial characters as the Mitford girls.

When she left school, Ciss wanted to be a florist. She soon discovered that sphagnum moss, which they used for making wreaths, often contained maggots - which she couldn't abide, so that idea was rather short lived. She was then taken on as an apprentice milliner at Maud Moore's, an exclusive and very expensive hat shop in Kensington, opposite Harrods.

Her hectic social life was a constant source of anxiety to her mother who used to stay up into the early hours, lying in wait with a broom to teach her a lesson when she eventually returned!

Mum's sister, Dot, worked as a nursemaid to Helena Lambton, daughter of Arthur Lambton, a cousin of the Earl of Durham. Apparently, he was quite a colourful character and a friend of Arthur Conan Doyle, creator of Sherlock Holmes.

Mum left school at 14 and her first job was as a mother's help in a large house in Redcliffe Gardens, Chelsea. Eventually, she managed to get a job with Ciss at Maud Moore's in Knightsbridge, but this entailed working long hours in an underground room for seven shillings and sixpence a week (37p). She was a hard worker and rose steadily in the business, first becoming an improver (matching up ribbons and dying felt) and then a copyist. She moved to their branch in New Bond Street and then, in September 1927, aged 16½, began working for Madame Adele in Curzon Street Mayfair as an assistant milliner.

Ciss had many men friends but, despite her hopes of joining the aristocracy like Aunt Alice, eventually married Billy Christy in 1929. Dot, Mum, and Eddie were bridesmaids. Bill was a sergeant in the Territorial Army and later worked as a bus driver for London Transport. They lived at 42, Longston Avenue, Harlesden.

Ciss & Bill's Wedding in 1929. Mum is a bridesmaid at the back.

Dot married Alfred Whiffen in 1931. He worked for London transport as a bus conductor, and often Alf and Bill would work together on the same bus. In the early 1930s, Britain had recovered impressively from a double-dip recession and there was a boom in housebuilding. Annie, Alf, and Dot decided to pool their resources and buy one of the new houses that were being built in Cheam, Surrey. They purchased 73, Priory Crescent, a nice three bedroomed terraced house for £750. The house was to be converted into two flats with Dot and Alf having the first floor and Annie, Mum, and Eddie living in the downstairs flat.

The move from their flat in Chelsea to the house in Cheam and its subsequent conversion caused quite a bit of disruption for the family. Mum needed to get to work in Mayfair, so Ciss suggested that she could stay with her for a while until things settled down. With hindsight that wasn't a good idea. Ciss still liked to go out on the town and have a good time, so wasn't the best influence for Mum, who was a respectable but impressionable 20 year old.

Joyce in 1931

"Now you can really start living!" Ciss declared. "No more restrictions – get out there and enjoy yourself!"

Mum was quiet and shy and, shielded by her protective mother, had led a comparatively sheltered life. Apart from Bubbles, who had been her best (totally platonic) friend from childhood and had now left home to pursue his career as an actor, she had never had a serious boyfriend. Ciss was determined to change that! There was a music hall, several cinemas and a number of pubs, some more sleazy than others. Ciss lost no time in introducing her to all her favourite haunts in and around Harlesden where she lived.

On one occasion, after spending the evening at the Picardy cinema watching the newly released film 'City Lights' with Charlie Chaplin, they popped into the Elm Tree pub next door.

"Don't look now, but I think that man over there fancies you!" Ciss said, with a twinkle in her eye. Mum couldn't help herself. She glanced sideways and caught the eye of a man standing at the bar. "No, it's you he's looking at," Mum laughed. "Everybody fancies you!"

The man came over. "Can I buy you lovely ladies another drink?" Mum was about to protest, but before she could say anything, Ciss replied, "Thank you so much. We'd love another drink."

The man returned with the drinks and Ciss indicated that he could join them at the table.

"I'm William Worrall," he introduced himself. "But just call me Bill. I live in Richmond and I'm a banker in the city." He was in his late twenties and quite good looking in a suave kind of a way.

"Will you be going to the dance at the Hippodrome on Saturday?" he asked. Ciss confirmed that they would be there but told him that she would be accompanied by her husband Billy.

"In that case," he said, taking Mum's hand, "Will you, dear lady, reserve the first dance for me?" Mum giggled. She had never met such a charming man and she could think of nothing else until Saturday.

They did indeed dance the first dance and spent the rest of the evening together. Mum was besotted. Never before had she known anybody who was so charismatic, sophisticated and self-assured.

Over the next few weeks, they went out together almost every other evening. Bill loved to watch horror films although Mum preferred a good romantic comedy. That year, there were many scary movies, but as long as she had Bill to protect her, she was just happy to be with him. Within a month they had seen both 'Dracula' starring Bela Lugosi, and 'Frankenstein' with Boris Karloff.

One evening, he turned up with a large bunch of flowers. "We're going to do something special tonight. We've got something to celebrate – but it's a surprise." Mum was excited and apprehensive, wondering if he was about to propose.

They took a trolleybus in the direction of Putney and eventually arrived at a small flat in a shabby looking house.

"Where are we?" Mum asked, suddenly feeling uneasy.

"This is my place," he said proudly, "And tonight we are going to celebrate!"

"Celebrate what?"

"That I have found the woman of my dreams – my true love!" he declared, gathering her into his arms in a warm embrace.

Mum stepped back. "I thought you said you lived in Richmond," she mumbled.

"I *almost* do," he laughed. "This is Upper Richmond Road – you can't get much closer than that and, before you ask, I'm not quite a banker either – just one letter out. I'm actually a baker and I work in Nottinghill."

Mum was stunned. "I expect you're married too?"

"Too much talking. Let's celebrate!" he said uncorking a large bottle of cheap bubbly.

Mum woke up the next morning with a really bad headache. She couldn't remember anything about the previous night.

She didn't see Bill again until the following Saturday. "How about going to my place again tonight?" he suggested with a grin.

"But you said you wanted to watch 'Dr. Jekyll and Mr. Hyde' at the Odeon," she reminded him.

They did go to the cinema that night but Bill was subdued and they hardly spoke. The following week he didn't turn up at all. Mum was distraught. What had she done to upset him? She constantly tried to contact him but to no avail. It was as if he had disappeared from the face of the earth.

A few weeks later, the family got together to celebrate Christmas. Mum wasn't feeling very well. She was frequently sick and felt weak and faint. Everyone commented on how pale she looked and they all put it down to a broken heart. Ciss suspected otherwise. "You don't think …?" Mum burst into tears. "I'm not sure, but it's possible – I don't know what to do," she said in despair.

"You stupid, stupid girl!" Ciss exploded. "How on earth did you let that happen?"

"It must have been that night when he took me to his house. We drank a lot of bubbly and he might even have put something in it. I don't remember what happened after that."

"Have you told him yet?" Ciss asked.

"I haven't even seen him," Mum replied weakly.

"Well, I suppose there's always the chance he'll do the right thing and marry you. After all, you did fancy him!"

"Not anymore. How could I marry someone who lives a lie? He told me he was a banker who lives in Richmond and it turns out he's a baker who lives in a sleazy flat in Putney. I expect he would deny all knowledge of even knowing me."

"I know his type," Ciss said. "Once they get what they want they dump you." He's probably chatting up some other poor girl right now and she'll end up in the same boat as you."

"But what do I do now," Mum sobbed. "You can't tell anyone. It would kill Mother if she found out!"

"Well the first thing you can do is drink half a bottle of gin and then have a scalding hot bath and hope it will go away. If that doesn't work I may be able to find someone who can help."

Mum might have been desperate, but she knew that wasn't the answer. "Will I be able to keep on living with you?" she pleaded. "I can't go back home now."

"I'll have to tell Billie and we'll see what we can arrange," Ciss said, but she knew that her husband, once he knew the situation, would not agree. It just wasn't acceptable for a young woman to have a child outside marriage, and attitudes to those that did so were frequently harsh and judgmental.

The solution lay with Billie Christy's older sister, Lillian, who was 44 and had married Albert Reade ten years earlier. She lived at 17, Denbigh Road Willesden and, despite the stigma, offered Mum a home for the rest of her pregnancy. She secretly blamed Ciss for Mum's predicament and felt sorry for Mum, knowing that she had been a naïve and virtuous young woman who had been taken advantage of by a despicable and devious predator. She was very fond of Mum and wanted to do everything she could to support her during that difficult time. She was angry with William Worrall for the way he had treated her and insisted that they go together to confront him and seek his help. As expected, however, he denied any misconduct.

Apart from Ciss and Lillian and their husbands, no one else knew about the pregnancy, and Mum wanted to keep it that way. She continued working until mid-April but then left her employment with Madame Adele before her condition became known to her employer and colleagues.

One day, while reading the News of the World newspaper, Lillian saw an article about the Foundling Hospital in London. It sounded wonderful; a benevolent, wealthy charity that would take the baby and give it a great start in life with a good education in a brand new, purpose built school that had recently been constructed in the countryside.

At the time, Mum had no idea what would happen in the future. She did know that with no home of her own, no prospect of marriage and no income other than what she herself could earn, she would have no choice but to make the hard decision to part with the baby. There were no welfare provisions, and the condemnation she would face from society in general and even her close family would make raising a child outside marriage almost impossible.

Lillian wrote to the Secretary of the Foundling Hospital on the 6th June to ask for advice on Mum's behalf. In response, they sent her details of the Rules of Admission and an application form with the information that no application could even be considered prior to the birth of the child. It was made clear that it wouldn't be an easy process and *if* the governors did agree to consider the application they would need to make many enquiries which would involve interviewing Mum's family, friends and even her former employer. They would only accept babies from girls with high moral standards who had been unlucky or had been taken advantage of in some way.

Mum's heart sank. She had hoped to keep the pregnancy a secret, at least for the time being. If her application was to be considered, she realised that everyone would eventually find out - and she was painfully aware of how the shock would affect her mother. Lillian was supportive and reassuring. "Let's leave things as they are at the moment. When the time comes I'll be with you. It wasn't your fault. It'll be a shock to them at first but when they know the circumstances, I'm sure everything will be fine!"

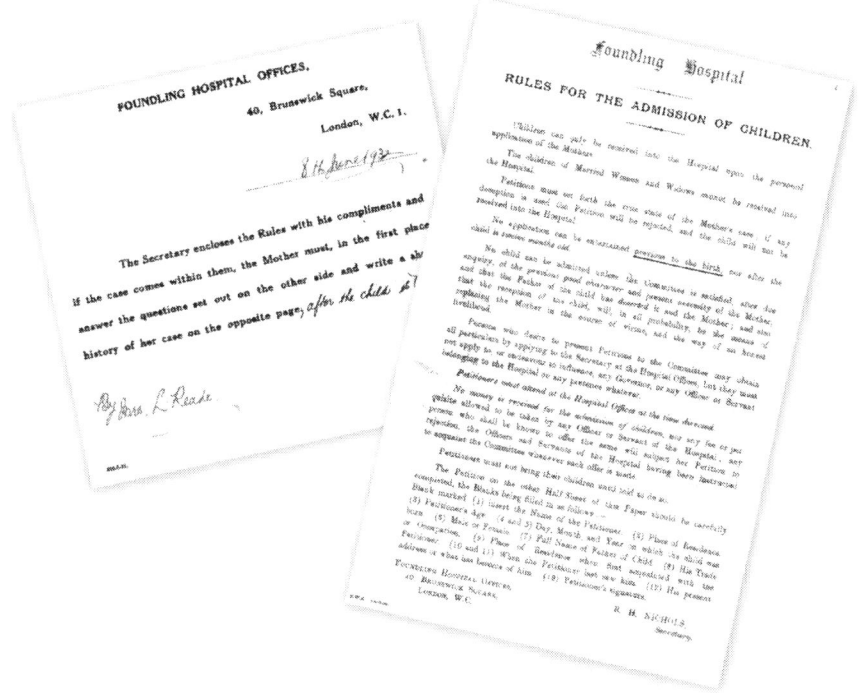

Mum's pregnancy progressed normally, although the weeks after she left work seemed interminable. She worried about the birth as she had no idea what to expect. Lillian, although reassuring, couldn't really offer advice as she hadn't any personal experience. The worst thing, however, was the constant anxiety about what would happen in the future if the Foundling Hospital decided against taking the baby into their care.

Finally, on Friday the 19th of August she was admitted to Park Royal Hospital, Willesden. It was the hottest day of the year with temperatures exceeding 33C. She had a natural, uncomplicated birth and the baby was a beautiful and healthy little boy. Mum had already decided that, if it was a boy, she would name him David John.

Lillian was her first visitor. After congratulating Mum on the birth and admiring the little bundle in her arms, she lost no time in revealing the true reason for her visit.

"I've bought you some notepaper, envelopes and a pen. You know what you've got to do. Now the baby is born you must complete that application form as soon as possible."

Mum looked lovingly at the tiny baby. "He's so precious and helpless. He needs me. I don't think I can go through with it. How could I bear to part with him?"

Lillian looked her straight in the eye and spoke firmly the words she knew she would have to say: "Joyce, please don't get too attached. You know that there's no way you can keep him. If you love him you must think about him and his future." She then added softly, "You *do* want what's best for him, don't you?"

Mum did want what was best for David and she knew in her heart that it was best for her too. She would be able to put the past year with all its mistakes behind her and have a completely fresh start. She hoped that when they found out, her family would forgive her and that she would be allowed to go back and live in the safe environment of her own home.

Now she had to focus on David's future; a good education in a fantastic new school, a healthy upbringing in the countryside, a satisfying and lucrative career and eventually, a loving family of his own. She knew that on her own she couldn't give him the wonderful opportunities afforded by the Foundling Hospital, so reluctantly she forced herself to fill in the application form which was very comprehensive. She had to explain how she had found herself in such a hopeless situation, how she had met the father and how long they had been going out together. In fact, they wanted to know about everything that had happened during the relationship and what her plans were for the future.

She was aware that the vetting process was rigorous, so her initial covering letter needed to make a good impression. When one finally met her approval, she asked Lillian to check it over and then post it, together with the application form – before she changed her mind.

~~~

It was the usual practice for the Governors of the Foundling Hospital to make careful enquiries into each application they received, in order to be sure that admitting a baby into their care would be the best way to help both mother and child. In particular, the Governors were anxious that fathers should be encouraged to accept their responsibilities because that might prevent the need for a baby to come into care.

In Mum's case, the father's whereabouts were known, so she was advised to consult a solicitor and take out a summons for an affiliation order. The Governors indicated that they would pay the legal costs of doing this. (An affiliation order was a court order for a father who was not married to the mother of his child to pay an amount of money towards the support of that child.)

Mum was feeling optimistic. If that was successful she wouldn't have to part with David, who had now become such an important part of her life. She took legal advice, and a summons was issued for William Worrall to appear at Willesden Police Court on 6th October 1932. After a long hearing in which he continued to deny responsibility, Mum's application for an affiliation order was dismissed on the grounds of insufficient corroborative evidence. She was devastated; without modern DNA testing, there was nothing more she could do.

Shortly after this, on the 10th October, Mum was interviewed at the Foundling Hospital Office and completed a more detailed application. This asked for details of the alleged father, his age, occupation, anyone who had seen the couple together, and his whereabouts. The mother also had to provide details of her previous employment, and supply the name of someone who could support the application.

Her hands shook and her heart sank; once this form had been submitted, her secret would no longer be safe and she would have a lot of explaining to do. She knew the time had finally come to reveal her situation to her mother and sisters and introduce them to little David – but she dreaded their reaction. She knew that they would be shocked and disappointed, but even worse was the possibility that she would be rejected and disowned by the family.

An officer from the Hospital then followed up the references. He first contacted the solicitor who had acted for her in Court and then interviewed Mum's sister, Ciss, (Mrs Gladys Christy of 42, Longstone Avenue, Harlesden.) She was able to give a full account of how Mum first met William Worrall when they were out together, and how he came over and introduced himself to them. She then confirmed that she had seen them together on a number of occasions. She described Mum as being a truthful and well-conducted person and she had no doubts that William Worrall was the baby's father.

The enquiry officer also interviewed Lillian Reade, who had originally written on Mum's behalf. She described herself as a relative by marriage. She said she had known Mum for about seven years and felt very sorry for her, which was why she had offered her a place to live while pregnant. She said she had accompanied Mum on one occasion when she went to speak to William Worrall to seek his help, but that he had denied misconduct. Mrs Reade hoped that the Governors would help Mum.

By this time, Mum's family knew the situation. They were obviously devastated by the news, but once they had got over the initial shock, they were prepared to help in any way they could. They couldn't understand why Mum hadn't had the courage to tell them earlier. They weren't in any position to financially support the baby but they agreed that she could move back home until David's future was decided.

They were now living at the newly built terrace house in Priory Crescent, which had been converted into two flats. Dot and her husband, Alf, lived upstairs and Mum's mother and her younger sister, Eddie lived below.

Mum's sister, Dot, was very kind and sympathetic but her mother, still traumatised by the news, made it clear that she wanted to distance herself from the baby and temporarily moved out to stay at the home of her niece in nearby Buxton Crescent.

The enquiry officer visited Mum at the address in Priory Crescent and also spoke to Dot who told him that she wanted to do everything to help as she knew Mum was a steady and honest person, worthy of help.

He also spoke to Mum's mother at her niece's house in Buxton Crescent. She told him that she had been a widow for eleven years and that, before his death, her husband had been the butler to Sir Robert Burnett. She explained she lived on a small widow's pension and could not afford to support Mum and a baby, but she spoke well of Mum and said her pregnancy had come as a great shock.

Finally, the enquiry officer spoke to Mum's former employer, Madame Adele, at 16 Curzon Street, Mayfair, who had by now come to hear of Mum's situation. Madame Adele said that she had employed Mum from September 1927 to April 1932 and that she had proved to be an excellent worker who had a good reputation with those that knew her. She said she felt very sorry for Mum and hoped to reinstate her as soon as arrangements were made for the baby's care.

The purpose of the interviews was to get additional confirmation of the mother's circumstances, and also to get personal references to show that the girls were deserving of help. The report of all the interviews was submitted to the Governors on the 25th October.

Mum would have to attend the meeting with the Governors on that day and her own account would be typed out for to sign. This must have been a very daunting experience for her and she had hoped that Dot would accompany her.

"This is something you've got to do on your own," Dot stated firmly. "I'll stay here and look after the baby. Just keep remembering that you want the very best for David – and that is something that only they can give him." She was aware that Mum had grown very attached to the child and was desperate to find some way she could keep him. She had been feeding and caring for the baby for two months now, and the thought of having to part with him was unbearable.

Dressed in her best clothes and feeling nervous, Mum arrived at the imposing looking building in Bloomsbury. She had come in good time, but as she waited in the grand oak panelled lobby, she became more anxious with every tick of the huge grandfather clock. Beautiful pictures in ornate gilded frames lined the walls. To calm her nerves she studied the faces of the men in the portraits. Some looked warm and friendly and others were more serious and austere. She wondered if these were the kind benefactors from the past who had turned Thomas Coram's dream into a reality.

Suddenly the clock struck eleven, a door opened and a woman appeared.

"Miss Mundon, please come this way." Mum followed her along the hall and up the magnificent sweeping staircase. She was shown into a large room with a long table running down the centre. Mum hadn't known what to expect, but she was surprised to be faced by eight important looking gentlemen who were sitting along one side of the table – the entire board of governors. The woman beckoned her to the single empty chair on the opposite side of the table where she was invited to sit.

One of the men began by giving a brief account of the history of the Foundling Hospital. He explained how it began in the 18th century when Thomas Coram, a philanthropic ship's captain, was appalled by the abandoned babies and children starving and dying in London. He campaigned for a hospital to accommodate them and was successfully granted a Royal Charter 'for the Maintenance and Education of Exposed and Deserted Children' in 1739. Three years later, in 1742, he established the Foundling Hospital at Lamb's Conduit Fields in Bloomsbury, London. It was the first children's charity in the country and the precedent for such charities everywhere. Of course, Mum already knew this as she had read about it in that article in the paper many months previously, but she said nothing.

The interview lasted for almost an hour. They asked many questions; some were very personal, and others were more about Mum's hopes and expectations for the future. She was surprised by this, as she had expected that they would concentrate on the baby rather than her own life and prospects. They assured her that although the child's welfare was, of course, their main priority, they also wanted to ensure that the mother, given a fresh start, would go on to enjoy a good and fulfilling life.

Occasionally, between the questions, the governors murmured among themselves, giving Mum, who by now was feeling a little more relaxed, the opportunity to appreciate the splendour of the room. It was like being in a palace, with an intricately moulded ceiling, huge Georgian windows, a magnificent marble fireplace and walls lined with beautiful paintings.

Eventually, the interview came to an end with the reassurance that, *if* they did agree to take the child, he would be guaranteed the best of care, a good Christian education in a fantastic school and the prospect of a great career. However, they warned her that he would be given a new name and she could have no further contact with him. They acknowledged that it would be difficult for her to part with him, but doing so would be in the best interests of both of them; he would be given the finest opportunities in life, which in her present circumstances she couldn't provide, and she could continue her life with a clean slate as if nothing had happened.

She went home with mixed feelings. It would be the ultimate sacrifice to part with her beautiful baby, but she knew in her heart that it really was the only option. She had no home of her own, no prospect of marriage and no income other than what she herself could earn. It would be impossible for her to give him the future that he deserved, and she forced herself to accept that she had no choice but to make the hard decision to part with him – *if* they would agree to take him. She felt that the interview had gone well, but she would have to wait for the final decision.

She didn't have long to wait. Just two days later, on the 27th October 1932, she received a letter confirming that the Committee of Governors had accepted that she had lived an honest and hardworking life and that they were prepared to take care of the child's future education and well-being. She was asked to bring the baby to the offices at 40 Brunswick Square, on Thursday the 3rd November at 10.30. She was asked to be punctual, as there were other children who were to be admitted on that day. The Hospital offered to assist with the costs of bringing the children to the Office if necessary.

There were usually one or two admission days each month, when between 4 and 8 children were admitted. Admission days appear to have been very organised. The Foundling Hospital's register indicates that there were 7 children admitted on the 3rd November 1932. On admission, all children were examined by two Medical Officers. They were then baptised with a new name and on the same day, they went to live with foster parents. Charles and the other children admitted on the 3rd November, all went to foster parents in or around Addlestone. Transport was arranged so that all the foster mothers could travel together on that day to collect the children.

The 3rd November was cloudy, but mild and dry. This was the day Mum had dreaded; the day when she would finally have to say goodbye.

This time Dot did accompany her. Little David was now almost three months old; a beautiful, happy little boy with blond hair. When medically examined he was declared to be 'a well-developed, well-nourished and healthy baby'.

(The Annual Report for 1932 states that 52 children were admitted that year to the Foundling Hospital. A total of 73 requests had been made, 8 of which were rejected and the rest were withdrawn).

~~~

Mum was distraught. All she had to identify her baby was the letter 'Y' and the date of his admission. She would never forget him, and all she could hope for was that his new foster Mum, whoever she was and wherever she lived, would be able to give him as much love and affection as she had.

She couldn't remember anything about the journey home. Despite Dot's constant reassurances that she had done the right thing, she just felt numb and empty, detached from the real world as if she was in some sort of a trance.

When they arrived back at the house later that afternoon, tea was already laid on the dining table and her mother had returned home. Everything was back to normal, and Mum would once again be sharing her bedroom with her younger sister, Eddie. Nobody mentioned the baby - it was just as if he had never existed.

Dot, Mum & Rex

After tea, which Mum couldn't touch, Alf came down the stairs carrying a large cardboard box, which he carefully laid on the floor in front of her. "Go on. Open it!" he said.

Mum gingerly lifted the lid and promptly burst into tears. Inside was a tiny black and white fox terrier puppy.

"His name is Rex," Alf said, as all the family looked on, wondering how she would react. They knew that nothing would ever compensate for her loss, but she had always wanted a dog and they hoped that this new life would give her something positive on which to focus in the coming weeks.

~~~

At that time, the governors did not allow mothers any further contact with their babies, and they were not encouraged to make enquiries about them. Despite that, however, Mum never forgot her little boy and he was always on her mind throughout his childhood. She regularly wrote many letters over the years, seeking news and showing concern for his wellbeing. Every birthday and Christmas time she included a special gift and a small sum of money, which was deposited in a savings account in his name. In response to her enquiries she was given reassurances that he was well but few personal details.

A typical letter that Mum would write on a frequent basis would say:

> *Dear Sir,*
> *I would be so grateful if you would let me know how my little boy is getting on. I am always thinking about him and how he is growing up. I shall always be so grateful to the hospital for caring for him. He was admitted on 3rd November 1932 and his letter is 'Y'.*
> *Yours respectfully,*
> *Joyce Mundon*

Almost without fail the curt reply would say:

> *Dear Madam,*
> *I am in receipt of your letter and am glad to tell you your little boy is quite well.*
> *Yours faithfully,*
> *Secretary*

~~~

Although Mum constantly thought of her son and imagined how he was growing up, life for the rest of the family returned to normal and Mum's pregnancy and the baby were never ever mentioned again.

Mum and Eddie went on holiday to Jersey in 1939 where she met James Banks – a very successful professional boxer who fought under the name Jimmy Pearce. They married in June the following year and she was convinced that it had only been possible because of the assistance she'd been given from the Hospital. She wrote to thank them:

Mum & Dad's Wedding 1940

> *I have married since I last wrote to you and I realise that this was only possible through the way you helped me and I shall always be grateful to you.*

She was constantly on the lookout for any news items relating to the Hospital and in one poignant letter dated 18th May 1941, she wrote:

> *I was naturally very interested in your article in the 'Picture Post' last week. One of the boys in the first picture is just as I imagine little David to be. I would so much like to know if it is he.*

Citizens of To-morrow: Choirboys of the Foundling Hospital
Among the most worthy of British institutions is the Foundling Hospital, home of 600 children whose fathers have deserted them. Here, for over 200 years, children have been cared for and educated first at temporary premises in Hatton Garden, then at the Hospital in Lamb's Conduit Fields —famous London landmark. To-day, they are in fine new premises set in the fields of Hertfordshire.

FOUNDLING HOSPITAL

One of England's most famous schools. Where 600 penniless girls and boys are cared for, educated and trained for jobs in surroundings equal to those of any expensive boarding school.

JUST over two hundred years ago it was a common thing in and around London to see "infants abandoned on dunghills."

The eighteenth century was a brutal age, and unmarried mothers had little to hope for when their children were born. With no one willing or able to provide for them, hundreds of children were left to die.

A retired sea captain, Captain Thomas Coram, with a warm heart and a strong belief in the future of the colonies, passed many such sights on his daily journey from Rotherhithe to London. The practice had become so prevalent, and seemed to him so injurious to the country's strength, that he made up his mind to end it. He started a campaign for a Foundling Hospital for England which should maintain and educate "exposed and deserted young children." Seventeen years later, at the age of seventy, he got his way.

On October 17, 1739, George II granted the Hospital's Charter. The following January, sixty children were admitted to temporary premises in Hatton Garden. But, from the beginning, the Governors looked about for a suitable site for a permanent home. In September, 1742, the foundation stone was laid of the Hospital in Lamb's Conduit Fields, which became one of the landmarks of London until its removal to the country in 1926.

At first it was planned to admit all children offered to them. But requests for admission were so heavy that women scrambled and fought to be first at the doors. To prevent unruly scenes, an unusual ballot by white, red and black balls was arranged. The women who drew the white balls were told to take their children for immediate examination; those who drew the black were turned away at once; the red balls entitled the mothers to wait in case there were any babies rejected from the first group.

Despite the ballot, the pressure on accommodation grew. By 1752, there were 600 children on the books whose maintenance cost many times more than the income of the Hospital. The Governors appealed to Parliament for aid.

This was willingly given, but with an unfortunate stipulation attached. The Hospital was told it must turn no child away from its doors. The evils that followed from the method of "indiscriminate admission" nearly killed the whole scheme. Sick children were brought among healthy; mortality rates rose to startling heights; the public complained that prostitution was directly encouraged. Four years later, indiscriminate admission was stopped and with it the aid from Parliament, save in respect of those children already admitted under its scheme.

From that time, the Hospital has been maintained by private efforts. Admission is governed to-day by the following rules: Children can only
Continued overleaf

PICTURE POST

David, at that time would have been nine – but she never found out if he actually was the boy in the picture. She just received the normal standard reply which made no reference to her question.

As time went by, Mum became aware that the Governors had relaxed some of their policies and in August 1948, when her son was sixteen, she wrote:

Dear Sir,

Would you kindly let me know how my boy is getting on? I am enclosing a postal order for 10 shillings for his birthday. I have heard about the new arrangements for visiting the children and I am wondering if I will have a chance of seeing my boy although he is over the age. How I have hoped it would be allowed when he was small.

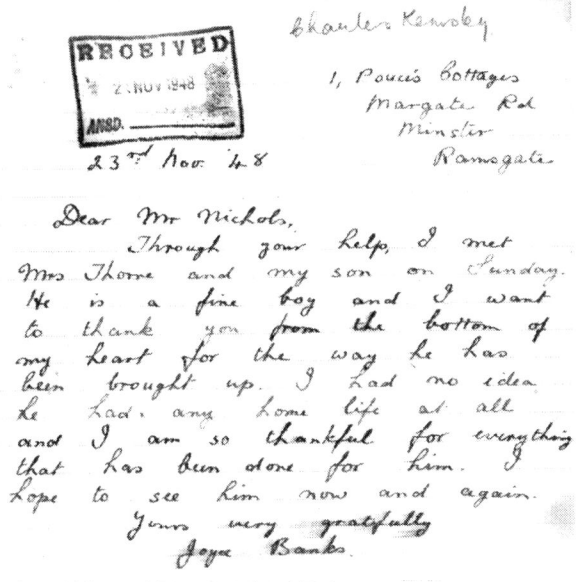

In view of her contact over the years, Mum was eventually told his new name, and for the first time, he was given details about his birth mother.

In November 1948 she met him and his foster mother, Mrs Thorne, for the first time

Although this was something that Mum had always longed for, it must have been very hard for Chuck, who harboured deep feelings of resentment and animosity toward her because of all the misinformation he had been given. He had no idea of the true circumstances of his birth and why he had been given up. Throughout his schooldays, he believed what he'd been told - that his evil parents had rejected and abandoned him to enjoy a selfish life of pleasure and luxury.

Mum had been assured that he would be given a loving and happy childhood with a good education in a beautiful school, and although she missed him so much, she was comforted by that promise. Little did she know that after spending the first five years of his life with his kind foster mother, he would be wrenched from her arms and placed in a vast and terrifying institution with no love, harsh discipline and constant bullying. She had no idea of the suffering he would experience, particularly during the war years, when male members of staff were called up and not replaced. Sadly, educational standards suffered during those years, and there were few teachers to hold in check the terrible bullying that occurred amongst the boys. But there will be much more about all that in the following chapters…

PART 3

CHUCK'S STORY

All we knew about Chuck was that he was listed on the internet as being a 'leading dog trainer and animal behaviour expert'. That was intriguing enough but we were very interested in finding out what else had happened during those eighty missing years.

On our first visit he gave us some tantalizing snippets and it was obvious that he had enjoyed a rather colourful and exciting life. He spoke of his time in the merchant navy; jumping ship and gun running for Fidel Castro's Cuban rebels; motorcycle stunt riding, including the famous Wall of Death and even working in Hollywood, training animals for some very well-known films.

He explained how his profound feelings of rejection, together with the brutal bullying endured at his pro-military boarding school had affected him deeply and compelled him to live a life on the edge – seeking danger and defying death. With a chip on his shoulder and a volatile temper, he had travelled the world, tough, fearless and invincible.

Our curiosity aroused, we wanted to know more – but he was tired and talking left him exhausted. However, he was able to use his lap-top and promised that he would let us know more about his life by e-mail. He was true to his word and, bit by bit, I received every installment.

Over the next year or so, we learnt about his traumatic schooldays, which he always referred to as his 'lost childhood'; his apprenticeship at the Lamerton Hunt Kennels in West Devon, where he was taught the time-honoured craft of traditional dog training and horsemanship; his dramatic seafaring days and his motor cycling exploits. We also discovered how, as a confirmed 30 year old bachelor, he met Yvonne – his true love and soul-mate and how, as a team, they dedicated the rest of their lives to the welfare and training of animals. Although Chuck was a formally trained professional, concentrating on working dogs of all kinds, Yvonne was more concerned about the wellbeing of misunderstood family pets, which she called her 'Cinderella Dogs'.

It is an amazing story and in the next few chapters I will share it with you – told in Chuck's own words, just as he sent it to me. If you think it a bit far-fetched in places, so did I, but he assured me that every word is true!

~~~

CHUCK'S STORY 1
FOSTER CARE
1932 – 1938

Obviously, Chuck didn't remember the time when, on the 3rd November 1932, aged just eleven weeks old, he was admitted into the care of the Foundling Hospital.

On that very first day, he was medically examined and found to be a well-developed, well-nourished and healthy baby. He was then baptized and given the new name, Charles Kemsley. It was the practice in those days to change children's names in order to protect the confidentiality of both mothers and their babies and to give them the opportunity for a fresh start in life. David John Mundon had now become Charles Kemsley, which explains why, in our search, we could find no records of his existence, other than his birth certificate.

The children would then be placed with foster parents in the country, where they would spend the first five years of their life before starting the main school in Berkhamsted, which would then be their home for the next ten years.

The foster parents were carefully chosen and usually lived in a small group of towns on the outskirts of London; towns which included Addlestone, Saffron Walden, and Chertsey. They would be good working class people, rather than from the higher echelons of society - they didn't want the children to grow up with ideas above their station!

~~~

Mrs Thorne of Addlestone in Surrey was chosen to be young Charles Kemsley's foster mother. She would have been told nothing about his background or the circumstances of his birth, the name and address of his mother or his own original name. To her, he was just Charles Kemsley from the Foundling Hospital, and she probably naively assumed that he had been abandoned on their doorstep like so many other babies had been, way back in the past. In fact, it was she who had told Chuck, in good faith, that he had been found on that particular doorstep – not through malice but because it was something that she genuinely believed.

Ellen Thorne was a 56 year old widow who lived with her 30 year old son, Ernest, who took on the role of 'foster Dad'. Her husband and her two daughters had tragically died of T.B a few years earlier.

They lived in a modest semi-detached Victorian cottage in Chapel Avenue, Addlestone in Surrey, and when her husband was alive, they used to breed show dogs. They still had a pet dog, Sally, a cocker spaniel, who young Charlie considered to be his very own 'official guard and companion'.

Ellen and Ernest were very kind to young Charlie. Although they received an allowance from the Foundling Hospital, which continued to be Charlie's official guardian, they brought him up as their own son in a loving family environment. They were the only 'Mum and Dad' that he knew and he always regarded them as such.

When he was three, in 1935, he had a problem with walking. He was seen by specialists at Weybridge Hospital who diagnosed a bad case of 'flat feet'. His feet were put in plaster, and when it was eventually removed, the doctors suggested that paddling in the sea would help to strengthen the muscles. So, being the kind and caring people that they were, Ellen and Ernest carried out the doctor's orders faithfully and took him by train from Addlestone in Surrey where they lived, to Bognor Regis in Sussex. They only had a very small income and could ill afford it, but they regularly made those monthly therapeutic trips to the seaside for young Charlie's long term benefit.

Chuck could remember little about his early years but he always thought of his beloved foster parents with great affection. He was forever grateful to them for kindling his love of animals which would form such an important part of his later life when he went on to become one of the world's most successful dog trainers and a leading authority on canine behavior and body language.

Chapel Avenue, Addlestone

CHUCK'S STORY 2
MY FIRST MEMORY
1937

Before he died, Chuck began writing a book in which he intended to give a step-by-step guide to his unique methods of dog training. It was to be called 'If Only Dogs Could Speak', but, unfortunately, he only managed to complete the first chapter.

This is an excerpt from that chapter which relates to a poignant memory from those early years in foster care:

~~~

Before I served my apprenticeship, taking in foxhounds, hunt terriers, gun dogs, sheepdogs, security dogs and police dogs, I would have certainly thrown my hands up in the air and exclaimed, "If only dogs could speak!" whenever I failed to understand them.

According to my dear foster parents, the first time this happened was when I was a little boy running errands for them. At 8 am I would often see an immaculately groomed beagle hound trotting along on its own. You could set your clock by it. My foster parents brought me up to respect animals, especially dogs, but, as they had not taught me to know that animals cannot speak as humans do, I did not know that they could not.

Therefore, as the beagle passed by one day, I said, "Good morning Mr Beagle!"

When he did not return my greeting I thought I had upset him and done something wrong. After all, I was only 4¾ years old!

When I told my foster Mum about this, she sat me on her knee and explained, "Animals can't speak as humans do, and so you haven't upset 'Mr Beagle' and neither have you done anything wrong."

"But Mum, why did he have such a haunted look in his eyes as if he was in terrible pain?"

"Well, he is in terrible pain - emotional pain that is… At times Charlie, I feel I'm fostering a young Einstein instead of a bright 4¾ year old child!"

Not knowing who Einstein was, I must have looked blank, because Mum said, "Never mind. After lunch, I will tell you the full story of the beagle's pain and what led up to it."

After lunch, she continued, "The man, who owned the beagle, used it as a vital part of his work. He was a professional hare and rabbit hunter. He and his beagle were inseparable and no one could ever recall seeing one without the other. That is until the man passed away.

As the beagle's master preferred the company of his beagle rather than that of humankind, the sole mourner at his funeral was his loyal beagle. His faithful four-legged friend followed the horse-drawn hearse that carried his master all the way to the local cemetery gates.

As his master's coffin was lowered into his grave, the beagle kept up a mournful howling from a safe distance until everyone had gone.

At 6 am the next morning, when the cemetery staff arrived for work, they were astounded to see the grieving beagle lying on top of his master's grave with every intention of defending it – come what may. Every attempt by the cemetery authorities to remove the beagle was met with fits of aggression. They, therefore, decided that the beagle should be shot!

However, public opinion decreed otherwise. There was such a hullabaloo about it that the mournful beagle was allowed to come and go as he pleased. What people could not understand, though, is why he always looked so spick and span, until it was discovered that another professional hare and rabbit hunter who lived nearby, took him in and cared for him until he could get over his master's death.

The new man, being another formally trained professional steeped in the ways of hunting dogs, as was his predecessor, gave the beagle all the support and space to do what it thought it had to do!

Three months after I had this conversation with my foster Mum I was wrenched from her arms and packed off to what can only be described as 'The military prep school from hell.' So, I never saw Mr Beagle again. And it wasn't until 10 horrific years later, when I was free of that dreadful place, that I received the good news from her that Mr Beagle had turned out to be a very happy bunny indeed... working for his new master, and carrying out the traditional tasks that beagles were originally bred for – just as he did for his first master.

What bliss this must have been for this faithful working hound, and the wonderful way that his dignity was restored!

~~~

CHUCK'S STORY 3
SCHOOLDAYS
1938 – 1947

From here onwards, the remainder of Part 3 - 'Chucks Story' will be written entirely in his own words, exactly as he sent it to me, chapter by chapter, (with just a bit of editing on my behalf in the punctuation and grammar department.) For the sake of clarity, any text or information which I have added and which are not Chuck's actual words will be written in italics.

In May 1938, when Chuck was approaching six years old, he had to leave his foster parent's home to go into the new Foundling Hospital School in Berkhamsted. This was not an easy move for children who had only known life in a loving family environment, and many children found the separation from their foster families to be a heart-breaking experience. At the time, society didn't understand the emotional needs of children and the impact that this kind of separation could have. It would have been distressing and very hard to be one of many small children trying to get used to a new way of life in a large institution. The school made sure that the children were fed, clothed and received good medical care.

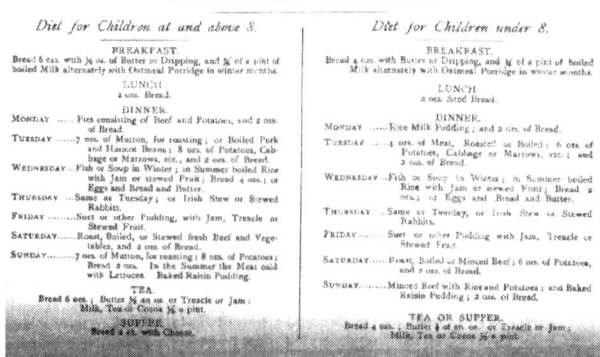

However, it was a harsh environment and physical punishment was regularly used, as it was in most schools and institutions of the time. There was also little scope for individual love or attention.

The school itself was a brand new, purpose built building in Berkhamsted, Hertfordshire. It was a beautiful and impressive building which was modelled on the original Georgian buildings of the Foundling Hospital in Bloomsbury, most of which by then had been demolished. The school was completed in 1935 and included a chapel, concert hall, dining room, indoor swimming pool, gymnasium and acres of landscaped grounds.

A good basic education in reading, writing, arithmetic, and scripture was provided, and this gradually broadened to include grammar, geography and drawing. Girls and boys were strictly segregated at all times for both lessons and day to day life. Music played an important role in the children's lives. When George Frideric Handel had been a governor in the eighteenth century, he had donated an organ and given a benefit concert every year in the Hospital chapel to raise funds for the charity, and had even composed the Foundling Hospital's anthem, 'Blessed are they that considereth the poor', which included the 'Hallelujah' chorus from Messiah. Ever since then, music had been afforded a special place, and many of the boys sang in the choir or joined the boys' band, which provided a steady stream of recruits to military bands over the following years.

The uniform was rather unusual and outdated and probably based on the predicted future expectations of the children; the majority of boys would go on to join the army and girls generally went into domestic service. The boys looked like smart little soldiers in their uniform of chocolate-brown trousers and scarlet waistcoats with brass buttons and a high white collar. On Sundays, they wore a bow tie and a military style cap. The girls were dressed like little serving maids with long dark dresses and white pinafores and caps.

Despite the wonderful building and amazing facilities, the regime was brutal, the discipline was merciless and bullying was rife.

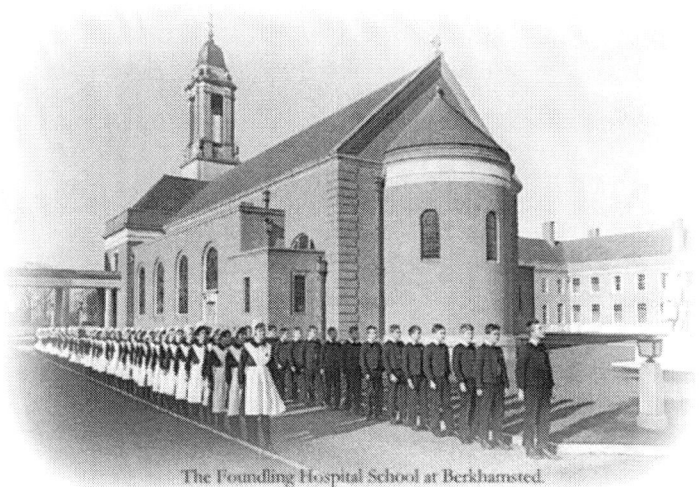

The Foundling Hospital School at Berkhamsted.

People, who knew me as a child, told me that I had a very happy early childhood, but I cannot remember much about it. This was because it was deeply overshadowed by the next 10 years of my life, which were filled with the harsh disciplined regime of a British pro-military type prep school.

I arrived at the School on my fifth birthday in 1937. On my arrival, I was taken to the infant's section and given a scalding hot bath by two rough, foul-mouthed nursemaids. They scrubbed me all over with stiff scrubbing brushes and strong carbolic soap which got into my eyes and made me scream with pain. Their reaction to this was to jeeringly call me a cry baby and hold my head under water until I thought I would drown.

When I was being taken to the bathhouse I could hear other children screaming in agony and I wondered why. When I met them later, they told me that they had been subjected to the same abuse as I had been. Still shocked and bewildered, we were taken to the parade ground every day and taught to march military style. 'Left right, left right' and so on! Naturally, as we were only 5 years old, we burst into tears when we were shouted at. Sometimes we were caned for crying and also for making mistakes, both on and off the parade ground.

The worst tanning I had when I was in the infants' section was actually on the parade ground. The drill instructor was shouting at my best friend, Robert Neighbour, for forgetting to call him 'Sir'!

"Where are your manners?" he roared, and poor Robert, who always got flustered when shouted at, thought the instructor had said, "Where's your flannel?" So he replied, "Hanging up on the hook next to my toothbrush!" To which I burst out laughing and couldn't stop.

In 1938, having done my year in the infants' section, I was duly enrolled into the main body of the school, as were all my classmates. We all thought that the infants' section was bad enough, but now we had to contend with the sadistic ex-Army NCOs that were employed to carry out the school's dirty work, such as beating us up when we didn't do what we were told. They were on our backs all the time. Then there were the older boys bullying us whenever they felt like it.

There was no escape from the tyranny. The school was surrounded by a ten foot high wall, with two gatehouses built into it, one for the main front gate and the other for the back gate. A gang of those sadistic ex-army NCOs, or 'Gorillas' as we called them, permanently manned both gatehouses.

1939 was not quite as bad as 1938; in fact, it was rather exciting. Every year the school held its summer camp, and everyone who was old enough went there. Summer camp was always set up on land owned by the War Department, or the Ministry of Defence as it is now called. This particular year it was on land adjoining Hawkinge Airfield near Folkestone in Kent, which was to become the famous Battle of Britain fighter base in World War 2. I thoroughly enjoyed Summer Camp. Discipline was a lot more relaxed than it was at school and there was a more holiday-like feel to it.

On my birthday, while I was at camp, I received a present from one of my biological parents; they didn't say which one. It was a tennis racquet. To my amazement, my housemaster told me that parents are strictly forbidden to send presents to us.

According to him, when I was born my biological parents were more concerned with enjoying themselves than bringing me up. He told me that they had decided to hand me over to the school at the age of five, to be educated to be a Cavalry Officer, thereby keeping up the family traditions. He said that the school had agreed to this, on the understanding that they had no contact with me whatsoever until I had completed my education.

In 1939, Britain was doing very well at tennis and many people wanted their sons and daughters to be tennis stars, so maybe that is why they broke the rules. Anyway, I was allowed to play with the racquet for two hours before my housemaster confiscated it. When I asked him why he said, "Cavalrymen travel light and they don't have room for toys. Your father should know that, he is one." What he said affected me deeply and, among other things, I thought to myself: 'surprise, surprise, the truth is coming out at last. The selfish rats, whoever they are, dumped me!'

I was walking around in a daze, trying to get my head round this, when suddenly all hell broke loose. Spitfires, Hurricanes and other aircraft were landing and taking off throughout the night. We boys were hastily loaded into Army trucks and taken back to school.

"What's going on?" we asked the drivers.

"World War 2 is going to break out in the next two or three days," they said.

Back at school, the doors were being reinforced with plywood sheets to help to protect us from bomb blast. Printed on these sheets, in big bold black letters, it said 'MADE IN POLAND', and so I asked my geography master if he could tell me where Poland is.

"Poland is just north of Germany and the Germans are attacking her with planes and tanks. That's why we are at war with Germany," he replied.

Then with his voice filled with passion, he went on to say: "The courageous Polish Cavalrymen, in a last ditch stand, attacked the German tanks and they and their horses were annihilated in the process!" Strange as it may seem, this revelation did not put me off wanting to be a Cavalryman. If anything, it made me want to be one even more.

In 1941, a platoon of Commandos was brought in to teach us jujitsu and other forms of unarmed combat such as how to kill our enemy without making a sound - with both the fearsome commando knife and our bare hands. We already knew such things as how to take a machine gun to pieces and put it back together blindfolded and, of course, use it with accuracy. Even at our tender age, we were rapidly becoming a force to be reckoned with.

I got on very well with one of the Commandos, who explained, "Although Churchill is putting a brave face on things, deep down he is thinking that there is a strong possibility that we might get invaded and lose the war! Personally, I think that's why you are being trained up at such an early age to learn how to do these barbaric things we are teaching you."

Amongst many other things that he told me, he said, "Every British Commando keeps a single ·303 bullet in a secret place, for emergencies." He then took a ·303 bullet out of his rifle and placed it inside a crack in the gymnasium outer wall, sealing it in with a wad of clay, and said, "There you are mate, you never know when you might need it." He was dead right - more about that later.

That was the last time I saw my commando friend. I missed him terribly and when I heard later that he was killed on a secret mission in Norway, I was angry, devastated, and dying for a fight; and I got one.

There was this nasty twelve-year-old boy that kept bullying my classmates, and as I walked into the cloakroom, there he was, beating up one of my friends. I hit him so hard that his head hit the wall and he collapsed at my feet. If he had been the same age as me, I would have let him get up before I hit him again - but he was almost two years older than me and this was war, my personal war! So, I proceeded to kick his head in, until one of the 'Gorillas' pulled me off him.

The bully spent several days in intensive care. As I nearly killed him and was also the one that started the fight, albeit under provocation, I got six strokes of the cane on my bare bottom, in front of the whole school. It hurt a lot but I was not going to show it and give them the satisfaction of thinking that they had won. After that, my classmates were not bullied by the older boys anymore. Okay, the 'Gorillas' were still bullying us, and there wasn't anything we could do about that until we were bigger and stronger.

After my fight with the twelve year old boy, nothing much happened until the Yanks came over here in 1942 to help us win the war, so they say! We played them at football. They lost to both our first team and our junior team, which I was in. The Yanks team came from the local United States Air Force bomber base. It was really funny to see these great big guys tripping up over their own feet. They had a great sense of humour though, and they thoroughly enjoyed themselves, and so did we.

Playing us at football became a regular fixture and they always insisted on providing the fruit at halftime, and also after the match. One day they gave us some bananas. This was a real treat, as no one in Britain had tasted bananas since the outbreak of the war. The Yanks at the bomber base were very kind to us. On hearing that we didn't have any toys, they sent us some!

Every boy in the school received a very expensive toy; mine was a scaled down Boing B7 Flying Fortress bomber. It was a marvellous piece of work, as was the Boing B7 itself. We were only allowed to play with the toys for exactly two hours, then, as usual, they were taken away from us and we never saw them again - just like the tennis racquet I received on my birthday, back in 1939.

When the Yanks got wind of this, they sent a stern letter of disapproval to Churchill, which was signed by everyone at the bomber base, including the Station Commander - but to no avail! Churchill wrote back and told the Yanks to mind their own business and that was that.

The highlight of 1942, as far as I was concerned, happened in the school dining hall at lunchtime, when Mr Holgate, the headmaster, overheard a boy dropping his T's when he asked another boy to pass the butter.

"Say butter, not bu—er!" Mr Holgate roared.

"Butter," the boy said, correctly.

Dropping his own T's, Mr Holgate replied, "That's be--er, boy!"

Someone tittered, and Mr Holgate stepped back to see who it was and immediately slipped up on a strategically placed banana skin. As everyone laughed fit to bust, we helped him up to his feet. He glared at me and spluttered, "Kemsley, if I find out you had anything to do with this, you will rue the day you were born." Although he suspected that I was the culprit, he could never prove it.

In 1944 I was twelve, and getting a reputation for being a bit of a daredevil and defender of the underdog - which I still am to this day. I was also developing a great passion for sport, and was doing very well at boxing, swimming and water polo. I was bigger than most boys of my age at that time, and the more sport I did the stronger I became, which didn't go unnoticed by Mr Gordon, the school's boxing coach. He was also one of the 'Gorillas!'

This one was more sadistic than all the others put together. Before coming to the school he was a PT instructor at the notorious Army Prison, at Colchester. Loads and loads of soldiers who were incarcerated there would have given a year's pay for a chance to put a bullet in his back! That's how sadistic and unpopular he was.

Every Saturday afternoon, he rigged up a makeshift boxing ring in a quiet corner of the parade ground and terrorised us, on the pretence of coaching us. One of his favourite tricks was to tell us to hit him, and when we did, he would knock us about. Earlier on, I noticed he had this funny nervous quirk of standing on the outside edges of his feet when he was riled up, which left him completely off balance.

So, when he said, "Hit me!" I refused over and over and, true to form, there he was standing on the outside edges of his feet, completely off balance. With my heart in my mouth, I brought my fist up in a powerful right uppercut to the point of his jaw, and down he went, hitting his head on the tarmac and knocking himself out. I hit him so hard that I fractured my wrist and had to have my arm in plaster, for several weeks.

Having lost face, you would have thought that he would have resigned, but no, he went around boasting to everyone, "What a great boxing coach I am! That Kemsley idiot didn't even know a right uppercut from a left hook until I taught him!" Like all bullies, he was a braggart to boot. The fact of the matter is that if the commandos had not taught me how to recognise my enemy's weakness and then exploit it, I would not have been able to do what I did.

Whilst I had my arm in plaster I was formulating a plan that would get Mr Gordon sacked. I knew he was supposed to write our boxing reports in longhand and then take them to the main office to be typed Instead he was borrowing Mr Holgate's typewriter without his permission, and typing them himself. I took into account that, as his office was just a small cubbyhole and his desk was quite large, he had to push his desk away from the wall before he sat down and then pull it back again towards himself before he could type.

One night, when I was standing in front of his desk getting a grilling, I noticed that when he was trapped behind his desk in this fashion, he was ten times easier to wind up, and, of course, more likely to throw the typewriter at my head - and hopefully, through the priceless centuries old stained glass window that was behind me.

The final part of the plan was to get Mr Holgate to witness Mr Gordon throwing the typewriter through the stained glass window. I was due to get another grilling from Mr Gordon at five pm on the Friday, which was the day after my arm was taken out of plaster. Mr Holgate always left his office at a quarter to five every Friday. This was when Mr Gordon would sneak in there and grab the typewriter.

Mr Holgate loved boys telling him what a great headmaster he was, and this type of flattery could always delay him. So, on this particular Friday, whilst some of my classmates were doing this, others were high up in the trees, monitoring what was going on behind and in front of Mr Gordon's desk. Then, on a given signal, another classmate rushed up to Mr Holgate and said, "Please sir, someone is breaking into your office." So Mr Holgate rushed back to his office, with all my classmates in tow.

When Mr Holgate got to his office, he found his office door was unlocked and his typewriter was missing. As Mr Holgate started to deduce what had happened, he heard Mr Gordon shouting at me. Then, as he came rushing up the stairs to investigate what was going on, he was just in time to see Mr Gordon throw the typewriter through the stained glass window. Seeing that I was on the floor, Mr Holgate asked me if I am alright, to which I blurted out, "I'm in shock sir, he went berserk, I don't know why!"

Mr Gordon was sacked on the spot and had to pay for a new window, which left him penniless and a broken man. He could not even afford the taxi fare to the station, which was a long way from the school. And just to add insult to injury, the school band played Colonel Bogy, as he made his way down to the main gate.

We all watched him struggling with his big heavy suitcases, as we sang along with the band, "Onions, they make a fine, fine stew … onions, they're very good for you … onions, those bloody onions … onions, and bollocks to you!"

~ ~ ~

My best mate at school was Sheldrake. He was nicknamed Shelly and I was nicknamed Kemo. We both liked to get up and sneak out into the school grounds before anyone was about, and run and run - just for the sake of running! One early morning, just before sunrise, we stumbled on a rope ladder, attached to a grappling iron. It must have been left behind by the commandos in 1941 when they taught us how to use it.

Having tested it out and finding it worked okay, we hid it in some long grass and went back to our dormitory to plan our escape. We didn't have a clue as to what things were like outside the school, so the only plan we could come up with was to put as much distance between us and the school - in the shortest possible time. We were also worried that the 'gorillas' might discover the rope ladder, so we decided to go over the wall just before dawn, the next day.

Once we were over the wall and had buried the rope ladder, we were off, covering mile after mile, until we were so tired and hungry that we had to stop. As we sat down, catching our breath, we could smell homemade bread being baked and we didn't have to go far to find out where it came from.

As we turned the corner, we caught sight of a housemaid putting six large loaves of bread outside to cool. We waited until she went indoors, then we sneaked up and grabbed four of the loaves and ran off into some woods. The loaves were very hot and burnt our hands, but we hung on to them, like as if our lives depended on it. We ate two of the loaves and kept the other two for later.

On the road again, we kept up a cracking pace until we arrived at a large town. The air was acrid with fumes compared to the fresh air at school. We were halfway through the town when Shelly started choking. I sat him down on a bench and gave him a drink out of my water bottle. He then said, "I feel a bit better, but I can't go on. Just leave me here and go on alone."

"No way Shelly, I never leave my mates in the lurch, it's part of my code. You know that - and I will carry you if I have to!" I growled.

I was so concerned about Shelly's condition that I didn't hear two big policemen come up behind us until they spoke to us the way that policemen do.

"What are you boys doing fifteen miles away from your school? Don't say you are not from there because your uniforms give you away!" They took us to the police station and gave us some tea and buns and they also called a doctor for Shelly.

The doctor gave Shelly some tablets and told him that he'd had a small asthma attack and if he kept on taking the tablets he should be okay. Then a policeman tucked us up in bed in one of the cells and said, conspiringly, "The next time you think about going over the wall, get yourselves some civilian clothes. Those school uniforms make you stick out like a couple of sore thumbs."

At 6 am the next morning, the 'Gorillas' came to take us back to school. As soon as we were handed over, they started pushing us around until one of the policemen snarled, "These are just two little scared kids, and if you don't take your hands off them, I will take off my uniform and beat you to a pulp!" Back at school, we were given two weeks solitary confinement on bread and water. As soon as we were released, our classmates picked us up bodily and ran around the school grounds with us on their shoulders, cheering their heads off.

Early in 1945, there was no doubt about it, we were definitely going to win the war, and there was a feeling of optimism in the air as our treatment started to improve dramatically. With the war in Europe drawing to a close, the School Governors were terrified that the Labour Party was going to win the next General Election. As soon as they were elected, they planned to close down all schools that used barbaric practices, which included deliberately lying and deceiving pupils as well as being extremely violent and cruel to them.

For starters, all the sadistic 'gorillas' were sacked, with the exception of just two who manned the gatehouses. Some of the masters that had deliberately lied and deceived us over the years were also sacked.

Then on Saturday afternoons we were given pocket money and were allowed to walk down to the town on our own and spend it on whatever we liked. This was the very first time that anything like this had happened since anyone could remember.

Making rude gestures and swearing at the 'gorilla' who manned the main gatehouse as we walked out the gate was very satisfying. He was not allowed to be sadistic or do anything unpleasant to us anymore, and by the look on his face, he didn't like it one little bit.

One Saturday afternoon I decided to go out the back gate, down Swing Gate Lane, for a change. As I walked past some bushes, a boy about my own age jumped out and started punching me. I grabbed his arm and twisted it behind his back and hissed in his ear, "Who the hell are you, and what do you think you're doing?" In a small pleading voice, he squeaked, "I'm Tommy Jenkins, I didn't want to do it, but the Swing Gate Lane gang told me to. They say that you boys up there are sissies, and so I thought you would be a push over and I would be accepted as a member of the gang!" And with that, he ran off.

Going out the back gate was a good shortcut to the town, so I used it for several weeks. Then one day I was confronted by an angry looking girl, spitting and screeching,

"You're the dirty bastard that twisted my brother's arm and made him cry!" Then she started hitting me with a stick. If she was a boy, I would have knocked her flat - but she was a girl and I didn't know what to do. I beat a hasty retreat back to school and not knowing what else to do, I told Mr Holgate about it. He just looked embarrassed and blurted out, "I don't know. Use your initiative boy!"

~~~

The war in Europe ended on the 5th of May. The Labour Party won the General Election with a landslide victory. Eleven weeks later, on the 12th July, the school was falling over backwards to get its house in order so as to appease the new Government. Eight days later, I was allowed to go and stay with my foster parents for six weeks. They held me in their arms and cried and cried. I felt safe for the first time since I was wrenched away from them all those years ago. It was wonderful! But I didn't cry. I was unable to. That had been knocked out of me by all the harsh treatment I had received.

On my return to school, I knuckled down to catch up with my studies and I was a star pupil. That was up until early in 1947, when it was revealed to me by the army careers officer, that all British Cavalry Regiments, including the one that I had set my heart on joining, were now fully mechanised and that they had been so for many years.

"Or, to put it more bluntly, Kemsley, horses were replaced by battle tanks!"

I was speechless. My heart was broken. I stormed out of his office with a red mist clouding my eyes. I wanted to kill all the lying swine that had deceived me over the years, leading me on to believe that, when my education was completed, I would become a true traditional cavalryman - or 'Horse Soldier' as the Americans call them. And now they're saying I will be cooped up in a smelly inanimate piece of metal!

Several of my classmates felt the same way. They also wanted to kill those lying swine that made monkeys of us and took away our childhood, just as much as I did. We wanted revenge and we wanted it so much that we could taste it. It was our main topic of conversation for several weeks.

Plan A was to break into the armoury of the local shooting club, down in the town, and steal guns and ammunition in order to kill the teachers and 'gorillas' that had lied and deceived us. Most of them had been sacked in the 1945 purge, but a few had reinvented themselves and survived. One of them became our woodwork master. As a sop to the Labour Party, the school was teaching us some non-military skills.

Plan A failed because someone snitched on us, so we had no other ordinance than the ·303 bullet, which my commando friend had stashed away for me, back in 1941. Plan B was to kill the woodwork master by placing the bullet in a vice and fire it by hitting the percussion end of the bullet with a hammer and a blunted four-inch nail. The difficult part was working out the angle of trajectory that the bullet would take to the target; the target being the woodwork master's head - and where his head would be at the time the bullet was fired.

The 'gorilla', cum woodwork master, loved his blackboard and he spent a lot of time writing on it, so that was the best time to fire the bullet.

The next thing to decide was who was going to fire the bullet. So we decided to draw straws on it, and whoever drew the short straw would do it. A boy called Ducket drew the short straw. He was an utter wimp and was bound to lose his nerve at the last minute and cock it up. So, on those grounds, and the fact that it was my bullet anyway, I took the short straw off him.

It was a bright summer day in August when the woodwork master held his next woodwork class. Although it was a hot day, I was as cool as a cucumber. Everything was set up, and at the precise moment he started writing on the blackboard, I hit the bullet. He crumpled and fell down, with blood streaming from his head. At the sound of the shot, teachers swarmed in from adjoining classrooms and an ambulance came and took him away. We heard that he was unconscious but unlikely to die. As for us, we were all put in solitary confinement for the rest of the day.

The next day, a preliminary enquiry was held. When we were individually questioned, we each claimed responsibility so no one could be charged with the offence. Two more enquiries were held, to the same effect. An Army Brigadier got up and said, "The way this attempted assassination was carried out with just a bullet, a vice, a hammer and a blunted nail, was nothing short of being the work of a blooming genius. And if it hadn't been for the woodwork master's previous battle hardened reflex to drop at the sound of a shot, they would have killed the bloody tyrant stone dead!"

Of course, everyone knew that I had fired the bullet and why I fired it, including the school governors. So, they decided to call in a high ranking army psychiatrist to straighten me out, a full Colonel no less. He asked me a lot of questions as to why I tried to kill the woodwork master. He then said, "Now then, Kemsley, if, you are a good boy, from now on, you will command a battle tank and if you are a very good boy, one day you will command a whole squadron of them!"

I replied, "You can give me all the tanks in the British Army and I still wouldn't be interested in what you have to say!"

After shuffling through his papers, he looked up and said, "Ah here it is… The best thing we can do with you is to send you to a foxhunting establishment where your thwarted, outdated passion for cavalry charges and the cavalryman's philosophy of putting the welfare of your horses and men before your own, will find a suitable outlet… Well, Kemsley, what do you think of that?"

I shrugged my shoulders and said, "Whatever."

I admit I didn't have a clue what he was talking about and I had to wait fourteen months to find out.

During this time I got into more fights than ever. Also, now I was an older boy, I was expected to bully the young boys, and as I refused to do so, I was called a sissy. Not by my classmates, but by the boys in the next class up. The first two times I let it pass, but every time after that I did not. The third time a boy called me a sissy I broke his jaw. The next boy didn't fare any better.

And so it went on until they all ganged up on me and gave me a real pasting, but that didn't stop me. I got each one on his own, when he least expected it, and gave them a taste of their own medicine! They got the message and left me alone, after that.

Fourteen months to the day after seeing the psychiatrist, I was woken up at the crack of dawn by Mr Kirk, the school's welfare officer, and taken to Waterloo Station. We boarded a train to Plymouth, en-route to Lydford, in West Devon, where we hired a taxi to take us to the foxhunting establishment that the psychiatrist told me about.

The train that took us to Plymouth was a crack main line express, so we were able to eat a hearty breakfast in the fully equipped dining car. Eating ham and eggs, with the scenery rushing by, was a new experience for me. This was in the nostalgic days of steam, and the rhythmic sounds and smells of it all were really something to remember.

At Plymouth, we caught a very ancient train to Lydford. Whereas the state of the art Plymouth train travelled at very high speed and only stopped at three main line stations, during its two-hundred mile journey, the Lydford train was very slow and stopped at every little station and 'halt' on its short twenty mile journey. 'Halts' consisted of just a small, unmanned platform, about sixty feet long, with no shelter at all from the bitter Dartmoor weather. If there were any passengers, milk churns, market produce, etc. on it, the train would stop and pick them up.

At the third stop a very large, smelly, old lady got on the train, carrying a baby pig. She sat down next to Mr Kirk, and then pulled out a grubby handkerchief which contained some cooked sausages, and said, in a very broad West Devon accent, "Excuse me zur, would e like one of these yere zausages - they be homemade yer know!"

Precisely, at that moment, the little pig farted and relieved itself all over the sausages. The smell was horrendous. We grabbed our bags and fled to the other end of the train, where we found an empty compartment. Once inside, we stuck our heads out of the window until we had cleared the putrid stench from our nostrils. Fresh air had never tasted better!

All this excitement was a bit too much for Mr Kirk; he slept like a baby, all the way to Lydford Town. As he slept, my nose was pressed to the window, watching the wild Dartmoor landscape slowly pass by. I was fascinated by the size and wildness of the place, and of course, the thousands of wild Dartmoor ponies that were free to roam where they pleased.

The little old steam engine that pulled the train was a very ancient one, with a tall funnel.

"A right little old Puffing Billy," Mr Kirk called it, just before he dozed off and began to snore. As the little old puffer climbed the hills it seemed to say, "I think I can … I think I can … I think I can," and then, as it went downhill, "I know I can I know I can I know I can." And so, puffing and panting along, over hill and down dale, it took us all the way to Lydford Town.

As I stepped off the train, I was captivated by the scene! There were horses everywhere; some drawing wagons, and scores of saddle horses tied to hitch rails on both sides of the street. It was just like the old Wild West in the cowboy movies. I was half expecting the Lone Ranger to appear at any moment!

But I had to go. The taxi was waiting. The taxi was a big old Austin, built like a tank. We climbed in the back and Mr Kirk immediately went back to sleep, leaving me to continue my perusal of the Dartmoor landscape, which after a minute or two became enclosed farmland. Here I could see great big heavy horses ploughing the land, drawing wagons and doing many other tasks. Just like it was in Lydford, the horse was King! This pleased me immensely!

After leaving Lydford, the road became steeper all the way up to the old A30 trunk road, where it flattened out. Turning left onto it at Lewdown and going west for a few hundred yards, we turned right at the Royal Exchange Pub, where we went down a very steep narrow country lane to Stowford. Stowford was, and probably still is, a small hamlet, just a manor house and a farm. The Lamerton Hunt Kennels was a mile further on.

On a score of one to ten for scenic beauty, the final mile downhill to the kennels would get a ten. The lane was getting even steeper, narrower and windier than ever, as we dropped down into the valley. The beauty of the unfolding valley, with the river Wolfe flowing through it, was breath-taking. Coming around the last bend, I saw the river flowing under the most picturesque little stone bridge I have ever seen. Then, as we passed over the little bridge there, low and behold in front of us, lay the Lamerton Hunt Kennels.

~~~

After leaving school, Chuck was given the opportunity to meet his birth mother for the first time. Although Mum was desperate to see him, her feelings weren't reciprocated. Because of all the malicious lies he had been told, he blamed her for abandoning him and harboured deep feelings of bitterness and resentment. This is what he wrote about it, many years later

On leaving school I was given my mother's contact details and on one Sunday in November 1948 my foster mother and I met her for the first time. That's when we gave her the photo of me as a baby. I remember thinking she was so pretty – like Vera Lynn. She was always very nice to me, treating me like royalty when I visited. She also came to see me on a number of other occasions. But we were never to grow close because by my teens my heart was already hardened against her. I was treated badly at the military school and never forgave my birth parents for leaving me there. When my mother said she had kept in touch through the Foundling Hospital, I didn't believe her. Now with hindsight and the proof that she never forgot me, I regret thinking badly of her. I realise that she did her best in very difficult circumstances.

It must have been a couple of years later, on a warm summer's day in 1950, when he came to tea with us. I was seven at the time and he would have been seventeen. We had recently moved to our brand new council house in St. Paul's Cray and Christine was just a tiny baby. We obviously didn't know who he was – and he had been told not to tell us. I was horse mad as a child and, because he worked with horses and knew everything about them, we got on really well. I noticed that in the picture of the three of us in the garden, my collection of toy horses is at my feet! I don't remember much about that visit but Mum must have asked him about the various presents and money she had regularly sent to the school and been very disappointed to discover that he had not received any of them. (In fact, his savings account was still active and in 2013 he was presented with a cheque for £40!)

As far as I can remember, I visited Mum and your family, somewhere near Orpington, on a new housing estate in the Green Belt. We had our tea ... and as far as I can recall there were two of you there besides Mum, maybe all three of you, but I can't be sure of that ... After we had tea we all walked to the train station and said goodbye ... there was a footpath or lane lined with beautiful trees ... it was a lovely Summer day and Mum was telling me it was a lovely place to live and I thought so too. I don't remember much about it because my memory was clouded by the trauma of coping with the real world after leaving that terrible school at that time. Your Dad wasn't around, and as far as I remember, I never met him.

St. Paul's Cray 1950

CHUCK'S STORY 4
APPRENTICESHIP
1948 - 1954

After a brief interview it was agreed that I was to be given a month's trial, and if my work and conduct were satisfactory, I would be granted a five-year apprenticeship as a trainee huntsman. It was also agreed that during my month's trial, I would stay at the Chalet Café in Lewdown and report for work at 6 am every morning. The Chalet Café was owned by Mr Bruce. He also owned three taxis, including the one in which we rode. He told me that the distance by road, from his place to the kennels was three miles, but across the fields, it was just over a mile.

Early the next morning, I set off across the fields. I was almost there, with the entrance to the kennels in sight, when I was confronted by a big black bull. Not knowing what else to do, I punched him on the nose and, to my amazement, he galloped off. Unknown to me, the owner of the bull was close by, hiding behind a haystack. And then, as his bull ran away, he appeared and in his broad West Devon accent said, "Well done boy, you've just passed your first trial by ordeal!"

I clicked my heels, stood at attention and answered, "What do you mean Sir?" He replied, "Well boy, you be the new kennel boy ain't e? And this be your first day of your month's trial. Around these yere parts this type of trial means 'trial by ordeal', and there'll be many more of those that you'll have to face during your month's trial period. Moreover, you'll have to show Mr Gerry and members of the hunt committee, like me, that you're worthy of succeeding him when he eventually retires."

He then went on to say: "We're looking for a boy that's fearless and has the guts and ability to do a proper job. The way you called old Samson's bluff just now, showed me that you could be the very boy we're looking for. We hope so, as we have heard a lot about your exploits at that school of yours. You may not know this yet, boy, but the Lamerton's hunting territory lays both in West Devon and Cornwall. To the west is Launceston, to the east, Okehampton and Tavistock in the south. We hunt twice a week to cover this extensive territory which encompasses hundreds of square miles, including the northern half of Dartmoor – it's one of the most formidable hunting territories in England, where only deeds count and nothing else. If you make the grade as the new Lamerton huntsman, you will ride the best horses that money can buy. These horses have a great turn of speed that they can keep up all day. This is so that the huntsman can keep up with his hounds for hours on end. There's no time for pussyfooting around; you're expected to ride straight across country, over high fences, wide ditches, five bar gates and anything else that crosses your path!"

Leaning up against the haystack all the while, he went on, "You would have met Mr Gerry yesterday. He's going to be your immediate boss and chief mentor. He's a very difficult man to get on with and he will try his utmost to break you. If he can't break you, he'll teach you everything he knows. This is the way that he was trained, as other huntsmen were trained before him in an unbroken line, for countless generations past. As he pushes you beyond the limits of your physical and mental endurance, he'll be looking to see if you will run back to Mummy or, even much worse, vent your spite on the hounds or horses. If you run back to Mummy you might get a second chance. If you vent your spite on the hounds or horses, you'll be dismissed immediately and will never be able to get a job with horses and hounds anywhere!"

Having said his piece, he looked me straight in the eye and said, "So, now I've told e you what to expect, do e want to go on, or do e want to go back from whence ye came?"

I replied, "I'm going on, Sir, and nothing is going to stop me doing what I have to do!" And with that, I clicked my heels and leapt over the kennel's back gate and into 'the lion's den'.

"Stop clicking your heels and stop calling me Sir," he bellowed.
"Yes Sir," I said as I turned and went on into the kennels to meet my new boss and chief mentor.

"Kemsley, why are you late?" thundered Mr Gerry. I clicked my heels, stood at attention out of respect and said, "Sorry Sir, I got held up Sir."

When I clicked my heels and called him Sir, he gave me such a black look that I thought he wanted to murder me on the spot. It wasn't until later in the day when I met Pamela, his daughter, that I found out why.

She said: "During the war, when my father was called up, he relished the thought of killing Germans, but instead of that they stuck him in the cookhouse at Aldershot and made him an instructor, teaching new recruits how to cook. Outside the cookhouse, so-called 'riding instructors', who didn't know their arse from their elbow, were trying to teach officers, how to ride horses!"

"I think I know exactly how he must feel," I replied. And I then told her what it was like at my school.

After discussing that, Pamela started teasing me to get me to chase her. After all, we were just a couple of kids enjoying some harmless fun after the drudgery of doing our chores and getting sworn at and scolded for any little mistake. I had Pamela pinned to the ground, to stop her tickling me, when her father came out of the kennels to find out what all the noise was about.

As we sprang to our feet, I could see Pamela was shaking like a leaf. It looked like he was going to hit us, so I stepped in front of her to protect her.

"Step aside, Kemsley," he snarled.

I looked him straight in the eye, and in a quiet voice, I said, "No Sir I will not. Not unless you promise me that you won't hit her."

"Hit her? I wouldn't touch the pair of you with a bargepole, you filthy brats," he growled, and stalked off.

With that, we went back to work, sawing up logs that were used to fire the boilers which boiled up the meat for the hounds to eat. After five minutes of sawing, Pamela started crying, so I asked, "What are you crying for?"

"Why was he so angry?" she sobbed.

"Perhaps it was because we had stopped working?" I hazarded.

"No" she cried, "It's more serious than that. Since the war he gets very moody and sometimes, dangerous."

"In that case, I'm going to stick around, until he cools down."

"Don't worry, I'll be okay," she answered, trying to put a brave face on it. So, with that, I went back to my digs.

The next morning, Mr Gerry was out collecting the carcass of a dead horse from a nearby farm. Pamela and I were left on our own to let the hounds out and clean the kennels. While we were doing this, I noticed that she had a big bruise on her face, so I stopped working and said, angrily, "I knew it, I knew it! What's he done to you?"

Just as she was about to tell me, we heard the kennel lorry pull up outside. Pamela squeezed my hand as hard as she could and whispered, "Please, please, Charlie, don't say anything. Everything is okay, I've sorted it out."

Mr Gerry came in with a big smile on his face and said, "Well little old boy, what's your digs like? And before you say anything, don't click your heels, and don't call me Sir."

I was about to hit him on the head with the shovel I was holding, when I saw Pamela shaking her head with such a pleading look in her eyes, that my temper melted immediately, and with tongue in cheek, I replied, "They are very nice Mr Gerry, thank you."

In the afternoon Mr Gerry gave me my first lesson in skinning and cutting up the dead horse. It was very interesting, especially in this case, because the owner wanted to know why the animal had died, so this was also my first lesson in anatomy. Once the skin was off, he told me to brace myself as he pushed a skewer into the horse's stomach. The released putrid air and gasses were nauseating. I was only just about able to put a brave face on it and not be violently sick!

"Still with us, boy?" Mr Gerry asked, talking around a smouldering cigarette. He was a heavy smoker. He rolled his own cigarettes and always had one when he was skinning and cutting up dead animals.

"Yep, still here," I replied.

He then cut away the breastbone and belly flesh, thereby revealing the heart, lungs and all the other major internal organs. By now I was so fascinated that I hardly noticed the awful stench. I had studied the anatomy of the horse at school, but now seeing it for real was much more interesting than a stuffy old textbook.

"See that mucus boy, that's TB," he said, after cutting into the lungs.

Seeing that we both shared a common interest in anatomy, and also the fact that I didn't keel over at the smell and sight of blood and gore, he said, "Looks like you won't have too much trouble with this important part of the job, boy. This animal is comparatively fresh though. Sometimes they can be dead for much longer and then they really do hum, especially, in the height of summer."

Changing the subject, he said, "Now boy, about that nasty bruise on Pamela's face. I admit I put it there. I know I shouldn't have, but I'm afraid my temper got the better of me. I thought the pair of you … hmm … were … trying to … hmm … you know, hmm…" growing beetroot red with embarrassment.

Seeing by my expression that I wasn't going to let him off the hook, he said, "Pamela has told me what it was like at your school. I now realise you hate the Army and everything about it as much as I do and, more or less, for the same reasons. By the way, from now on try to stop clicking your heels and calling people Sir, you're making us nervous. My name is Frank; make sure you use it from now on."

"Yes Sir, I mean Frank, Sir," I replied.

At that moment, the owner of the dead horse rode up on a handsome bay hunter. Apparently, he owned a large mixed farm, next door to the owner of the bull that I punched on the nose.

"Ah-ha!" he cried, followed up with, "This must be the new little old kennel boy that's so handy with his fists. Farmer Davy was giving us a running commentary about it in the pub at lunch time! He told us that he was working on his haystack when he spotted the boy hurrying along, lest he be late for work. He said that old Sampson, the bull, had also spotted him and rushed up to confront him. Bellowing and stamping the ground, he stood there blocking the boy's path. But, the boy didn't stop. He just walked up to him and, without saying a word, punched him right on the nose. He said it was one hell of a humdinger of a punch and he wouldn't have liked to be on the receiving end of it. Neither did Sampson, he was off like a shot!"

After Farmer Davy's next door neighbour had gone, Frank said, "So why didn't you tell me about the bull yesterday?"

"I thought you might think I was making it up, as an excuse for being late," I replied.

"Well boy, I reckon there's a lot more to you than meets the eye," he said, as we resumed the gruesome task of cutting up the dead horse. Half of it was hung up on hooks to be cooked later, and the rest we fed to the hounds raw.

Watching hounds tearing the raw flesh off the carcass is always an exciting sight to behold. After twenty minutes, there's nothing left but bare bones. No sloppy toothless lapdogs here, only a professional hunting pack of canine athletes, all muscle, sinew, skin and bone. Seeing the interplay of muscles as they ripped and tore off the flesh was a sure indication of their fitness to do the tough job they were bred for and schooled to do.

"How can just one man control so many hounds when their blood is up, as it must be at times like these?" I asked.

"There is no quick answer to that, boy. Least, not one that you could understand until you are well into your apprenticeship and that is subject to you getting through your month's trial period, and also the many trials by ordeal I set you after that," he replied.

Looking me straight in the eye, he continued, "If, and only if, you get as far as that will you be privileged to know how to do this, and many other such powerful things. If on the other hand you do not, then all this knowledge will be intentionally withheld from you, as it is from anyone else that is not formally trained in this traditional way."

After waiting a moment for this to sink in and, still looking me straight in the eye, he stated with a very serious note in his voice, "Remember that what I'm talking about is the fountainhead of all canine and equine knowledge, passed down in an unbroken line from master to apprentice for over a thousand years. It started in Normandy and was brought to England shortly after the days of the Norman Conquest in 1066, when the Norman's brought their hunting hounds to England, along with their exclusive disciplines and knowledge. Not just in hounds and hunting, but also in horses and horsemanship too. It was all written down by monks for safekeeping!"

~~~

The first two weeks of my month trial period passed slowly. I was up at the crack of dawn and worked hard at the most boring and menial tasks all day long. Nothing I did was good enough, and I had to do it over and over again. No praise or encouragement for doing anything right, just relentless swearing and abuse. My mind harked back to Farmer Davy's words: "He's a very difficult man to get on with, and he will try his utmost to break you!" There was no way I was going to give him the satisfaction to do that!

On the fifteenth day of the month, I helped Frank and Pamela prepare the hounds' food. We filled the feeding trough with cooked flesh, meat stock, root vegetables, oatmeal, barley meal, wheat meal and maize. After removing the bones, we mashed it up with a big masher, a bit like a potato masher only much bigger and with a T shaped handle.

Finally, we plunged our bare hands into the trough, right up to our elbows, and meticulously picked out any small bones that had escaped us earlier. This is done, not only to prevent hounds choking on them, but also to prevent them from secreting them behind their teeth and fighting over them later, when they are back in their lodges.

Usually, after I had helped Frank with this job I was given another one, but this time he pointed to the wall behind the feeding trough and said, "Stay there boy and don't speak unless you are spoken to! I am now going to give you your first lesson in hound management and pack leadership so, mark, learn and inwardly digest!"

At this point, Pamela appeared and opened the bitch hounds' door and let them out. I stood there fascinated as sixty-five bitch hounds rushed flat out down the corridor to the feed trough - each hound vying to get as much food into its belly in the shortest possible time!

Frank knew exactly how much food the pack needed on any particular day, and also how much food each individual hound needed on that day. The ones that needed less food were removed from the trough after they only had a few mouthfuls, while the others were left longer.

The first hound told to leave the trough was Audrey. The words of command Frank used were: 'Audrey, Leave-it', which she did immediately. Next was Primrose, next Harriett and so on. As each hound was ordered to leave the trough, Pamela let it out into the communal exercise paddock, until all the bitch hounds were out there. Then it was the turn of the sixty-five dog hounds, and the same procedure was followed to the letter. What impressed me the most was that not one single hound refused to leave the feeding trough immediately when ordered to do so.

~~~

The last two weeks of my trial period went much faster; in fact, a lot too fast for my liking. I had to learn the names of over one hundred and forty hounds and be able to identify and name them from any angle and in all weathers. So far I could only name seventy-two, and if I couldn't name them all, I wouldn't win the apprenticeship. I would have failed - just like the other twenty-seven boys that had tried to win it.

And that wasn't all. On the first day of my month's trial period, I was given a hunting crop and told to practice cracking it in my spare time. Not an easy task, by any means.

The type of hunting crop huntsmen and their assistants use has a fairly stiff stock that is twenty inches in length. The thong is made of tightly plaited, high quality leather, which is over fifty inches in length by approximately half an inch in diameter, tapering down to one eighth of an inch. The lash is attached to this. The lash is just a few inches in length, and looks a bit like a small piece of thick bootlace. The lash is what gives the whip its crack. The Americans call this the cracker!

Two weeks later, feeling a bit cocky with my progress, I asked Mr Gerry to give me his honest opinion on my progress so far. In response to that, he said, "Not bad boy, but that's just the easy part."

He then, took me to the flesh house and said, "Do you see those three big black blowflies, on the wall, three feet away from you?"

"Yes I do," I replied.

"Now, I want you to stand exactly where you are and cut the middle one in half with the tail end of your whip, as you crack it," he said.

I tried and tried, but missed every time, and then huffed, "It's not possible."

"Not possible, boy," he roared as he took the whip off me and effortlessly cracked it ten times, cutting ten blowflies in half in as many seconds!

"So, what's that on the floor boy, chicken shit? You've got two weeks to learn, or else," he said, icily.

When I was at work I was told to drape my hunting crop over my neck, like you see some modern doctors do with their stethoscopes when doing their hospital rounds. At first, I thought this must be some sort of practical joke that Frank was playing on me, like telling an engineering apprentice to go to the stores and ask for a left handed screwdriver!

When I asked Frank, "Why do I have to do this?" he said, "Just do it - until I tell you differently."

Then, seeing that Frank and Pamela carried their hunting crops in the same fashion for most of the time, and that the hunting crops are so well balanced that you hardly know they're there, I surmised that there must be a very important reason for this, and it wasn't something you joke about!

Every day Frank and Pamela took the whole pack of hounds out of the kennels' gate for road exercise. This started with Frank waiting outside as Pamela opened the door and let them out. Then, in a cheerful voice, he cried, "Yere Little Fellers," as he walked on with his pack of Foxhounds following on behind him, through the gate and up the lane towards Stowford, with Pamela keeping up the rear.

While I was standing by the door, in readiness to shut it after Pamela had let out the hounds, I noticed that she had her hunting crop draped around her neck, right up until she had passed through the door. Then, a split second later at the speed of light, it was in her hand ready for use, as she hurried along to catch up with the pack.

"Wow, serious stuff!" I thought out loud.

On the seventeenth day of my month's trial period, Frank told me to follow on behind Pamela. For a mile and a half, not a word was spoken and nothing untoward happened. Then, suddenly, a hound called Gory saw a rabbit and went to chase it, but Pamela had also seen the rabbit and, quick as a flash, she shouted, "Gory Leave-it," as she cracked her hunting crop alongside and barely half an inch away from his ear a split second later.

In a cheerful voice, without breaking stride or even looking round, Frank cried out, "Yere Gory, there's a good little fella," as Gory melted back into the pack.

"Wow, that's neat!" I thought to myself.

After lunch, Frank prodded, "Well little old boy, what are your thoughts as to what happened this morning?"

"It all seemed to happen within a couple of seconds … as if by magic!"

"Magic, that's not magic boy. That's highly skilled teamwork, handed down from master to apprentice in an unbroken line, over countless generations. And it's never seen anywhere other than in Foxhounds and Staghounds. But that's not to say that a properly schooled pack of hounds doesn't think that hunting crops don't have magical properties, or that formally trained huntsmen don't have eyes in the back of their heads, and must be obeyed at all times!" he quipped.

With that, he took Pamela and me to the flesh house. Then, pointing to the end wall, he said testily, "Out of the two of you, I want to see who can cut all five of those blowflies in half with the tail end of your whip as you crack it."

Pamela got five and I got four. Two days later I got five and Pamela got five. Pamela congratulated me, but Frank just said, "Not bad boy, but don't let it go to your head."

On the last day of my trial period, and much to my surprise, Frank grudgingly proclaimed, "You have won your apprenticeship. But don't think for one moment, boy, that you are out of the wood yet. You now have another five years of trial by ordeal to endure under my mentorship before you can become a qualified huntsman. So, do you want to run back to Mummy, or can you take it on the chin like a man?"

I replied, defiantly "I disowned both my mother and father several years ago and if you reckon that you can break me, you can think again because many tougher men than you have tried and rued the day."

I knew I was pushing my luck with this tough talk, bearing in mind that the Lamerton is run and financed by West Devon farmers for West Devon farmers, and that twenty-seven West Devon farmer's sons had tried to win the apprenticeship before I came. Frank was a farmer's son but I'm not, and if I couldn't keep a civil tongue in my head, then the apprenticeship might be taken away from me. Despite all that, I still couldn't help myself. Everyone in authority so far had either deceived me or let me down.

Frank looked at me thoughtfully for quite a while and then said, "Yes boy, there is definitely more to you than meets the eye. Now get back to your digs and get a good night's sleep because tomorrow is the first day of your apprenticeship, and it's going to be a very long, busy day."

Earlier in the day Frank gave me one of the Lamerton Hunt's information sheets and told me to read it before coming to work the next day. After I had my tea, I read it and this is what it said: -

The Lamerton Hunt is run and financed by West Devon farmers for West Devon farmers, and should not, for any reason, be confused with snob Hunts, run by hoity toities, solely for sport.

The main purpose of the Lamerton is conservation: keeping the fox population down, to a reasonable level.

The fox's natural prey is rabbit, but if the Lamerton does not kill enough foxes, then there will be too many foxes, with not enough rabbits for them to eat. Therefore, they will kill the farmer's lambs and other small livestock. On the other hand, if the Lamerton kills too many foxes, then there will not be enough foxes left to keep the rabbit population down to a reasonable level. Therefore, in turn, there will be a plague of rabbits, devouring the farmer's crops!

The Lamerton's kennels are set in sixty acres of fertile land, deep in the glorious West Devon countryside. Seventy couple of Foxhounds (that's one hundred and forty hounds) eight Hunt Terriers and four magnificent Hunters are kept there.

The hounds are housed in four lodges, line abreast. The dog hounds live in the first lodge and the bitch hounds in the second. Bitch hounds that are in season live in the third and hounds that are sick or injured live in the fourth. The walls of the lodges are made of quarried stone and are three feet thick, as are all the walls of the kennel complex. The floors throughout the kennel complex consist of ultra-smooth concrete, of the highest quality.

The floor space of each lodge measures, approximately, thirty-nine feet by twenty-five feet. The sleeping area of each lodge takes up twenty-five feet by nine feet of this. The remaining thirty feet by twenty-five feet of floor space is used by the hounds to relieve themselves if they need to, or drink from the running water trough when they are thirsty. Each lodge's sleeping area consists of a wall to wall wooden slatted bed, filled up to the brim with best quality wheat straw, which is changed daily.

All the woodwork throughout the kennel complex is made of top grade seasoned oak. Each lodge's sleeping quarters has a stable type door, and each lodge's yard has a plain standard type door, opening into a corridor. Halfway down the corridor there's a wrought iron gate, opening out to a large exercise paddock. The top half of the corridor wall, on the exercise paddock side, is also made of wrought iron. This allows an unobstructed view of the hounds, when they are in the exercise paddock.

At the end of the corridor, in its own space, is the hounds' communal feeding trough, which is made of stainless steel and is specifically designed for foxhound kennels. It's approximately ten feet long by three feet wide and eighteen inches deep. To the right of this is the cookhouse.

There's another plain door in the dog hounds' yard, opening out onto the 'kennel plat' and the main kennels gate beyond. Plat, or Platt, is a centuries' old word for a large lawn that's constantly grazed by the kennels' billy goat, which naturally keeps the turf in good shape. A billy goat's presence has a therapeutic calming effect on packs of hounds, when kennelled. A donkey has the same effect on racehorses.

The kennel plat is used for social events such as the annual hound puppy show, when they come back to the kennels after being 'walked' for several months by local farmers. It's also where apprentice huntsmen are initially taught to ride.

Five hunt terriers are kept; they live in one of the haystacks. The hay is for the hunters to eat and when one stack is depleted, they move into an adjoining one. Besides, being used to help dig out foxes, when they go to ground, they kill hundreds of kennel rats every year.

The Hunters that carry the Huntsman and his Assistants live in the stables, behind the kennels. Three are kept. Two of these are thoroughbred Hunters and the other one is three-quarters thoroughbred and one quarter Cleveland Bay. This gives him the extra strength and stamina to carry the First Whip, who's a bit on the heavy side.

~~~

The next day I was at work bright and early, with a spring in my step. I had won my five-year apprenticeship and was looking forward to learning all those exclusive disciplines in hounds, horses and horsemanship, which the Norman's brought to England in 1066.

I admit I was also inspired and excited by the stirring words that Farmer Davy gave me on the first day of my month's trial period. So much so, that I decided to tell Frank what he said.

I emphasised the bit where he said: "As a Lamerton huntsman, you ride the best horses that money can buy. These horses have a great turn of speed that they can keep up all day, so that you can keep up with your hounds which also have a great turn of speed that they can keep up all day. There's no time for pussyfooting around, boy, you're expected to ride straight across country, over high fences, wide ditches, five bar gates and anything else that crosses your path!"

After getting me to repeat what Farmer Davy had said over again, Frank crowed, "That's just about right boy, it's all part of the job!"

"So, when am I going to learn to ride?" I asked.

"Didn't that school of yours teach you?" he prodded.

"Only in theory. They fobbed me off by telling me the Army would teach me the Army way when I was old enough." I replied.

"Hah, just like the chinless wonders I saw at Aldershot when I was stationed there during the war, bloody idiots!" he raged.

I then added the bit where Farmer Davy had said, "Mr Gerry is a very difficult man to get on with and he will try his utmost to break you. If he can't break you, he'll teach you everything he knows."

"Yes that just about sums it up, boy," he replied.

Later in the day, still wanting to know when I was going to be taught to ride properly, I brought the subject up again. He looked at me with a painful expression on his face and retorted, "Well I'll be damned, you and your passion for horses! Now you get this straight, boy. Horses, as far as I'm concerned, are just a means of keeping up with the hounds and nothing else. So the quicker you get this into your thick skull, the better it will be for all concerned. I'll teach you when I'm good and ready."

Two hours before I was due to finish work, Frank said, "Go round to the stables and help Fred Cole.

Seeing a man grooming a big bay horse, I asked him, "Are you Mr Cole?"

"I suppose I am boy," he said, "but as you are now an apprentice and a member of staff, you should call me Fred."

"Yes, Mr Fred," I replied.

"No, boy, just Fred," he corrected.

"What's the horse called?" I asked.

"His name is Warrior, he's a heavyweight hunter and he's a bit wild at the moment!"

"Why is that?" I asked.

"It's because he's just up from grass," he replied.

"Oh, I see," I nodded.

"So, now you're here boy, you can hold his head, while I finish grooming him," he said.

I knew a bit about Fred Cole, from what Farmer Davy had told me. Fred was one of the best horsemen on the planet at that time. Before he came to the Lamerton, he had reached the dizzy heights of Stud groom and

Stallion man to both King George the Fifth and King George the Sixth, respectively. So, while I was holding Warrior's head, I ventured, "Hey Fred, can you give me some proper riding lessons?"

"No boy, I'm not allowed to. Frank will teach you himself, when he thinks the time is right. My job, as far as you are concerned, is to teach you everything about horses, but not how to ride them."

The following day, Frank told me that he had a little test for me after I finished work. When I badgered him to tell me what it was, he refused to tell me. He was on and off the phone all day and laughing a lot, as were the people on the other end of the line, which led me to believe that I was being set up for something.

Around about six o'clock, Kenny Harris arrived, riding his little son's tiny Exmoor pony. Kenny was well over six feet tall and the pony was only 13.2 hands high, so Kenny's feet were almost touching the ground. Kenny owned a small mixed farm and was also the Lamerton's part time 2nd Whip. I liked Kenny a lot, he was always laughing and joking, but seeing him like this, was too funny for words.

Hearing me laughing, Frank's wife, Dorothy and Pamela, his daughter, came out of their cottage to see what was going on. They were just in time to see Kenny handing the pony over to Frank, who looked at me and growled, "Stop laughing boy and come over here, I'm going to give you your first riding lesson."

"What, on that little thing!" I sneered.

"Ah, so you're a top class rider eh? In that case boy, you won't need a saddle," he goaded, whilst taking it off the pony's back.

"Seeing that everyone was laughing at me, I gritted my teeth and spat out, "What do you want me to do?"

"Well boy, do you see that post and rails fence over where Dorothy and Pamela are standing?" he asked.

"Yes," I replied.

"Get up on the pony and jump him over that little baby fence," he prodded. I did what I was told, and promptly fell off in the process, amidst roars of laughter.

What everyone else knew, but I didn't, was that this clever little pony didn't like strangers getting on his back and over the years he had come up with a few tricks of his own to deal with the situation. In my case, sensing that he wasn't saddled and my feet must be dangling in mid-air, he skimmed the fence with his legs tucked in under his body, thereby hooking my feet under the top bar of the fence and dragging me off his back.

I jumped back on him, but he wasn't going to give in and neither was I. He kicked and bucked like crazy, arching his back and jumping straight up in the air with all four hoofs off the ground. Then he reared up on his hind legs, punching the air with his forelegs whilst snorting down his nostrils with anger. His blood was up and so was mine so, as soon as I got him pointed in the right direction, I galloped him flat out at the fence on the assumption that he would not be able to skim it and hook me off. It was a crazy idea I knew, but I felt I had no other choice.

It worked like a dream, but as I wasn't used to riding without a saddle and stirrups, I came down heavily when we landed. The pain was so excruciating that I had to get off the pony and sit on the ground with my head between my knees and be violently sick.

"What's up boy?" Kenny quipped.

As I was about to tell him what was wrong, I saw Pamela coming towards me with a worried expression on her face, so I squeaked, "It's nothing Kenny, I'll be alright in a minute." Well, you just didn't discuss things like that, in the presence of young ladies!

In the morning, at work, I asked Frank if I had passed yesterday's test. "Well, boy, you did manage to get over the little fence on your second attempt without falling off, but next Thursday I have another little test for you. After all, it's only fair that you let the little pony have a return match on his home ground!" he exclaimed.

Next Thursday, Frank took me over to Kenny Harris's farm for the little pony's return match! We saw Kenny in a big ten-acre field where he was watching his twelve-year old son riding the little pony, so we quickly hastened over to join them.

"Hello Frank," says Kenny, "I see you've brought the champion jockey with you!"

"Yes, here he is, but he says he's still a bit sore, so we will let him have a saddle and we won't get him to do any jumps this time," Frank said mockingly.

"What do you want me to do?" I asked, testily.

"Same as Kenny's little boy was doing - gallop him up and down the field," he replied.

"I shrugged my shoulders and mounted the pony. Before I could get my feet in the stirrups, Frank gave him a great big slap on the rump and off he went like a rocket! Where the little pony thought he was going I cared not; neither did I worry about getting my feet in the stirrups. I was having too much fun to bother about such niceties as I spurred him on.

Then, straight ahead of me I saw a great big bomb crater coming up fast. It must have been at least twenty feet deep. I pulled on the reins with all my strength, but to no avail. I thought to myself that this crazy pony must have a death wish like me, but he hadn't. He chickened out and skidded to a halt at the very last moment, jettisoning me over his head, straight into the bomb crater.

As I flew through the air and hit the ground, I realized that I had been duped again. But this time I was already planning my revenge, not on the little pony but on Frank and Kenny. Luckily for me, I had been trained to fall by experts and so I didn't break any bones; I just had a few bruises. To get my own back, I decided to make out I was dead.

Seeing that I wasn't moving, Kenny ran back to the farmhouse to get a long rope and a stretcher.

After lowering Frank down to the bottom of the crater, he cried out, "Is he dead?"

"No. He's still breathing, but he's unconscious. I've put him on the stretcher and I'm climbing back up the rope to help you pull him up."

By the time they had pulled me up and stretchered me halfway to the farmhouse, they were puffing like a couple of old broken down nags. On top of that, they were sweating buckets, partly from their exertions, but also because they thought that I was seriously injured and they would get the blame.

I smiled to myself and let them suffer until we had almost reached the farmhouse. As I couldn't contain my laughter any longer, I sat up and quipped, "Thanks for the ride chaps, but I must get back to my digs, or I will be late for my tea!" The look on their faces was priceless!

As I started work the following day, Frank came up to me and said, "Do you want the little pony to be put down, after what he did to you?"

"No I don't," I snapped, "he was only doing what he had to do to get me off his back. I would have done the same if I had to,"

"Well, little old boy, that just about wraps it up. You've passed both of my little tests," he said.

"Piece of cake," I said, quietly.

"What's that boy?" he asked.

"Nothing, I was just thinking back to what someone said at school," I replied.

~~~

Every day at feeding time, throughout the next month, my initial lessons in hound management and pack leadership continued with: "Don't speak until you are spoken to, and mark, learn and inwardly digest." That was also the case when Frank and Pamela took the pack out for road work exercise, with me still tagging along behind.

After another month of this, I asked Frank if I could have some time off.

"Time off, boy! What do you think this is - a holiday camp? ... How much time do you want, and what do you want it for?" he huffed.

"I need a month off to go to Okehampton and take some riding lessons," I replied.

"So you want some riding lessons eh. So why didn't you say so in the first place?" he asked.

I was flabbergasted! I just stood there with my mouth wide open. Time after time I had asked him to give me some proper riding lessons, and each time he had refused.

"Have you lost your tongue boy? Go and ask Fred to give you a horse, and be on the kennel plat every evening for the next six weeks," he spluttered.

On the last day of those six weeks, Kenny brought his best hunter over for me to ride. Past experience should have warned me that Frank and Kenny were up to something, which they were, but this time in a kindly way. Not that I would have thought so, as the hunter acted up like a bucking bronco in a rodeo show as soon as I got up on its back.

Frank and Kenny watched and waited until the hunter realised that it couldn't throw me off and stood still and refused to move! Kenny then came over to me and offered me his whip and said, "Take it," which I did. As I took the whip, the hunter's ears pricked up and he did everything perfectly, like the thoroughbred he was.

After I handed Kenny's hunter back to him, Frank declared, "Well boy, now you know why you always carry a whip when riding a horse. It's as I keep telling you - a whip is not an instrument of torture, it's a signal to the horse to carry out the task that it was originally schooled to do, just as a hunting crop is, when you're handling a pack of hounds. Furthermore, when you have ridden horses at professional level as long as Kenny and me, you will know that horses and other animals suffer more cruelty by so called 'kindness' from well-meaning people than anything else. So next time I tell you to do something, you do it without question!"

My face was beetroot red with embarrassment, but I had learnt a very important lesson that I would never forget.

Seeing that I was thoroughly ashamed of myself for behaving like some anthropomorphic, 'do-gooder', Kenny gave me a pat on the back and said "Don't take it too hard Charlie, we all have to learn.

Frank chimed in, "Well, boy, do you now understand what I have been telling you all along?"

"Yes, I do Frank, sir," I replied.

Turning to face Kenny and throwing his hands up in the air, he exclaimed, "What are we going to do with him?"

"Shoot him?" Kenny offered, with a wry smile on his face.

~~~

After completing my course of horse riding lessons, it was August and time to start schooling the young hounds that had been puppy walked by pro-hunting farmers. So far, I had only seen highly schooled hounds with perfect manners, but seeing this wild bunch of unruly young hounds, I wondered how on earth they could be licked into shape in time for the next hunting season that would start in just a few weeks' time.

As if reading my thoughts, Frank laughed and said, "No worries boy, no worries! The puppy walkers have done a proper job, with this lot. They were told to allow them to grow up without any form of restraint, and they've done just that."

"But how are you going to train them in such a short time?" I asked.

"Train them, boy. What do think they are? Rose bushes! You don't train hounds; you *school* them. And the same thing applies to all canine beings," he thundered, as he walked away from me, shaking his head.

After putting the young hounds in with the old hounds, he said, "When we go in to see them in about two hours' time, they will rush forward and try to jump up on us, in an endeavour to lick our faces. The old ones will stay back, as they were taught to do when they were the same age as those young ones!"

"What do you do to train … sorry … I mean, *school* them, not to do that?" I asked.

"Damn me, are you trying to wind me up, boy?" he roared.

"No Frank, it was just a slip of the tongue," I said, apologetically.

"It had better be, because if you ever use that ridiculously uncouth word in my presence again, I'll ring your scrawny neck!" he growled.

"Now then, boy, you pay full attention to what I say. When a Foxhound, or any other breed of dog for that matter, is allowed to jump up on us and lick our faces, it is hardwired by nature to feel that it is of a higher status than the people that allow it to behave in such a way. Unknowledgeable people exacerbate the situation further by sticking their hands out to protect themselves, whilst babbling out useless phrases such as 'get off, get down', etc. Do you understand, boy? Because if you don't, you don't belong here!"

Seeing that I was paying full attention to what he was saying, he went on, "As part of my overall schooling plan, these young hounds have been deliberately allowed to habitually get away with jumping up on people. As a consequence, when they jump up on you, they will do so at great speed, and under the mistaken belief that they will land on a very soft target, such as your chest or stomach. Their front feet will hit you in those vulnerable places with tremendous force if you don't take effective action."

"Wow, Frank! All those hounds coming at you all at once sounds rather scary," I said.

"Yes, it is, if, you don't know what you're doing, and so I had better tell you what you must do, in no uncertain terms. Not just for your own protection, but also so you don't ruin these young hounds' prospects at this very critical stage of their schooling, before it's even started. Mark my words, boy, because, if, you get it wrong after all the time and effort that has gone into the preparation for this moment, I will have your guts for garters! This is what you do boy: You stand perfectly still until the very precise moment that they are in mid-air, then you turn sideways, causing them to miss their supposedly 'soft target' and land heavily on their front feet. Then, before they recover from the shock, you give them the command, 'Get back,' in a gruff tone of voice. They won't know what 'Get back' means, but seeing the old hounds have wisely stayed back and are staring at them as if they are stupid, they will feel awkward and out of place and they will have no other alternative than to get back into the pack."

Two hours later we put this awesome, centuries' old piece of schooling into practice, and it worked perfectly. It was very exciting, with an element of danger thrown in for good measure, which pleased me immensely. It was also very hectic too. At one moment the young ones were coming at us, thick and fast from all directions and at great speed and velocity, as they leapt through the air. Then at the next moment, with the exception of one or two stragglers, they were all back with the old ones, with respect for us written all over their faces.

We repeated this exercise at two hourly intervals throughout the day until they stayed back with the rest of the pack when we appeared.

"Not bad, not bad, so what do you think of that?" Frank crowed, after it was over.

This was indeed a first - he forgot to call me 'boy' - so I was thinking to myself that he must be pleased with my progress this time!

"Cat got your tongue, boy?" he prodded.

"Err … n…no … it was pure magic," I stuttered.

"That's not magic, boy, that's pure old fashioned logic, and it's only part of the exercise, as you will see tomorrow," he replied.

Over the next three days, Frank concentrated on the final part of this exercise, which was to teach the young hounds to stay back until their name was called. To do this, Frank called a few of the older hounds to him by name with the jolly cry of 'Yere Vulcan', 'Yere Archer' or whatever the particular hound's name was.

Initially, as these older hounds came to him, some of the young rooky hounds tried to follow suite, only to be sternly rebuked by Frank with a well-timed, 'Get back', which stopped most of them in their tracks. The more persistent ones were either dragged back or driven back with a well-placed crack of the whip.

This was my job, and whilst I was doing it I noticed that some of the old hounds were not only giving these young delinquent hounds black looks, but they also growled at them the next time they were about to get it wrong. I also noticed that some of the young ones sported a few cuts and bruises, so it was obvious that the older, higher status hounds had disciplined them during the night for upsetting the status quo the day before.

While all this was taking place, I was thinking that this Frank was a very clever man!

Two days later, as if reading my thoughts yet again, he said, "The clever ones, boy, are the people that worked it out in the first place, all those centuries ago. If they were here today, they would tell you that, as far as schooling hounds is concerned, any fool can knock them back, break their spirit and ruin their hunting instincts in the process, but bringing them on and channelling those instincts is the job of a highly qualified professional. Stop dreaming, boy, and come with me, we've got work to do. These young hounds won't school themselves, you know."

All the hounds, both young and old, were assembled and were waiting expectantly. Then, as we approached them, they all moved back from us and waited to see what was going to happen. The young hounds were expecting Frank to call a few of the old hounds to him, but instead, he started calling the young hounds to him, one at a time.

The first three to be called were Sailor, Sinbad, and Bashful. "Yere Sailor!" cried Frank cheerfully, but Sailor was too scared to move. I was half expecting Frank to raise his voice, but he didn't. Instead, he lowered it, lower and lower, until he was speaking so quietly that I could not hear him at all. But Sailor could and was heartened by it. So much so, that he came to Frank and lay down at his feet. "There's a good little fella, there's a good little fella!" he whispered so quietly that I had to strain my ears to hear what he was saying.

Sinbad was next. As he was Sailor's litter brother and they had both been puppy walked by the same farmer, he wanted to be with him, so the moment he was called he was off like a shot. But poor Bashful went to pieces when it was his turn. He started off all right, but then Valiant, one of the old hounds who had it in for him, growled at him, which caused him to panic and hide behind the other hounds.

"Valiant Leave-it damn 'e!" roared Frank. Then in a much kinder and quieter voice, he said, "Yere Bashful." Bashful, seeing that Valiant was slinking off with his tail between his legs, came to Frank and was told that he was a good little fella! Taking heart from this, the rest of the young hounds had no trouble with this after that.

After schooling the young hounds in this exercise several times during the next two weeks it was time to move onto the next one, which was to take the young hounds out with the rest of the pack for road exercise. The first one to be taken out with the pack was a young hound called Barrister, who was coupled up to a steady old hound called Victor.

After Frank had double checked the couples to make sure that they were adjusted correctly, a quick good luck kiss from Pamela, and a cheery, "Yere little fellas," from Frank, we were off - out of the kennel's main gates and down the lane. For half a mile nothing untoward happened, and then Barrister saw some rabbits. But, I had seen them before he did and as he went to chase them, I shouted, "Barrister 'Leave-it'!" Knowing full well that he would ignore my command, I cracked my hunting crop alongside his ear a split second later.

This procedure was not only to teach him not to chase rabbits but also to remind him that when Frank cries, 'Yere, little fellas', he must follow him, regardless of anything else. We walked on for another mile without seeing any more rabbits, so we turned back. On the way back, Barrister stared at some rabbits and when I shouted, "Barrister, Leave it," he quickly averted his gaze and trotted on like a good hound should!

Hearing me ordering Barrister to 'Leave-it' without putting a crack alongside his ear, Frank picked up on this. He presumed, correctly, that Barrister had now ignored the rabbits and praised him with a cheerful, 'There's a good little fella!' He did this without turning his head or breaking his stride as if to say that body language is everything when schooling hounds, or any species of animal for that matter.

Three more young hounds were taken out with the old hounds that same day, with the same results. The next day, four more were taken out and so on, until all sixteen young hounds had been taken out. This procedure was repeated until they had all been out twice. Then it was time to test them without couples. Some of them tried to take advantage of this, but their heart wasn't really in it; the previous schooling had taken the fire out of their bellies, and so they were easily persuaded to conform to the status quo.

With this part of the young hounds schooling complete, Frank and Pamela took them out with the rest of the pack, for road exercise. When they got back, I asked Frank how the young hounds behaved and grudgingly he said, "Not bad, boy, not bad."

Pamela then reared up on him and growled, "Not bad! They were blooming marvelous - the best we've ever had!"

With that, he glared at her and roared: "You hold your tongue girl and only speak when you're spoken to," as he stormed off into the woods.

Now that the young hounds were well into their schooling, they were much more subservient, which made feeding time a lot less strenuous for both Pamela and me. Instead of having to drag them away from the feeding trough when Frank said, "Leave-it", they now left the trough immediately and without any hassle. There was also a remarkable change in their bearing and in the dignified way they carried themselves, just like soldiers after receiving basic training.

I commented on this to Frank and he said, "Yes, boy, they've had just the right amount of schooling; firstly in kennel discipline, then in exercise discipline, to prepare them for their field discipline, which will complete their schooling and turn them into proper hunting hounds!"

Watching me like a hawk and seeing that I was hanging onto his every word, he continued, "Under my tutelage, over the next five years, you will learn exactly how much schooling in kennel discipline you must give young hounds before you school them in exercise discipline. And then again, exactly how much of that you must give them before you can start schooling them in their field discipline. Moreover, always school them in that order, boy, and never ever try to school them the other way round!"

Quickly recognizing that he was in a reasonable mind, I asked: "Does the field discipline start with cub hunting?"

"Yes, it does," he replied. "We start cub hunting in three days' time. You won't be taking an active part in it until you have more riding experience, and that won't be until you are in the second or third year of your apprenticeship. Until then, boy, you mark, learn and take in what's going on. This time, Kenny will take you and keep an eye on you, so that you can see for yourself how much riding experience this entails. That's if he can find a horse for you."

Three days later, Kenny arrived on his hunter leading his son's little pony.

"I'm not riding that! I'll be a laughing stock. Both you and Frank are laughing at me already," I complained.

Seeing I was about to blow my top, Pamela said, "You take Messerschmitt, Charlie. I'm not going. I wouldn't be seen dead with these two clowns after the way they've treated you!"

Her pony was named Messerschmitt after a German Messerschmitt fighter plane crash landed in the field where he was grazing. A piece of metal flew off and damaged a small nerve in his right foreleg. This was in World War 2 when he was a three year old foal. I was very fond of Messerschmitt and so, of course, was Pamela. He was quite big for a pony, just under fifteen hands high, and despite his previous injury, he was very surefooted and very bold over fences, though he did flip his fore left hoof sometimes.

A few minutes later, Frank mounted Mischief, his big chestnut hunter, and trotted off with his sixteen young hounds following on behind him. Fred, the Lamerton's first whip, who was already mounted on Warrior, his heavyweight bay hunter, immediately took up his place behind them. Kenny was mounted on his big bay hunter, Beethoven, and I was on Pamela's Messerschmitt, riding beside him.

We rode in silence for almost half an hour, when Fred turned in the saddle and exclaimed, "You've done a really good job helping Frank school these young hounds, Charlie."

"Thanks, Fred. Pamela said the same thing," I replied.

"That's enough of that," Frank snarled. Kenny laughed and said, "You're in for it now Charlie!"

Fifteen minutes later, we arrived at a large sheep farm where the new owner of the farm was waiting to welcome us. He had lost so many lambs to foxes that he was almost bankrupt. On top of that, the foxes had killed and eaten all the wild rabbits that his family and his workers' families relied on to feed themselves.

On the way to the farm, Kenny had already declared, "The previous owner's way of dealing with his plague of foxes was gassing and shooting them, which had backfired on him, leaving him more overrun with them than he was in the first place!" Warming up to his subject, he continued, "Gassing foxes is a hit and miss affair and smacks of Hitler's horrific death camps. Shooting is not much better either; it takes an expert marksman to kill foxes cleanly, so more often than not, they are wounded and die a very painful death."

We didn't have to go far to find foxes; they were everywhere. When the young hounds saw the foxes, they weren't sure what to do. Their instincts told them to chase them, but their previous conditioning not to chase rabbits held them back.

My heart was in my mouth. "What if, they don't give chase? Because if, they don't - I'm bound to get the blame." I said, to Kenny.

"That's for sure, but don't worry Charlie, just sit tight," he said. The words were hardly out of his mouth when they were off after a big dog fox. Frank was tooting his horn whilst galloping his horse alongside them, which really set them alight!

Unfortunately, this one was too big and powerful for them and easily got away, leaving them somewhat disheartened. Then they spotted a young, half-grown vixen and took off after her. They soon caught up with her and killed her. With their hunting instincts now fully aroused, they went on to kill two more half-grown foxes and one three-quarters grown one, before going home.

We visited the same farm several times over the rest of the week and killed all the half-grown and three-quarters grown foxes; also seven fully-grown sick ones that had been maimed by the previous owner of the farm. All the full grown foxes, with the exception of just a few breeding pairs, were hunted down and killed when the Foxhunting season started in earnest, six weeks later.

These few breeding pairs would kill enough rabbits to prevent the rabbit population devastating the farmer's crops, but would also leave enough rabbits for them and their offspring to eat, thereby curbing their need to kill the farmer's lambs. This would also leave enough rabbits for the new sheep farmer's family and his workers' families to eat.

In conclusion: The new sheep farmer reared a bumper crop of lambs the next time around, thereby saving himself from bankruptcy. The young hounds which I came to think of as 'my hounds', became some of the best the Lamerton had ever seen.

Frank's reaction to this was to half my wages on the grounds that 'I might be about to become too big for my boots,' as he put it. Personally, I didn't care two hoots, because I found other ways of reimbursing myself.

My best mate at that time was a boy called Harry. He was the oldest son of the sheep farmer who had the fox problem. Adjacent to his father's farm there was this old retired Admiral who went pheasant shooting on his country estate with his Labrador. The Admiral was a crack shot and never missed his target, but as far as handling a gundog was concerned he was totally useless. When he shot pheasants he often sent his dog in the wrong direction, so we would send one of the farm sheepdogs in to steal them. Butchers paid a lot of money for pheasants in those days – and they still do, so I've been told.

Another good little earner was pulling tractors out of the unforgiving West Devon clay with our dependable heavy Shire horses at £5 a time - when these unwieldy 'new-fangled' machines got bogged down. £5 was a lot of money then, and I admit I had no scruples regarding ripping off this new flashy generation of farmers who were putting my traditional ploughmen friends and their horses out of work. They didn't earn much money in the first place, and now that the tractors were coming in they were having their wages cut again and again.

The more I ripped those spoilers off, the more money I had to share with my old friends now they were falling on hard times. I knew I was fighting a lost cause, trying to help them in any way I could. I also knew that, just as when the Cavalry was mechanized, traditional farming, even in West Devon, would soon go the same way. However, I was not prepared for the traumatic way it would happen.

The Ministry of Agriculture, which had become overly powerful during World War 2, was more or less forcing farmers to replace their heavy horses with tractors, irrespective of whether or not they were suitable for that purpose. In the case of West Devon's heavy clay and patchwork of tiny fields, tractors were absolutely useless. They were also informing everyone that the horses would be painlessly destroyed, but what they actually did was to have them shipped off to glue factories and slaughterhouses all over Europe.

During those long traumatic journeys, the horses were not fed or watered; neither were they painlessly destroyed when they finally reached their destinations. When the ploughmen heard about this, they were shocked to their inner core. I had just turned nineteen, and seeing these great big strong macho men sobbing their hearts out, cut me to the quick. But there was worse to come when two of the best friends I ever had went and hung themselves. This gave me yet another reason to hate and distrust the British Establishment and its deceitful ways.

Forcing farmers to tear down hedgerows and making the fields bigger so that tractors would have more room to manoeuvre, was spoiling the beautiful West Devon countryside and damaging the soil structure in the process. It certainly was not a good idea!

Yet another way to make money was to go to rodeos in Okehampton, and ride unbroken Dartmoor ponies. You got large sums of money for staying on them for a full five minutes. Numerous men and boys stayed on for two or three minutes, and some for three or four, but very few indeed stayed on for the full five.

Those of us that stayed on the ponies for the full amount of time were paid handsomely, but those that didn't weren't paid anything at all for their pains and, sometimes, broken bones. The owners got their ponies broken in at a fraction of the cost than if they did it themselves and, of course, without risking life and limb.

Frank ranted and raved when he found out about this, but there was nothing he could do about what I got up to in my spare time. I was also spending a lot of time hanging out with ploughmen and draymen who were showing me how to handle their big heavy horses. These horses were mainly Shires and Clydesdales which I adored, and still, do.

What annoyed him even more was that, as far as he was concerned, horses were no more than a means of keeping up with his beloved hounds, and as soon as I got that into my thick skull, the better it would be for all concerned!

Don't get me wrong, I liked the hounds a lot and worked hard at looking after them and learning all about them but, as far as Frank was concerned, that wasn't enough. He felt that, deep down inside me, there was a smouldering passion for hounds yet to be released.

So, in a desperate attempt to kick start that passion into action; he came up with a plan. This was to have me formally trained in all aspects of breeding and training gun dogs and sheepdogs, as well as that of hounds and hunt terriers, which I was already doing under his personal tuition. However, knowing that the Germans were fifty years ahead of Britain in police dog breeding and training, he decided to add that to my curriculum.

In exchange for taking on this extra work, he promised he would get me on a six-month scholarship in advanced horsemanship at the prestigious Spanish School of Equitation, in Vienna.

Because I was already 'going through the mill' with foxhounds and foxhunting, I didn't have to wait years to learn the good stuff, though I still doubted that I would master all these disciplines in time to go to Vienna.

But then I hadn't counted on those giants whose broad shoulders I was so privileged to stand on; those venerable head gamekeepers, master shepherds and German police dog Gurus. Thanks to them I eventually mastered all of the above disciplines and Frank kept to his end of the bargain - I got my six-month scholarship to go to the prestigious Spanish

School of Equitation in Vienna.

~~~

I had just a few weeks of my apprenticeship left to serve after I came back from Vienna, but despite all Frank's efforts, my passion for horses had not abated at all. If anything, it was even stronger. He was philosophical about it and said, "Well boy you can take a horse to water but you can't make it drink, so I suppose you'll soon be moving on."

"I'm afraid so Frank," I replied.

Although I led him to believe that was the only reason why I decided to move on, it wasn't - far from it. The main reason was that I had fallen deeply in love with his daughter, Pamela and she felt the same for me. Her father would never approve and I knew I had to move on before Frank came down on her like a ton of bricks.

After my farewell party, Frank took me to one side and said in his broad West Devon accent, "Well, little old boy, we're all sorry to see e go but, with all this stuff you've been learning, you'll never be out of a job. And, if I'm sure about one thing, boy, it's that one day, when you get this childish horse thing in perspective, you'll become a great man with hounds and a great huntsman and kennel man to boot!"

He wasn't exactly right, but he must have seen something in me that I didn't know I possessed because I went on to successfully train thousands of dogs, of all breeds and types, for both work and companionship; to the highest standards of excellence.

Lamerton Foxhounds

CHUCK'S STORY 5
AT SEA
MID 1950s

After leaving the Lamerton I went back to stay with my foster parents in Surrey. They were very pleased to see me and so proud that I had completed my apprenticeship as a professional huntsman. They could see that I had something bearing heavily on my mind, although they never pressed me as to why I threw away my great opportunity of becoming the Lamerton's next huntsman after having worked so hard and enduring so much.

They just supported me the best way they could, knowing full well that I would tell them why I did such a crazy thing in due course.

Ellen, my foster Mum would have been sixty five years old at that time and Ern, my foster Dad who was her son, would have been forty five years old. Ellen's husband and their two daughters died of TB in the 1920s. Her husband was a big strong chap and never had a day's illness before that. He worked as a drayman, driving a team of six heavy work horses for R. Whites, the soft drinks people. Their daughters were big and strong too. They must have taken after their father, whereas Ern must have taken after his mother, who was quite small.

I loved my foster parents very much. They were the kindest people I had ever known and I always thought of them as my real Mum and Dad. They were always there for me and always stood by me, whatever I did.

Unfortunately, I hated my biological parents and had disowned them many years ago. Without knowing the true circumstances of my birth, I held them fully responsible for robbing me of my childhood.

As I mentioned earlier, I did not know much about my early childhood until my foster Mum told me about it. When she did, she said that from two months through to five years of age, I did indeed have a very happy childhood. I finally told her all about my ten years at school and my five years with the Lamerton.

She became very angry and said, "No wonder you've got such a great big chip on your shoulder! You were such a happy, contented little boy when I was fostering you. That nasty school has certainly messed you up, but despite that, I see you have still retained your defender of the underdog attitude that you had as a child."

"I often wondered about that Mum," I cried, but before I had a chance to ask her, she suddenly changed the subject.

"So what are you going to do about Pamela?" she asked.

"I don't know Mum, I think I will go to Paris and join the French

Foreign Legion and try to forget her," I replied.

"Charlie, have you got a death wish? You will get killed and die a terrible death in the desert - and if the Arabs don't torture and kill you, your fellow legionnaires surely will. They are the scum of the earth – murderers and rapists that have fled their own countries to avoid capture. Please promise me that you won't go," she pleaded.

"I'm truly sorry Mum, but I can't promise you that. I've already been to Paris and tried to enlist, but couldn't find their recruiting office. I think I now know where it is and I am going to try again next week - and yes, I do have a death wish. I've also got a great thirst for danger and adventure and, of course, the adrenalin fix that danger and adventure can deliver," I confessed.

"I'm telling you, Mum, I need to do this, not just to take my mind off Pamela, but also to deal with my low tolerance to boredom and the crazy stuff in my head that's tearing me apart," I added.

Throwing her hands in the air, with despair written all over her face, she tearfully sobbed, "Oh Charlie my dear little boy what have they done to you! I am so sorry for you - I just don't know what to say."

I knew I had hurt Mum real bad, so I asked Dad what he would do if he was in my shoes, and he advised, "Well Charlie I don't think much of your idea of joining the French Foreign Legion, I think you should get a big powerful motorbike. I tell you what, I'll get you one and while I'm at it, I'll get me one too!"

We spent half the night talking motorbikes and I quickly recognised that my Dad was a great authority on them. He had ridden many different makes - until Mum became scared that he might kill himself.

"Wow Dad, are they that dangerous?" I asked.

"Yes, they are, son, especially the big ones, if you intend to ride them flat out all the time, as I'm sure you will. Mum won't like it, but I suppose she will definitely think it's a better way of dealing with your problems than joining the French Foreign Legion."

"Sounds good to me. I think that would be the perfect solution," I chuckled.

So after a great deal of discussion, I eventually chose a 500cc Matchless and Dad chose a 350cc Douglas for himself. Dad was dead right. I did need a big powerful motorbike, and just as he expected, I was thrilled to bits with it. It wasn't long before I could handle it like an expert, thanks to his tuition.

As I roared around the countryside on the Matchless, I felt as free as a bird. Although I liked doing this, I liked roaring around London even more so, especially around Marble Arch. That was a real buzz with all that traffic coming at you from all directions. Getting up at four o'clock in the morning and roaring off to work was good too. With empty roads and not a soul about I could really open her up.

Matchless

Two weeks after I came back to live with Mum and Dad, I had taken a job with United Dairies at Walton-on-Thames, looking after their carthorses - all twenty nine of them. I know I was very much over qualified for the job, but there were no other horse jobs available within a twenty five mile radius of where I lived. Anyway, I loved those cheeky little rascals. They were very clever and looking after them could be quite challenging at times.

The Depot Manager was an old retired Cavalry Major of the old school when the horse was 'King' and cavalrymen did their fighting on horseback! We got on just fine, but some of the antics that I got up to made the hairs on the back of his neck stand up on end. As each milkman and his horse had two rest days every week, there would be eight horses to be taken out for some mild exercise in order to keep their muscles supple and their digestive systems working properly. Until I arrived on the scene, the method used to exercise them was to take each one out singly, drawing an empty milk cart.

I considered this to be a stupid way to exercise horses, so I queried it with the Depot Manager. I pointed out that exercising the rest horses this way was not only cutting into quality care time in other essential areas but also that there was a strong likelihood of the horses suffering from pressure sores; they weren't getting any respite from the constant daily pressure on vulnerable areas of their bodies from the harnesses, while drawing the milk carts.

After patiently hearing me out, he exclaimed, "You are the first stableman we have ever had who could ride, so go and use your initiative." As I was halfway out the door, he added, "By the way, what are you going to use for a saddle?"

"I don't need one. I will ride bareback just like I was taught by those Lamerton Hunt experts," I replied.

"Good man, you would have made a great Cavalryman back in the old days," he said with a glint of reminiscence in his eyes.

So, all I needed now was a suitable pair of reins to use for the horse I would ride, and three leading reins for the three horses I would lead. Rummaging around in the tack room, I soon found what I was looking for - a complete set of saddler's tools and some discarded carthorse driving reins.

Carthorse driving reins are far too long, heavy and unwieldy for riding and leading horses. Using the saddlers' tools with basic skills that I had picked up here and there, plus a fair amount of ingenuity, I soon had just the right sort of reins suitable for exercising the horses.

After attaching the customised pair of reins to the bridle of the horse that I would ride, and a leading rein to each of the three bridles of the horses which I would lead, I mounted up, and off we went out of the Depot gate and down Walton High Street, as good as gold! That's until an overzealous policeman jumped out in front of us and shouted, "STOP!"

"What's up," I growled, reining the horses in as quickly as I could, but almost trampling him underfoot in the process!

"You're under arrest for breaking the law."

"What law is that?" I asked, looking down at him from my higher vantage point.

At a loss as to what law he could charge me with, he kept blowing his police whistle until another policeman came puffing up. After conferring with each other, the second policeman dashed off and came back with their sergeant.

Meanwhile, the traffic came to an abrupt halt and people were gathering to watch the slap stick drama unfold. After a while, my Boss, the Depot Manager, arrived on the scene and conferred with the sergeant about what horses and their care professionals are lawfully allowed to do.

After apologising profusely to both my Boss and I, the sergeant stormed up to the first policeman and bellowed, "You useless idiot." Then pointing at the snarled up traffic, he roared, "Get this mess cleaned up."

"B… b… but Sergeant, it's my lunch break," he whined.

"Don't push your luck Constable, your lunch break is cancelled and when you have finished up here, report back to me at the Police Station," he snarled.

On the front page of the local rag on the following Friday, there was a full report and some photos covering the above fiasco. Naturally, with newspaper photos being in black and white, they couldn't capture the deep beetroot red colour on the first policeman's face, but clever journalism more than made up for that.

After that, everyone except for the overzealous policeman was delighted. Milk sales were up, the horses were groomed and toned to perfection, harnesses gleamed and people stopped to stare at 10 am and 11 am each day when my two strings of rest horses came trotting down the High Street on the way to the green fields beyond!

I had been in the job for five weeks, when I received a letter from United Dairies' head office offering me the job of Stables & Horse Assessment Manager at their main depot at Nine Elms in London. I was trying to make up my mind whether to take the job when a very large buff envelope with, 'On Her Majesty's Service,' stamped on it, came crashing through the letterbox. Fearing the worst, Mum said, "That's a very sinister looking letter. What does it say?"

"It's probably my tax return," I said absently. Working my way down through the red tape, I added, "It says I have to report to the Army Medical Officer at Guildford to have a physical and mental examination to determine whether I am fit to do my two years National Service now that I have completed my apprenticeship."

I passed the physical part okay, but the Medical Officer was not sure that I was mentally fit enough to serve in the British Armed Forces. I was kept waiting for ages and then he called me into his office and said, "Mr Kemsley, it says here on your file that you kill people!" I replied, "Isn't that what soldiers are supposed to do?"

Looking over the top of his half-moon glasses as if inspecting something that had crawled out from under a rock, he said, "You are supposed to kill the enemy, but definitely not people on your own side." Then, tapping my file with his pen, he added, "I am talking about your woodwork master, for example, when you were at school."

Pausing for effect, he went on to say, "Mr Kemsley, the bottom line is we don't really want you. But listen, have you ever considered going into the Merchant Navy rather than having to do all that square bashing all over again - like you did at school?"

"No I haven't, but I wouldn't mind doing that with all that fresh air," I replied.

With that, his eyes lit up and he remarked, "Remember, if you do go into the Merchant Navy you cannot come out."

"It's Hobson's choice, but I will do it," I replied.

~~~

The first ship I signed on to was a very old rusty tramp steamer, homeward bound for her home port of Calcutta, but stopping at practically every other port along the way. She was a typical old rust bucket, so old that her engines were fired by coal. The Captain, the Deck Officers and the Deckhands were mainly English. The Chief Engineer was a Scotsman from Glasgow, as they usually are on these old rust buckets, and the stokers that shovelled the coal that fired the ship's boilers were Lascars.

Old Jock, the Chief Engineer, was interested in anything mechanical and when I told him about my Matchless motorcycle and how thrilled I was with it, he slapped me on the back and said, "That's a real fine machine laddie - you made a splendid choice there, but do you know how to tune it up and keep it in tiptop condition, because if you don't I will have to teach you."

"Would you really, that would be great," I said.

"No worries, laddie. I'll make an engineer out of ye yet," he said in his funny Glaswegian accent.

Most of the crew had hobbies such as model making etc. to combat boredom throughout these long voyages. My way of combating boredom was to study for my Third Mate's ticket. That's the way I was going till old Jock persuaded me to study for the equivalent ticket in engineering on top of my Third Mate's in navigation, which I was already doing. Thanks to my studies, I got through my first voyage and also my second without blowing my top.

My second voyage was also on the same old rust bucket, but this time she was outward bound to London.

Thanks to old Jock's tuition throughout these two voyages, I got my third engineer's ticket and was more than half way to getting my Third Mate's ticket in navigation.

Jock was pleased as punch about this and chortled, "Come on me wee laddie, let's see you in your shiny new uniform." After I put it on, he exclaimed, "Well I never, you remind me so much of myself all those years ago when I was a young Third Engineer and got my first shiny gold braid ring on each sleeve."

"But that's the problem, Jock, they look so shiny that they make me look like I've just started," I said sheepishly.

"Well you have, laddie, but I know what you mean," he said with a glint of distant memory in his eye. He then rubbed some soot into the gold braid and said, "Now everyone will think you've been a Third Engineer for ages, so get yourself down to the pool and sign on to another ship."

Texaco was looking for a Third Engineer to serve on the S.S. Texaco Oslo, which was one of their oil tankers, so I went to their office to apply for the job. After having had my credentials checked out by a clerk sitting behind an enormous desk, I was told to take a seat next to two other young applicants who were looking at me as if I was something the cat dragged in!

The first one said, condescendingly, "We have been waiting here since nine o'clock and its now almost twelve o'clock and we have been totally ignored."

The other one chimed in, "You would think we were invisible."

"And for good reason," I thought, as I watched them showing off in their new over-tailored uniforms as if to signal to everyone that they were God's gift to seagoing engineering.

Five minutes later, the clerk called me up to his desk and I duly signed on as the Oslo's Third Engineer. Turning to the other two, he looked at them disdainfully and said, "As for you two popinjays, you can shove off - the position is now filled."

As I left the office I was thinking that perhaps someone should have told them to have their uniforms tailored according to the fledgling rank of Third Engineer, and maybe rub a wee pinch of soot into the gold braid on their sleeves!

Ten hours later, I was onboard the S.S. Texaco Oslo, sailing with the tide down Southampton Water out of Fawley oil refinery into thick freezing fog. She was fully laden with 60,000 tons of petroleum spirit bound for Havana. Thick fog is always a danger to ships at sea at the best of times and when you are sitting on 60,000 tons of petroleum spirit it does up the ante, somewhat. Two days later, we emerged out of the fog into bright sunlight and it got a lot warmer for the next three days.

Then on the following day, a 115 mile an hour hurricane with 100 foot high waves came out of the blue and hit the ship on her port side almost capsizing her. The ship was in mortal danger of sinking as she was tossed around like a small toy.

Every ship has its own morbid pessimist who likes nothing better than to spread doom and gloom, and the Oslo was no exception. This one was the Second Engineer. He had already scared most of our shipmates half to death when we were sailing in thick freezing fog three days earlier by saying: "If we collide with another ship we will all be blown to smithereens, or even worse, be burned alive in the flaming seas should we decide to jump overboard."

And now the ship was being battered mercilessly by the hurricane, he was down in the engine room wringing his hands and blathering about tankers breaking up in hurricane force winds and that we were all going to die a horrible death.

"Why don't you put a sock in it, Yank?" I said.

"What's that you said, you goddamn Limy," he snarled.

"You heard," I said quietly.

Seeing that we were about to come to blows, The Chief Engineer, who was a Scandinavian, shouted at us, "Knock it off you two. You are going to need all the energy you've got to get through the next twenty four hours."

I was on duty down in the engine room when the hurricane hit. Five seconds later, the ship's telegraph rang down for full speed ahead, as the ship's helmsman was obviously trying to turn the ship into the hurricane force wind. It seemed like an eternity but was probably three or four minutes before the ship responded to the helm. In the meantime, the engines screamed and the ship's hull creaked and groaned like she would cave in under the intolerable pressure. With the ship's bows eventually coming round and the ship heading into the hurricane, we were out of immediate danger - but still under red alert as she rode the gigantic hundred foot high waves as if she was on a roller coaster.

During the night, the hurricane strengthened and the Chief Engineer received an emergency call from the bridge informing him that the bridge electrics were going haywire and needed urgent attention right away. Turning to the Second Engineer, he said, "Get up on the bridge right away and sort out the bridge's electrics."

"I can't go, Chief. I'm too busy here," he whined.

Sensing danger and adventure and pricking up my ears with interest, I said, "Can I go Chief?"

"Off you go then, lad, and watch your step," he cautioned.

When I came up on deck, I was met by the full force of the hurricane, now gusting at well over 140 miles an hour with 150 foot high waves crashing onto the deck - so I had no other alternative than to cling onto the ship's deck rail to stop myself from being swept overboard. Taking a deep breath and clinging onto the deck rail like grim death, I made my perilous way, hand over hand, to the bridge. Under fair weather conditions this short journey would take two minutes at most, but with these extreme rough weather conditions, it took ten times as long. My arms felt like they were being pulled out of their sockets as the hurricane did its utmost to blow me away.

When I reported to the Captain on the bridge, I was told to fix the faulty electrics, starting with the ship's twelve massive heavy duty windscreen wipers that had broken down under the intolerable pressure imposed on them by the hurricane. As soon as I had repaired the wipers, the Captain's face lit up. He could now see out of the windscreens properly and keep the ship pointed in the right direction more accurately. For the past twenty five minutes he'd had to keep his nose pressed to the windscreen whilst giving orders to the helmsman over his shoulder which, by the time they were received and carried out, were almost useless. I fixed a few other electrical faults and was told to stand by in case the wipers failed again, which they did three more times in the next eleven hours before the hurricane weakened its grip on the ship.

When I returned to the engine room, I was just in time to overhear the Chief Engineer giving the Second Engineer a right old wigging. "I am going to report you to the Captain for refusing to carry out an order and also being a useless lily livered coward," he growled.

Feeling rather embarrassed, I coughed politely and said, "May I go off duty now, Chief?"

"Yes, Third Engineer you may, and by the way, the Captain was very impressed by your conduct and efficiency," he praised.

"It was a piece of cake, Chief," I replied.

"Did you here that, Second Engineer?" he sneered.

The Second Engineer gave me a black look and stood there speechless.

With the hurricane out of the way, we were favoured with a following wind and soon made up the time lost riding out the hurricane, which had blown us off course. As we came out of the Atlantic Ocean and sailed into the Caribbean Sea, the climate became much warmer and by the time we docked in Havana it was very hot.

Havana, before the revolution, was a very pleasant city. That's if you were one of the idle rich people who lived or visited there. The rest of the people were so poor and downtrodden that they lived in hovels and couldn't even afford to send their children to school to better themselves. This sad state of affairs, not only in Havana, but also throughout the whole of Cuba, was exploited by their next door neighbour, the United States of America - not just for cheap labour, but also as their own rich man's playground.

I would have liked to have spent more time there so that I could help those poor unfortunate people, but modern tankers take just fifteen hours or so to turn around. So we were soon on our way again to pick up another 60,000 tons of petroleum spirit - this time from Texaco's Port Arthur oil refinery in Texas, lying in the Gulf of Mexico. It took just a few hours sailing time to get to Port Arthur, plus fifteen hours turn-around time and then we off again, back to Havana. Over the next eleven months, the Oslo delivered over ten million tons of petroleum and aviation spirit to many other Caribbean islands.

As we only had a mere fifteen hours in port on each turn-around, we spent most of those eleven months at sea. I got along fine with most of my shipmates and thoroughly enjoyed working with them. But each time we docked, I liked nothing better than to be with my girlfriends who were scattered around many of the Caribbean islands that we docked at! This didn't go unnoticed by the Second Engineer, who still bore a grudge against me for causing him to lose face in the presence of the Chief Engineer during the night of the hurricane. He was also extremely jealous of my ability to attract beautiful women.

I was in the recreation room with the rest of the off-duty watch one night, when he said to me in a loud sneering voice, "Hey Limy, are you a fighter or are you a lover." This was an American smart Alec expression that was going around at that time. It was meant to depict that men who are good at picking up women are sissies and don't fight! Some of the other Yanks tittered. So, thinking that he was some sort of smart arse comedian, he turned to his audience and made a mock bow.

That was his first big mistake because as he bowed I kicked him up the backside so hard that he went sprawling. His second mistake was in believing that all Englishmen (or Limies as he called us) never kicked a man when he's down. He was so wrong! My pent up temper flared up and I followed up by kicking his head in and didn't stop till my shipmates pulled me off him. Anyway, he was a great big hulking brute and would have killed me if I had let him get up. He was in sickbay with concussion for the next nine days and so I had to work his watch as well as my own. I was also logged and fined fifty dollars for fighting.

It wasn't long before I was promoted to Second Engineer and the original Second Engineer was demoted to Third Engineer. My British Board of Trade's Third Engineers' qualification is equivalent to the American Second Engineers' qualification. The Chief Engineer was fed up to the teeth with the original Second Engineer's sloppy work and so he considered that I was more qualified for the job.

As Second Engineer, I was allotted a larger cabin which had a bigger and more comfortable bunk and more space and better facilities for studying. My original cabin was not bad though, when compared to what's allotted to a Third Engineer or indeed any other junior officer on British Merchant Navy ships. During those eleven months when I was sailing around the Caribbean I had plenty of time on my hands to continue my studies and get my British Board of Trade Third Mate's ticket, to add to my British Board of Trade Third Engineer's ticket.

The Captain of the Oslo congratulated me and said, "Well done lad! I suppose you do realise that your British Third Mate's qualification is equivalent to a Second Mate's qualification on any American Mercantile Marine ship, including the Oslo?"

Yes, sir, I do sir," I said.

"Well, I wish you luck in whatever you choose to do and always remember, there will always be a good job here for you on the Oslo," he added.

"Thank you, Sir," I beamed with pride.

On my next voyage, I signed on as Second Mate on an American freighter. The freighter's Third Engineer was an Australian. He was another loner with a big chip on his shoulder like me; so naturally, we hit it off quite well and quickly became best mates. I also suspected he had a death wish like me!

The first time I spoke to him was two hours after we shoved off from New York. He was leaning on the stern safety rail, sweating like a pig.

"What's up mister?" I said.

"It's alright for you deck officers, out in the fresh air all day," he grumbled.

"Yeah, I know how you feel; I was Third Engineer like you on my last ship. You should do what I did," I said cheerily.

"What's that?" he said, perking up a bit.

"I studied for my Third Mate's ticket when I was Third Engineer on the Oslo and I got it in just over year. That's why I'm out here in the fresh air all day instead of being cooped up in a stuffy old engine room," I explained.

"Thanks for your advice cobber, but studying for my Third Engineer's ticket almost done my head in. I don't think I could go through that again," he responded.

"Hey, my name is Chuck, what's yours?" I asked.

"Just call me Aussie," he said.

"Come on, what's your real name?" I persisted.

"Promise me you won't tell anyone if I tell you?" he said.
"I promise!"
"Well, it's Wilberforce," he said, sheepishly.
"Is that what your Mummy calls you?" I blurted out without thinking, trying not to laugh.

A picture flashed in my imagination of this six foot, six inch Australian muscleman being called Wilberforce by his Mum when she told him not to forget to brush his teeth and wash behind his ears.

"You Pommy bastard!" he roared, as he threw a punch at my head with all his weight behind it. I automatically ducked and deflected him over my shoulder like I was taught at school by the British Commandos. He landed heavily on his back and hit his head on a metal stanchion, which knocked him out cold.

I'm just beginning to get worried, when he muttered, "What happened and how did you do that? In one second I'm on my feet and the next I'm flying through the air."

"I'll tell you later," I said.
"No, tell me now. I really want to know," he demanded.
"Okay, I'll tell you."

And so I told him how the Commandos had taught us unarmed combat, and all that stuff about Churchill having us boys trained up as his last ditch stand against the Germans when he thought we might lose the war. "This was when I was ten," I added.

"Well, I'll be jiggered! You were only ten years old when you learnt all that stuff, eh? I think you and I would make a good team," he said thoughtfully.

"Team, what are you talking about?" I asked.
"Tell you tomorrow, same place same time." he cried.
"Ok Aussie, see you then," I replied.

The next day he showed me a picture of a fifty foot speed boat.
"Wow! Isn't she a beauty" I said.
"She's berthed at Havana and the owner wants 70,000 dollars for her but will accept 10,000 as a down payment," he said excitedly.

"So how much have you got?" I asked.
"Just over 2,000," he replied.
"Is that all? I suppose you've been spending all your money on women?" I said.

"Yeah, don't you?"

"No, I don't. The women I go with pay their own way. Looks like I'll have to teach you a thing or two about that. Anyway, how do you intend to keep up the payments?" I enquired.

"Once I've saved up enough money for the down payment, I was thinking about jumping ship at Havana and using the boat for gunrunning and paying off the balance with the proceeds of that," he stated.

"Wow! That sounds exiting and very dangerous too. A bloke could get himself killed doing that!" I said matching his excitement.

"Yeah, it's all of that, and it's also very lucrative. Just ten runs and the boat will be paid for," he said.

"So when do we start?" I asked.

"I knew you would say that!"

"Look, I've got almost 20.000 dollars stashed away in a London bank. Adding that to your 2,000, we should have more than enough for the down payment and getting started," I prodded.

~~~

With us now being the rightful owners of the speedboat, we signed on a British cruise ship that was outward bound for Havana, where we jumped ship and picked up the speedboat. When I say speedboat, I'm not talking about a tiny plaything, but a customised ex World War 2 MTB, seventy feet long with a twenty foot beam. Originally, she had a top speed of forty knots - fast, but not fast enough for gunrunning.

So the previous owner had stripped out the heavy torpedo firing equipment and other World War 2 stuff, including, the crew's living quarters and all the bulky paraphernalia that goes with it. As a motor torpedo boat, she would have had a crew of two officers and fifteen men, so the reduction in weight was considerable. This also made extra space for carrying more contraband. He had also replaced the original engines with even more powerful ones. Overall, this beefed up the power to weight ratio and gave the boat a top speed of sixty knots, which was almost fifty per cent faster than any of the Cuban Navy's patrol boats that he and his crewman would have to contend with.

They had only done two runs with the boat. The first one was dead easy.

They had picked up eighty crates of rifles, ninety machine guns, ten crates of hand grenades, fifty-seven crates of ammo and one and a half tons of dynamite from a Panamanian freighter. This was fifteen miles off the Cuban coast in the middle of the night. Fifty-five minutes later, the cargo was unloaded on a deserted Cuban beach by a bunch of Fidel Castro's rebels.

These rough, tough looking blokes were armed to the teeth and if they decided not to pay for the goods there was nothing that the boat owner or his crewman could do about it. For all they knew, the rebels could blow their brains out, take the boat and feed them to the sharks. But they just gave the boat owner the money and told him to count it. There were ten thousand dollars, which was the full amount of his fee.

But then the boat owner became greedy and tried to earn even more money by carrying twice as much contraband than he did on his first run. Although the boat was still able to do sixty knots with this extra load of contraband on board once she got going, she didn't have enough acceleration to make a quick getaway if they got in trouble. The trick was to pick up the contraband and drop it off before the Cuban patrol boat people realised what was going on. But he wasted so much time picking up the extra contraband that they were onto him like a flash.

He was a thousand yards or so away from the freighter when he spotted the lights of a patrol boat coming up fast. Then as the patrol boat came into gunshot range, it immediately signalled him to 'heave to or you will be blown out of the water!' The boat owner and his crewman knew they were in big trouble, but they decided to carry on regardless. Two minutes later, the patrol boat fired a warning shot across their bows, but they still did not heave-to.

The patrol boat fired again, this time blowing half of the boat owner's left arm clean off and also killing his crewman, who was monitoring the boat's speed and progress. The crewman's dying words were, "She's up to fifty knots skipper, and we're drawing away." The boat owner felt no pain in his arm; it was completely numb. The pain and also, the grieving for his crewman came later.

The patrol boat fired two more salvos that landed harmlessly in the water several hundred yards behind the boat, which was now running at sixty knots. With the boat now running at top speed, he soon reached his destination before he blacked out. The rebels knew exactly what to do - they had years of practice. The crewman's body was spirited back to his family, the boat owner's injuries were treated by the rebels' doctor; all the evidence of what had happened at sea was removed, and the boat was taken back to her moorings before anyone discovered she was missing. All this took place under the cover of darkness. It was obvious that these rebel blokes were incredible.

Aussie did a couple of cartwheels and cried out, "Wow, what an amazing adventure! I wonder if he would like to come with us!"

Aussie wrote to the previous owner and got a letter back by return of post. In the letter, the man wrote: "Not blooming likely. I've had enough adventure to last me a lifetime!"

Our first gunrunning trip was more or less the same as the previous owner's first one, as were our next twenty four runs. On our twenty sixth run, however, someone must have grassed us up because the patrol boats were waiting for us.

We were halfway back to our drop off point with our illicit cargo of guns, ammo and explosives, when we spotted a patrol boat's riding lights shining dimly out of the darkness, nine hundred yards directly ahead of us. I immediately swung the helm over to starboard and sped off on this new course for approximately two minutes, only to see the riding lights of another patrol boat eight hundred yards ahead of us. I swung the helm over to starboard for the third time, only to see the lights of yet another patrol boat ahead of us, this time even closer. There were now four patrol boats looming out of the darkness and closing in on us from all sides.

"What do you think Aussie?" I shouted.

"Ram the slimy toads! With all these explosives on board we can blow them to kingdom come!" he shouted back.

Taking him at his word, I swung the helm over to port and aimed our boat at the nearest patrol boat. They were expecting us to pull a stunt like this and the boat behind us opened fire, taking away our radio mast along with a large part of our substructure.

They obviously wanted to capture us alive because the next shell blew our rudder off, and the one after that buckled the propeller shaft, causing the engine to stop. We still didn't surrender, even then. When the first six officers tried to climb onboard, we pushed them back into the sea. Four others ended up the same way when they tried to climb up the other side of the boat and jump on us from behind.

"Well done, Aussie. I see you have been paying attention to the jujitsu that I've been teaching you!" I shouted.

"Look out, Chuck! There are three of them coming up behind you," he shouted back.

But his warning came too late. They slammed me down on the deck and handcuffed my hands behind my back. Aussie drew his big sword-like knife from its hidden scabbard, which nestled under the back of his shirt, and rushed to my aid. Quick as a flash, an officer drew his revolver and shot Aussie in the arm, thereby, disarming him. Four other officers jumped on him and slammed him down on the deck and handcuffed him, same as they did to me.

"Steady on. Can't you see my mate is bleeding to death?" I said to the officer in charge. I heard him bark an order in Spanish to his men. They immediately jumped to attention and took Aussie away. The officer looked at me and said in broken English, "Your amigo will be okay. They are taking him to hospital."

I ended up in jail and the next time I saw Aussie was two days later when he was put in the same cell as me.

"Well Aussie, my old mate, how have they been treating you?" I said cordially.

"Well Chuck, you would never believe this. I've been chatting up the night nurses with some very good results!" he cried.

"How did you do that then - they all speak Spanish?" I asked.

"It's like you said. That cocky, funny stuff that you taught me works with women of all nationalities - and as those nurses don't speak English, I used gestures and body language like you also taught me and it worked great. One of the night nurses could speak a little English though, and she said she could help us get out of this hellhole," he replied.

"Aussie, you are incorrigible. You were bleeding to death and I let you out of my sight for just two days and you're making out with half the nursing profession…," I trailed off.

"Yes I know," he said lamely.

As we had been supplying guns and explosives to the communist rebels, we were treated as communists and subject to torture and the worst treatment the Cuban fascist government could inflict on us.

But Aussie's courageous night nurse was as good as her word. Her name was Maria and she was our only contact with the outside world. She was getting messages in and out of the prison for us at great risk to herself.

The first thing Maria did was to inform the British Embassy that one of their British subjects was being held and tortured in a Cuban prison, which resulted in a British Embassy official being put on my case. The official could get me out but he couldn't get Aussie out because he wasn't a British subject. There was no way I was going to leave Aussie behind in that hellhole, so that was that.

Maria then turned to the Cuban rebels for help, on the grounds that we might crack under torture and grass them up. In reply, the rebels said that they were happy to help, not just because of that, but also because of the grave risks we had taken on their behalf and the brave fight we had put up before we were captured. They promised that they would get their top lawyers working on it right away.

Their original plan was to sell the boat and use the proceeds of that to bribe the top Cuban Government officials to get us out of jail, but the Law Enforcement Agency which had confiscated the boat wouldn't release it. So it took all of the 40,000 dollars that we had stashed away in an offshore bank to spring us, which left us penniless. Not that it worried me unduly with my championing of the underdog attitude - the underdogs this time being the multitudes of poor oppressed people of Cuba, who lived in hovels and were deprived of even the barest amenities of life under successive fascist Governments and jackbooted Military Juntas.

We were given twenty four hours to sign on a ship and leave the country. The only ship sailing that night was an ancient beat up banana boat outward bound for San Francisco. So, after saying goodbye to Maria and thanking her for everything she had done for us, we sailed away.

~~~

The only remarkable thing about the banana boat was that it was crawling with spiders; some being extremely dangerous. There was an old bloke on the boat who collected them; he had sailed on banana boats all his life because they fascinated him.

We sailed to San Francisco where we were able to rejoin my old ship, the Texaco Oslo. I introduced Aussie to Hank and John, and some other shipmates that I knew from the last time I was with them. They all wanted to know what I had been up to since then. I gave them a full account of everything that had happened and they listened intently to every word I said in stunned silence.

Up on the bridge, the Captain had stayed on to ask me how I had been getting on since I last saw him. Not wanting to sound immodest I just told him the bare bones.

"Come, come, lad, I know there's more to it than that. You were causing quite a stir in the recreation suit when I passed by, so out with it," he ordered.

So I repeated all of what I said to the others. After I finished he said, "Well done lad, I knew you had guts the first time I set eyes on you." Then in his formal Captain's voice, he said, "Carry on Mr Kemsley!"

"Aye aye, sir, thank you, sir," I replied.

I thoroughly enjoyed being back on the Oslo again, and I think Aussie enjoyed being on her too - but all too soon we were saying our goodbyes to our friends, never to see them again. Aussie hated goodbyes as much as I did and was feeling a bit down in the dumps, so I said, "Come on me old mate, let's have a holiday. We can stay with my Mum and Dad for a bit if you like."

"Sounds good to me, let's do it," he said cheering up a bit.

When we arrived, Mum said, "You must be Aussie!"

Dad chimed in, "Charlie has written a lot about you in his letters." After hearing Dad calling me 'Charlie', Aussie biting his lip and trying not to laugh said, "I'm ever so pleased to meet you both. He has told me a lot about you too!"

As soon as Mum and Dad were out of earshot, Aussie burst out laughing and sneered, "Charlie eh, that's a girl's name!"

"No, it isn't," I said, defiantly.

"It is, from where I come from," he replied, cockily.

"If you say so, Wilberforce."

"I suppose I asked for that," Aussie acknowledged.

I grinned at him and said in my best Australian accent, "No worries cobber, no worries!"

Mum poked her head round the door and said, "Lunch is on the table boys, so stop squabbling and come and eat it before it gets cold."

After lunch, Dad took us out to the shed where my motorbike was kept. We entered the shed and my eyes almost popped out of my head when I saw my big Matchless motorbike all polished up like she had just come out of the showroom. Next to my bike there was another one exactly the same and equally as shiny.

"What's going on Dad?" I asked.

"Well son, when you kept mentioning what a great mate Aussie was in your letters, I knew you would be bringing him home sometime. So I bought another motorbike, exactly the same as yours, so that there would be no squabbling over who should ride pillion. I also made doubly sure that both bikes were exactly the same, so there would be no squabbling over which bike is the better of the two," he explained.

"Dad you shouldn't have!" I said breathlessly. I couldn't believe it!

"It's the least I could do, son, after all the expensive presents you keep sending us from all over the world," he said graciously.

Poor Aussie was gobsmacked. "What a generous bloke!" he exclaimed.

"Yes, he's the best Dad there is," I replied.

Then looking the bikes over, I quipped, "Hey Aussie… I suppose you do know how to ride a motorbike?"

"Of course I do. Out in the outback, you learn to ride motorbikes almost before you can walk," he said scathingly.

"Horses too?" I questioned, raising my eyebrows.

"Yes, those too. Why did you ask me that?"

"Because I'm into horses just as much as high powered motorbikes," I replied.

"Wow, Chuck, you're a deep one."

"Yes I know, but all I want us to do at the moment is to fire up these motorbikes and go for a spin," I said impatiently.

"Yippee let's go!" he cried - and off we went.

We spent the next three weeks roaring around the countryside on our high powered motorbikes, reaching speeds of up to one hundred miles an hour on roads that were designed for doing a mere thirty to sixty miles an hour at best. Looking for even bigger and better kicks, I suggested that we go and race around the streets of London.

"Have you done it before?" he asked, excitedly.

"Yeah, every time I'm back in the UK - and I'm still in one piece," I assured him.

"But what about all those black cabs coming at you from all directions and cutting you up, and all that other heavy London traffic?"

"That's part of the fun. Those cabbies are only bluffing and trying to intimidate you. I just call their bluff and play them at their own game. What gets their goat more than anything is when they've been waiting in a long queue of traffic for ages, say at traffic lights for example, and you speed past them as free as a bird and give them the finger. Then, as the traffic lights turn green, you take off like a rocket leaving them still sitting there fuming."

I then explained London's heavy traffic to him, because it really doesn't matter how heavy it is; there's always tiny gaps left between vehicles where you can nip in and out of at high speed without getting crushed. It's the high speed and the guts to use that speed which makes it possible.

"Sounds highly dangerous Chuck!" he exclaimed.

"Yes I suppose it is, Aussie, but don't worry, it just takes a fearless bloke on a high powered motorbike and a bit of practice. A death wish like we have thrown in for good measure might also help, but it's not essential. We will start off slow until you get the hang of it, then we can speed it up until you're cutting through London traffic like a knife through butter."

"What do you think Aussie?" I asked when he got the hang of it.

"Well, it definitely beats the hell out of seeing London from the top of an open-top tourist bus, and just you wait till I tell my mates back home in Australia! They'll be green with envy, and that's for sure," he chortled.

After some exciting escapades bombing around London on our bikes, we realised that Aussie's driving licence was out of date, so we went back to sea. We served on five more ships together over the next seven months and had many more exciting adventures in all four corners of the world.

Towards the end of those seven months, I received two pieces of supposedly good news. The first was when I was listening to the BBC World News in Hong Kong. I heard that those of us that had stayed in the Merchant Navy for two years or more instead of doing National Service, were free to leave if they so wished. But I had no intention of leaving the Merchant Navy for at least another year or two.

The second piece of news came through a letter from a firm of London solicitors, informing me that an anonymous benefactor had left me £27,000 in his will!

After that, all my shipmates with the exception of Aussie started to shun me. I was no longer 'our good old mate, Chuck' but 'the bloke with all that money'. Certainly, £27,000 was a considerable sum of money in those days, but I would have been a lot happier without it, just earning my living as a junior Merchant Navy officer.

Aussie held the same views as me, and he angrily pointed out to the rest of them: "Chuck will always be Chuck, however much money he has got. You don't know him like I do. He will probably end up giving it all away like he always does. That's the sort of bloke he is. He's also got more guts than all the rest of you slimy weasels put together - and if you don't stop treating him like a leper, I will clobber the lot of you!"

"How do you know so much about him then?" one of them asked, pushing his luck.

"Because I've been in more dangerous situations with him than you've had hot dinners, and he never left me in the lurch when the chips were down," he said, rolling up his sleeves as if to say: "anyone else got anything to add?"

I overheard the last few words as I passed by, and asked, "What's going on Aussie?"

He told me the rest of what he had said and I replied, "It isn't going to work is it?"

"No," he said, heavily.

Aussie and I had often talked about settling down deep in the glorious English countryside to breed and school horses for a living, as well as gundogs, sheepdogs, and police dogs. And that's exactly what we did - until Aussie's visa ran out and he couldn't get it renewed. We spent a small fortune on solicitors, but the authorities refused to renew it. The solicitors surmised that it had something to do with our gunrunning exploits in Cuba.

We were both shocked at this outcome, which meant that Aussie would have to leave the UK and go back to sea. When this finally sunk in, I turned to Aussie and said, "If you have to go back to sea then I'm coming with you."

To which he replied: "No Chuck, as much as I would like you to come with me, you have to stay here and continue what we started. That would make me feel really good and very proud too."

Not a word was spoken as I drove Aussie to the dock gates. After all we had been through we could read each other like a book. We both knew that there were no words we could say to each other to ease the bitter sadness of parting. So when we arrived at the dock gates, we squared our shoulders and took one last long look at each other. We stayed that way for a few seconds until I nodded my head ever so slightly and Aussie did the same. He then threw his kitbag over his shoulder and marched off through the dock gates. He didn't look back and I didn't expect him to. We had planned it that way.

~~~

With Aussie gone, the days dragged by as I went about my work like a zombie. Horses were schooled and dogs were trained, but my heart was no longer in it so I decided to get my motorbike out and go for a spin. When I went to get it, I froze on the spot as I was so used to seeing Aussie's motorbike there next to mine. I slammed the door and locked it and went back to work, with a huge lump in my throat.

I had completely forgotten that before Aussie went away he had decided to give his motorbike back to my Dad, but Dad insisted that he should keep it as a memento. He also offered to pay for it to be shipped to Australia for him, if that's what he wanted. After a great deal of argument, Aussie had finally agreed, on the understanding that he would pay Dad the full cost of the shipping and also his time and out of pocket expenses for doing it.

After a few days, I pulled myself together and jumped on my Matchless and roared off on it. I rode it flat out all night and didn't come back until daybreak. I can't remember where I went, but I know it made me feel a lot better in myself. So much so, that I decided to employ a fulltime stableman and a fulltime kennel maid to carry out menial tasks such as feeding, grooming and mucking out my client's horses and working dogs and also to be there for them when I was out on my motorbike for hours on end.

Schooling and training my client's horses and dogs usually took me just a few hours each day, five days a week. Knowing that they were being properly cared for when I was absent took a great load off my mind. This left me free as a bird to take off on my motorbike whenever I felt the urge to do so without getting behind with my horse and dog work - which I still enjoyed as much as my messed up mind would let me.

After all this time, I was still deeply in love with Pamela and couldn't get her out of my mind. Also, I still had that great big chip on my shoulder that I had since my school days - and the death wish that went along with it was just as strong as ever.

~~~

Five weeks after Aussie went away, and still smouldering at the despicable treatment that he had received from the immigration authorities for not renewing his visa, I took up show jumping. In those days, show jumping was a lot more dangerous and exciting than it is today, with all the safety regulations that are now in place. Back then, show jumping was a rich man's sport and there wasn't the big prize money or the corporate sponsorship to make it financially viable. But as I had a lot of money that I wanted to get rid of, I decided to have a go at it anyway.

With my usual devil may care attitude and my bold horses to match, we were soon a force to be reckoned with, winning event after event. This didn't go unnoticed by four top members of the British Establishment who wanted their sons and daughters to win at all costs, creating the prestige that went with it. They were also aware that I was rapidly running out of money.

I blamed the British Establishment for messing up my childhood with their lies and deceit, so I wasn't surprised me when those four offered me large sums of money to let their sons and daughters win. In all four cases it gave me grim satisfaction to tell them, in no uncertain terms, what I thought of them, and what they could do with their stinking money. It was probably the first time that they had come up against anyone or anything that they couldn't buy, and they were absolutely gutted - which pleased me immensely.

As well as giving those members of the British Establishment yet another good kick up the backside, I was also highly delighted several weeks later when all the money that had been left to me – and had caused me so much grief - was gone. I could now concentrate fully on my client's horses and dogs and of course my motorcycling again.

~~~

CHUCK'S STORY 6
THRILLS & SPILLS
MID 1950s

I was out on my motorcycle one day, when I came across another motorcyclist who had broken down. I stopped to help him, which we all did in those far off days – 'knights of the road' they used to call us. His motorcycle was a 650cc Triumph 110, and when I asked him what's wrong with it, he said, "The engine cut out and though I've tried everything I know, I still can't get it to go."

I reset the contact breaker points and made a couple of adjustments to the carburettor and said, "Try it now."

It started first kick. He grinned and said, "Thanks, mate."

"I'll follow you for a couple of miles to make sure you're okay," I offered.

I tried to keep up with him but failed to do so. I just couldn't believe how much faster his Triumph was than my tuned up Matchless. I had heard a lot about these Triumphs, but I hadn't realised that they were as fast as that. After a while, he stopped to let me catch up with him and when I did, he cried, "Gee it's faster than ever; you try it and see!"

After I tried it out, I said, "Wow, I'm highly impressed. So much so that I'll get down the motorcycle shop first thing tomorrow morning and buy one!"

"Hey, I've got a great idea. I'm on my way to Rye House speedway track. I'm learning to be a speedway rider - and I thought you might want to come with me. We could swap motorbikes, which would give you another chance to ride my Triumph," he said graciously.

When we arrived at the speedway track, I muttered, "I've never ridden a speedway bike."

"Neither have I. It's my first lesson," he replied nervously.

"In that case, I think I'll have a go too," I said excitedly. I signed up for ten lessons, but only needed five. I did speedway for two months but gave it up to do scrambling, or motocross as it is now called.

Speedway motorcycles are usually raced on dirt or loosely packed shale. They have no brakes and on the straight sections of the track, they reach speeds of up 70 miles per hour. This is very dangerous and exciting, but once I got the hang of it I got bored with it and found that scrambling was just as dangerous, if not more so, and also a lot more interesting too.

The day after meeting my new friend with the Triumph 110, I went down to my local Triumph dealer to see about trading in my Matchless. After talking to the man who owned the shop, I decided to get a 500cc Triumph

Tiger 100, instead of the 110 that I originally intended to get.

Although the engine of the Tiger 100 was 150cc smaller, it was possible to tune it up to go even faster than the 110. The man who owned the shop also pointed out that although both the 110 and the Tiger 100 were much faster than my Matchless, the Matchless was a great deal easier to handle on wet and slippery roads.

Whilst I was in the shop, he told me about Motocross or Scrambles as it was still called in the 1950s, and he showed me the scrambler on which he won many races. It was a Triumph Trophy TR5 which had the same beautiful lines of the Tiger 100, but looked more rugged, as you would expect from an off-road racer. Seeing that I was deeply interested in what he was saying, he showed me a film of him winning several races on his TR5 at Chobham Common.

Chobham Common was one of the British Army's toughest battle tank testing grounds, and I could see from the film that it took a lot more skill and guts to win races over this sort of terrain with a TR5 than it would with any other make of scrambler. As I watched the enormous power being transmitted through the TR5s rear wheel, which caused it to whip viciously from lock to lock as he stormed up each steep slippery slope, and then watched it taking off and leaping thirty feet high up in the air and landing halfway down the downhill slope, I knew I just had to have one.

Certainly, there were many other makes of scrambler that were tamer and a lot more easier to handle than the wild TR5, just as there were for Triumph's road machines, but I bought a TR5 for doing Scrambles and also bought a Tiger 100 to ride on the road, both of which suited my wildness to a tee.

Riding the Tiger 100 home was a really exhilarating experience, but it was even more exhilarating after I had tuned it up to its absolute limits. Then it was time to go and test it against my friend's 110 on the same piece of road where his bike had put my Matchless to shame on the way to Rye House speedway track.

This time it was my tuned up Tiger 100 that put his 110 to shame. When I eventually stopped to let him catch up, he said, "Wow Chuck, what happened? My 110's engine is 150ccs bigger than yours and so I can't understand how you got it to go so fast!" I told him what the man in the shop told me, and he said, "If I traded in my 110 for a Tiger 100 like you've got, would you tune it up to go as fast as yours?"

"Yes, of course, but don't go breaking your neck on it!"

"I'll try not to," he promised.

My TR5 scrambler arrived two weeks later, straight from the Triumph works at Meriden. It didn't need any special tuning as this had already been done by the race mechanics at the works. All I needed to do now was to fill in an entry form and turn up at my chosen scrambles track. There were no specialised tuition courses in those days. You just jumped in at the deep end and hoped for the best and, of course, that's what I did.

My first scramble was a total disaster. I came last in every heat and fell off five times. However, after racing on several tracks and breaking a few bones, I started to get quite good at it. Certainly, breaking your bones hurts, but the worst part of it was the boredom that sets in whilst you are waiting to heal, which in those days took a long time.

We didn't have the benefit of the modern surgical procedures that we have today. But what we did have were Convalescent Hospitals where you were sent to recuperate after the main hospitals had patched you up.

There were three nurses for every patient and most of them were very attractive with the exception, of course, of the old traditional dragon type matron, who tried her utmost to make sure that there was no hanky-panky going on. Most of her patients were young men in their twenties or early thirties, so the matron faced an impossible task - especially at night time when she wasn't about!

Although the nurses that helped us to recuperate adored us wild bunch of scramblers, the surgeons who patched us up time after time did not. I can't say that I blame them. We kept getting stretchered into their squeaky clean hospitals, covered with slimy mud from head to toe, only to return again and again in the same muddy condition every few months or so after they've cleaned us up.

The first time this happened, the surgeon said, "I see from the muddy state that you are in that you are one of those rough tough scrambles chaps." I nodded my head in reply.

"In that case, I won't need to anesthetise you before I set this fractured bone in your leg will I?" I just shrugged my shoulders and said, "If you say so, doc!"

The pain was excruciating, but I said nothing - I wasn't going to give him the satisfaction. I just gritted my teeth and let him get on with it. I suppose what made matters worse was that scrambles meetings were always held on Sundays. They would have a dozen or so scramblers stretchered in with broken bones, which meant that the surgeons had to work when they would rather be off fishing or something.

Within six months of getting my TR5 scrambler, Scrambles had taken over my life. I was hooked on the danger, excitement and everything about it, like a junky on cocaine. So much so, it became my number one passion and cost every penny I earned over the next five years or so.

The first thing I did to fund my new passion was to sell my stables and dog training kennels and move to London to work as a precision engineer.

The space race had just started, and if you had precision engineering skills which I had - thanks to old Jock the chief engineer on my first ship - and were prepared to work in London, you could earn a lot of money. If you were prepared to work permanent nights, as I was, you could earn twice as much again.

The advantage of working permanent nights in the aerospace industry was that there was hardly any supervision. What there was could be easily fooled into believing that I was making aerospace parts, when most of the time I was making replacement parts for my scrambler.

Before any job was given out, the planning department wrote up their instructions as to how they thought the job should be done. Then, on the strength of that, the dayshift rate fixers estimated how long they thought it should take. Neither the planning nor the rate fixing departments had a clue about how much time we required to complete any job or operation. More often than not, we could find a much quicker way of doing the job - but of course we didn't tell them that!

On top of that, we could always bully the nightshift rate fixer into giving us more time to do the job, which gave us even more spare time to do as we pleased. Where the dayshift rate fixers could get away with putting the lowest rate on each job and thereby please the boss, our nightshift rate fixers had to deal with a wild bunch of mavericks who would tear him apart or walk off the job if provoked.

When you were happy with the rate for the job, you studied the blueprint and got on with it. If you were not, you stormed up to the rate fixer's office, kicked his door in, slammed the paperwork on his desk and roared, "What stupid moron put this crazy rate on my ticket!" After several of us carried out the same action throughout the night, he soon got the message and gave in to our demands. If he didn't, we kept it up until he did. It's fair to say that there was a massive turnover of rate fixers due to heart attacks and mental health problems!

On an average twelve hour nightshift, we spent approximately four hours on aerospace work and the rest of the time sleeping, playing cards and using the machine shop facilities to make our own personal bits and pieces - 'doing your homers' as it was called.

One bloke wanted to buy a top of the range motorised go-cart racer for his boy's birthday, but couldn't afford to pay the high prices that the manufacturers demanded, so we helped him make one to the manufacturer's specification, but even better. Go-cart engineers are only capable of working to low tolerances whereas precision engineers habitually work to tolerances of plus and minus one thousandths of an inch. Consequently, his boy's go-cart went faster and was more reliable than the other boys' go-carts, and he won more races without breaking his neck.

We made everything to our higher precision engineer's standards, including the engine, gearbox and everything else, right down to the last nut and bolt. The only things we couldn't make were the tyres, so we all chipped in and fitted new ones.

Two days before we finished making the go-cart, the machine shop manager paid us a visit. He suspected that we were up to something, but he wasn't sure what it was. After looking around and asking a lot of questions he went home none the wiser. Little did he know that a great big slice of the evidence he was looking for was staring him straight in the face or to put it more accurately, right under his feet.

The go-cart was tucked away under the closed-in steps and landing of a gigantic milling machine. When he was questioning the man who operated the machine, the go-cart was literally just two inches underneath his feet. How the operator managed to keep a straight face when he was being questioned, I really don't know.

Finding no evidence, and seeing that we were all working flat out making aerospace parts when he came in, he sacked the night rate fixer on the spot for wasting his time. The rate fixer tried to explain what we had been up to, but the machine shop manager wouldn't listen. If he had, he would have found out exactly what was going on, especially with that whacking great big go-cart stashed away where it was. That was the first and last time that the machine shop manager came in to check up on us - and it was also the last time that any night rate fixer ever tried to grass us up.

Having access to a fully equipped machine shop on a regular basis helped my scrambles career tremendously. With these facilities, I could make almost anything for my scrambler, and what I couldn't make I got from my mate Johnny Jakes for next to nothing. Johnny was one of Triumph's top works riders and one of the best friends I ever had. Then there was old Jock, the Chief Engineer on my first ship, who taught me my precision engineering skills along with my general seagoing engineering ones. Without this background, I would never have been able to keep going, let alone compete at championship level.

The stresses and strains on man and machine when competing at championship level are enormous. For two days after each race meeting, I ached in every muscle and bone and it took me every ounce of willpower to drag myself out of bed and ride off to the factory. I worked four hours or so, and then crashed out for the remaining eight hours of my shift. And then it was a race against time to prepare my scrambler for the next meeting in a few days' time. This might involve rebuilding an engine and gearbox or even rebuilding the complete machine.

Professional Triumph works riders like Johnny Jakes didn't have to spend huge amounts of time and effort preparing and maintaining their machines because Triumph's race engineers did it for them. So when the Triumph factory asked me to ride their new prototype scrambler at Pirbright Heath, I jumped at the chance.

Their new prototype was faster and more powerful than any other scrambler at that time, but they had a really big problem with its rear wheel viciously whipping from lock to lock when climbing steep slippery slopes. The resulting loss of traction in this area slowed it down dramatically. For some unknown reason, they had decided to launch the prototype before they had resolved this problem.

After much deliberation on their part, they eventually chose Pirbright scrambles track for the launch. This was probably because the track started off with a great long straight, which would enable their man to get well ahead of the pack and stay there. I say 'stay there,' because when your rear wheel viciously whips from lock to lock it leaves no room for other riders to overtake, especially up Pirbright's great big steep hill that's not just slippery with slimy mud, but very narrow too.

Although I lived a long way from Pirbright, I always thought of it as my local scrambles track. All my mates and fans were there to cheer me on. Some of my mates, including Johnny Jakes, were riding in the same heats as me. As I write, I remember quivering with excitement as forty two of us were all lined up waiting for the starter's flag to drop. As the flag dropped there was the usual almighty roar as we all took off, fighting neck and neck for the lead. With this particular track starting off with its great long straight, this deafening ear splitting roar usually lasted for a good forty-five seconds, only to die down somewhat as the field evened out. This time I only heard it for about twenty-five seconds so I was pretty sure that I was well ahead of the pack.

With a quick glance over my shoulder, I could see that I had a forty yard lead and was still gaining more. I know I shouldn't have done it, but I just couldn't resist taking another longer glance back to see how much of a lead I had, before slowing down to take the first bend, which was a left handed hairpin.

As I brought my eyes back on track, I was travelling at over seventy mph on slippery slimy mud with the hairpin coming up fast. I tried to power slide the big Triumph around the hairpin, knowing full well that only a miracle could save me from clouting a huge oak tree that lay directly ahead of me.

Obviously, no miracles were handed out that day - at least not to Triumph works riders! The next thing I knew, I was waking up in hospital with a fractured skull and a fractured wrist. The prototype was a complete write off. Triumph's bosses sacked me and told me that they would make sure that I would never get another works ride from them or any other motorcycle manufacturer – apparently my recklessness and devil may care attitude was not becoming of a works rider!

The day before I came out of hospital, Triumph's bosses relented and wrote to me saying: "We are making another prototype to the exact specification of the one that you smashed up. And, after a great deal of consideration, we have chosen you above everyone else to ride this new prototype, but only if you do exactly as you are told." Everyone else had refused to risk their neck on riding such a dangerous machine and now Triumph's bosses were saying that they have chosen me above everyone else to ride this latest prototype!

I admit I was crazy enough to want to ride this brute of a machine flat out up Pirbright's steep slippery muddy hills and to leap higher up in the air than anyone had ever done before - that's if the damned thing didn't throw me off before I got that far – but my answer was an emphatic "NO!"

They hadn't chosen me 'above everyone else' – everyone else had refused!

When I told my mate Johnny why I turned down Triumph's bosses offer to ride their latest prototype, he said, "There's another way you can do it if you really want to and without having to say 'Yes sir, no sir three bags full sir' to those chinless wonders."

"There is?" I asked, eagerly.

"The first thing to remember is that this so-called 'prototype' is just a standard TR5 like the one you own, but with a more beefed up engine," he

replied,

I studied the list of modifications that he handed me and said, "Ah, now I see what they've done, I can do all that stuff at work in about fourteen days - if you can get copies of the blueprints."

"No problem! I can even get you a brand new TR5 engine that you can strip down and use for the work," he said.

Twenty days later, I had completed the work just in time for the next race meeting at Pirbright. We all lined up, the flag dropped and we were off and just like last time, I was well ahead of the pack. Ninety seconds later, I was round the first right hand hairpin and trickling downhill in readiness to accelerate up the much bigger and slipperier hill that towered above me. By easing the throttle off ever so slightly and moving my body weight around each time it was about to whip, I was able to get enough wheel grip to get the TR5 up the hill. At the top of the hill, I snapped the throttle wide open and blasted the TR5 a good thirty feet high in the air off the top of the hill and then landed three quarters of the way down it.

While I was losing precious seconds fighting for wheel grip as I climbed the hill, many riders on better road holding machines had caught up and were about to overtake me, only to be thwarted at the very last moment by my crazy aerobatics. This cat and mouse game continued throughout the first lap. At the start of the second lap, I rode my TR5 flat out down the overlong starting straight, quickly leaving them all far behind.

Everything seemed to be going extraordinarily well as I went round the hairpin and trickled downhill in readiness to accelerate up the big slippery hill that towered immediately ahead of me. When I opened the throttle to gun the beefed up TR5 up the hill this time, its rear wheel started to whip from lock to lock much more viciously than it had ever done before. I gritted my teeth and tried to regain control of the bucking brute, but it was no use - I was thrown off into the middle of the track.

The TR5 had slid under the safety ropes into the spectators. I was just in time to crawl under the ropes before the rest of the pack came thundering up the hill. Fortunately, no one was seriously hurt, just a few cuts and bruises here and there.

I stayed on to watch the rest of the race. My mate Johnny won it, and I won the cup for the fastest lap. We had a couple of beers and then went home. In those far off days, if you were not a works rider, you rode your scrambler to the track. If it was still in one piece after the race you rode it back home. My TR5 wasn't seriously damaged, so after some minor repairs were carried out by Johnny's works mechanics, that's exactly what I did.

Johnny, being a works rider, didn't have to do that. So after changing into nice squeaky clean clothes and then making a rude gesture in my direction, he jumped into the passenger seat of one of the Triumph's works' motorcycle transporters, put his feet up on the dashboard and dozed off. I waited a while to let him get settled and then I took off after him.

It wasn't long before I caught him up and did a wheelie alongside the transporter's passenger door where he was dozing. It was pouring down with rain with a gale force wind blowing in the direction of the passenger's side window. Johnny woke up with a start and wound down the window to see what was going on, only to get smothered with great big goblets of Pirbright's thick slimy mud, coming off me and my TR5!

The driver slammed on the brakes and stopped, and so did I.

Johnny jumped out of the transporter, dressed in his no longer nice squeaky clean clothes. Wrinkling his nose, he said, "Phew... You stink like you've just come out of a sewer."

Laughing fit to bust I just managed to squeak out, "You don't smell so sweet either, me old mate!"

I didn't hear what Johnny said next because we were interrupted by the driver coming up behind me and shouting, "You got a flaming death wish or something, you stupid idiot; coming up like that on my inside!"

Johnny chimed in with, "As a matter of fact he has a death wish, and not only that he has a great big chip on his shoulder to match, didn't you know that?"

Scratching his head and shaking with rage, the driver retorted, "I don't know what this younger generation is coming to."

"Hey Pops, there's no need to get excited, I was just having a bit of fun," I croaked. Then letting in the clutch I disappeared into the night.

"LIGHTS, where's your bloody lights, you bloody maniac?" The driver screamed after me.

The truth is - I didn't have any! Scrambles motorcycles don't have lights; it's all part of the fun. Moreover, it's truly amazing how sharp our reflexes were after a day's racing on a scrambles track with the adrenalin pumping through our veins.

Two hours later, soaking in a nice steaming hot bath whilst sipping a large rum & coke, I thought about all the fun I had experienced without jumping through hoops and saying, "Yes sir, no sir three bags full sir" to those chinless wonders that run the country and, of course, the motorcycle industry.

There was an account of the race in the next week's Motorcycle magazine. The chief motorcycling correspondent reported on the astonishingly high speeds that I had travelled on Pirbright's starting straights, my record breaking leap off Pirbright's biggest hill and also the vicious lock to lock whipping behaviour of my TR5 on the hill where it threw me off.

There were several photos depicting this and also there was a close up of me and Johnny sitting astride our scramblers. In the photo, you could see him looking down in the direction of my beefed up TR5's engine, with a wry smile on his face. The caption under the photo read: 'Does he know something that we don't?'

The chief motorcycling correspondent, who also wrote the caption, fancied himself as a bit of an investigative journalist - so maybe he thought there was a bit of skullduggery going on that he needed to investigate. On the other hand, he also fancied himself as a bit of a comedian, so maybe he wrote the caption as a joke. Whether he did or not, I never found out. Anyway, it fired up the imagination of the fans. As there was a lot of speculation about how I had managed to get my 'standard' TR5 to go so fast, I decided not to race at Pirbright until all the fuss had died down.

I missed racing at Pirbright, but there were other tracks such as Tweseldown, Canada Heights, Biggin Hill, Haverhill, Beenham Park, Knockholt, Dodington Park, Brill, Brands Hatch and several others where I had just as much fun and excitement.

Several months later, I returned to Pirbright. Ten minutes before the first race started I was geeing up my mate Johnny about the last practical joke I had played on him when, over the public-address system, the presenter proclaimed, "The mystery man has returned and is racing here today. His race number, as usual, is number 13 - so look out for him, because when he's around there's bound to be plenty of thrills and spills!"

Raising my eyebrows and looking at Johnny accusingly, I said, "Did you hear what she just called me?"

"Yes I did and who can blame her. You know, Chuck, with your attitude and the great lengths you go to avoid publicity - you are bound to seem 'mysterious' to people who don't know you," he said, laughing his head off.

"Yes, I suppose so," I sighed. Then a sudden a thought struck me and I asked, "You put her up to that didn't you?"

"Yeah, gotcha!" he squeaked.

"You cheeky beggar," I growled.

"Sorry, but after that last practical joke you played on me, I couldn't resist it. You not only soaked me all over with your stinking slimy mud, but I had to listen to that grumpy old driver moaning about the younger generation all the way home!" he cried.

"By the way Johnny, why have the race organizers decided to run the track clockwise today instead of the usual anticlockwise way round?" I asked.

"Perhaps it's because they are having a go at you lazy blokes that can't get out of bed in time to get here for practice!" he replied.

"I know the track like the back of my hand, so I don't need practice. If I had known that it was going to run in the opposite direction, I would have been here at the crack of dawn," I said lamely.

"I'll tell you what, when the flag drops you tuck in behind me and stay there for the first lap. That might help you get some idea of how the track is laid out," he whispered in my ear.

"Thanks, Johnny. I'm glad you said that because I want to try something here today that I have done on some other tracks," I informed him.

"So what have you been getting up to then?" He asked.

"I have been changing gears in midair, just before landing back on the track, rather than piddling about changing them after landing. This saves precious seconds when you think about the hundreds of times you change gear during a race. After all, aren't you always telling me that time wasted in flying so high in the air, like I do, doesn't win races?" I replied.

"Brilliant. I will have to try that!" he said, eagerly.

"There's more: Where the track at the top of steep hills veers off to the right or left instead of going straight on, everyone, including me, used to slow right down before speeding up again as soon as the track straitened up. I don't do that anymore. If, for example, the track veers off to the left at the top of the hill, I get on the right hand edge of the track well before I reach the top. Then at the top of the hill, I slide my back wheel ever so slightly to the right as I turn on the extra bit of power that simultaneously raises the front wheel. This spins the motorcycle round to the left as I launch it into the air," I informed him.

"Seems to be highly dangerous to me," he muttered.

"Yes, I suppose it is - if you get it wrong."

Johnny crammed as much information into my head as he possibly could in those ten minutes before the race started. Then we were off. Johnny was in second place and I was right behind him, trying to stay with him and memorise the layout of the track at the same time. By the end of the first lap, I had a fair idea of how the track was laid out and I started to race in earnest.

On the second lap, I overtook Johnny just a few yards past the top of the first steep hill, where the track veered off to the right. He had slowed down at the top of the hill in order to cautiously negotiate this tricky section of the track. I flew through the air and landed on the track twenty feet ahead of him.

Three minutes later, on the next steep hill, I overtook Kenny Haynes in the same fashion. The only difference this time was the track veered off to the left. Kenny was in the lead and had been from the start. I stayed in the lead for the remainder of the second lap and also throughout the third and fourth. On the fifth and final lap, there was so much adrenalin pumping through my overloaded brain that I could no longer remember which hill was which. With four more hills to go, all I could do was guess, like playing a deadly game of Russian roulette. On the first one I guessed right, on the second one I also guessed right, but on the third one, I guessed wrong.

As this particular hill towered above me, I had no way of knowing which way the track veered off at the top until I was flying through the air and looking down on scores of upturned faces behind the safety ropes. Ironically, attached to those ropes, for the benefit of the spectator's safety, there was a mandatory eye catching sign proclaiming: 'MOTORCYCLE RACING IS DANGEROUS. YOU ARE HERE AT YOUR OWN RISK'.

By the worried looks on their faces, I could see that none of them disagreed with that as a maniac on a motorcycle passed over their heads with a deafening roar, and crashed down thirty feet behind them. I was stretchered off with a broken collar bone and three cracked ribs.

Johnny visited me in hospital and thanked me for helping him win the race. Looking at him in sheer amazement I said, "What on earth are you talking about?"

"Well Chuck, it's like this. Kenny took the lead at the start of the race and was going like the clappers until you put him off his stroke by flying through the air and landing in front of him. He wasn't able to pick up the pace after that and so I got ahead of him and stayed there and won the race," he replied.

The next day Johnny came in to see me grinning from ear to ear and said, "Guess what?"

"Your rich uncle has died and left you ten million pounds," I said, drolly.

Shaking his head and waving a finger at me he said, "There's a small engineering company in Northern Ireland that are making tailor made bolt on rear wheel swinging arm systems for scrambles motorcycles. These swinging arm systems are very expensive to make, but they will definitely solve your vicious rear wheel whipping problem if you get one."

"Sounds good to me. I'll order one right away," I replied.

Lowering his voice, he went on to say: "Now you can reinstall that beefed up engine I gave you into your TR5, and then you would be invincible."

"I don't know about being invincible, Johnny, but I certainly won't get thrown off like when I installed it before," I quipped.

"Well anyway, it would be a shame not to install it after all your meticulous and painstaking work," he said, sincerely.

There's no doubt about it, the new bolt on swinging arm system was a godsend. My TR5 no longer whipped from lock to lock on steep slippery hills, and with its beefed up engine installed, it was the fastest thing on the track again. But I still hankered for even more speed like a drug addict hooked on cocaine.

In my quest for more speed, I came across a crazy guy who fancied himself as a bit of an amateur petro-chemist. His name was Jake and he was developing an ultra-high octane racing fuel that he called 'Jake's Jungle Juice'. He was a very timid man and I had seen him hanging around the pits at scrambles meetings on several occasions. At first, I thought he might be some sort of spy until I found out that he was hoping that one of us would test his jungle juice under race conditions. So far there were no takers, which was not surprising bearing in mind that this was very volatile stuff.

Eventually, he plucked up enough courage to ask me if I would run my beefed up TR5 on it the next time I raced at Pirbright. When I agreed he was delighted and stammered, "Thank … you Sir … thank … you … I will …p … pay … you… h … handsomely."

"No need for that, just have the stuff here in time for practice, and if it is as good as you say it is, I will pay you," I replied, as I watched him gambolling away as if all his birthdays had come at once.

Next time at Pirbright, with a full tank of Jake's Special Jungle Juice, I was off to a flying start and stayed in the lead throughout the first four laps. It was raining cats and dogs, but I had never leapt so high off the top of the hills or raced at such high speeds as I did on that day. This new racing fuel was amazing. I was breaking lap records with ease, including one of my own. On the long starting straights, I was reaching speeds of up to ninety miles per hour before shutting down to take the left hand hairpin. That's almost twenty miles per hour faster than I had ever been on these straights, but I still thirsted for more speed.

Ignoring the rev counter as it hovered on the danger mark, I roared down the last straight at ninety three miles an hour on my fifth and final lap. Then, at the precise moment I was about to shut down to take the hairpin, my engine blew up and burst into flames. The front wheel dug into the ground and with the motorcycle travelling at ninety miles an hour, it catapulted itself high in the air and continued to cart wheel, end over end down the track until it finally hit the old oak tree that marked the hairpin and set it alight.

I was thrown over the handlebars in front of my flaming motorcycle, which somersaulted over me, missing me by a mere couple of inches as I rolled over and over in front of it. Although I was in a lot of pain, I couldn't help watching in fascination as the flaming motorcycle went careering off down the track in such spectacular fashion.

"Great balls of fire!" blurted out one of the two St John's Ambulance men as they snatched me off the track in the nick of time, before the rest of the pack came thundering down the track.

The ambulance men threw their coats over me to douse the flames and carted me off to Woking hospital with a broken ankle, superficial burns and a bunch of bruises and deep lacerations. The A&E doctor did a double take and exclaimed, "Oh no, not you again!"

Then after the ambulance men told him what happened, he examined me and proclaimed, "You are lucky not to have been killed!"

"Not lucky that way Doc, just lucky to have been taught how to fall by experts when I was small," I quipped.

When Johnny came to see how I was getting on, he said, "Your TR5 is a complete write-off and just a burnt out mass of twisted metal. The ACU scrutinizers say that you must have been doing over ninety miles an hour when your TR5's cylinder head disintegrated. The pushrods went straight through the petrol tank like torpedoes, turning it into a fireball. Your front wheel dug into the ground causing the bike to somersault over and over at high speed down the track until it hit the oak tree, setting it on fire."

He looked at me wryly and said, "That's the same oak tree that you collided with when Triumphs gave you that works ride several months ago. The first time you hit it at seventy miles an hour. This time you set the poor thing on fire - don't you like that oak tree for some reason?"

"I like oak trees and it was an accident both times," I retorted.

"Gotcha!" he said, just before my medication kicked in and I drifted off to sleep.

~~~

While I was in hospital I was offered a job by Cytrax Inc., the famous American motorcycle stunt riders display team. Apparently, a talent scout had sent them a photo of me sailing through the air in flames when my engine blew up. When I accepted the job, their rep came to see me and signed me up for a six weeks tour of California, Texas and Oklahoma, starting in eight weeks' time.

Most of the stunts I was called on to perform were to do with crashing motorcycles through large piles of rotten old chicken houses after they had been set on fire. These rotten old chicken houses were piled up on top of each other, then painted and papered over to look like real houses or shops, like on film sets. There was a six foot wide by ten foot high tunnel running through the centre of the structure that was also painted and papered over to look like the real thing.

When the structure was set on fire, the trick was to leap the motorcycle high in the air and crash through the soft papered opening and come out the other side - with your front wheel pawing the air in spectacular showman fashion. This might seem to be extremely dangerous, but the only real danger was if the support crew didn't hose you down quick enough after you performed the stunt or, of course, if you missed the soft papered-over opening.

When I was in Oklahoma, towards the end of the tour, I met a guy who ran a 'Wall of Death' show. I told him I was interested in having a go at it and he gave me a few lessons. After three lessons, he told me I was a natural and hired me on the days when I wasn't doing stunts. I was thrilled with riding the wall of death and getting highly paid for it, so when I went home I took a job with a British wall of death show.

All went well for a couple of months until the other riders got jealous when I started pulling more birds than they had ever had between them. Then one night, to make matters worse, a wild bunch of girls came to see the show. It wasn't unusual for members of the audience to lean over the top of the wall and hold out pound notes for us to snatch as we passed by. Instead of that, one of the girls pinned the notes to her knickers and held them out for me to catch - which I did, and stuffed them down my shirt. After that, each time I passed by her and her mates, I rode right up to the rim of the wall and blew them a kiss.

Faster and faster I rode, and the faster I went, the more excited they became. Then, as the show was closing, the master of ceremonies started his farewell spiel as we all lined up and bowed to the audience. After that, we all did our individual bows. When it was my turn, I bowed to each section of the audience but left the section where the wild bunch of girls was standing till last. Then, as I looked straight up into the eyes of the one that gave me her knickers, I dramatically drew them out of my shirt and bowed deeply like the Courtiers in Elizabethan times used to do. As I did this, the other wild girls became overexcited and threw their knickers down onto my head and shoulders. Each pair of knickers had a crisp one pound note pinned to it.

As far as the other riders were concerned this was the last straw. They all glared at me with bitter hatred written all over their faces and walked straight out the door, with the master of ceremonies running after them, shouting "Come back, come back you lot, I haven't finished my farewell speech".

The next day I went to see what the boss was going to do about the other wall of death riders walking out on him. I had hardly set foot in the door when he said: "I've got to let you go, Chuck. The other riders won't work with you and if I keep you on they won't come back, and then I'll go broke." I tried working in another four more different wall of death shows but, wherever I went, the same jealousy problems arose. I had given up my engineering job and sold my Willesden flat, so I moved back home with my Mum and Dad.

After a couple of weeks, I was thoroughly bored and wondering what to do next, when Johnny came roaring up on a motorcycle and vigorously knocked on the front door.

Thinking I was in trouble with the Old Bill again, I wrenched open the door and said, "Whatever it is - I didn't do it!"

But it wasn't them. It was my mate, Johnny. Seeing that he was very agitated, I pulled him through the door, sat him down in the lounge with a large rum & coke and asked, "What's up mate?"

After he had gulped it down, he blurted out, "Where have been? I've been looking for you everywhere. One moment you are in hospital - then the next you've disappeared!"

I told him about the stunt riding and the wall of death shows.

"Wow, Chuck, whatever will you get up to next?"

I opened my mouth to say something, but he was off again with, "You remember that bloke Jake, who put that revolutionary racing fuel in your tank?"

"Yes," I said.

"Well, he blew himself up in his garden shed, and that's not all - he demolished half of the house next door with the stuff he was working on. There's more! While you were in hospital, he ordered and paid for a brand spanking new TR5 scrambler direct from the factory, to replace the one that blew up." Then, without stopping to catch his breath, he went on to say, "He also left a tidy sum of money with them to pay for modifications to it, as per your instructions. You know Chuck; poor Jake was running around like a headless chicken trying to find you, so he could tell you this."

"Well, I never!" I exclaimed. "He didn't have to do that. It wasn't his fault that it blew up. If I hadn't been selfish and let the rev counter indicator go past the danger mark, it wouldn't have blown up."

Johnny held his hand up and said, "You're missing the point, Chuck, as usual. As far as I can gather, he was extremely grateful to you for risking your life trying out his experimental racing fuel and refusing to take money for doing it.

Johnny changed the subject by saying, "Have you still got that big old Tiger 100 road bike."

"Yes, as a matter of fact, I have," I said with pride. Puzzled as to what he was getting at, I said, "What about it?"

"Fire it up and come with me. I think you need some more excitement to cheer you up a bit," he said.

So off we roared on our motorcycles and went to a busy transport café called 'The Better 'Ole" in Isleworth, where a wild bunch of café racers hung out. Johnny introduced me to everybody. They all looked up to him because he was a scrambler and didn't scare easily, and when he told them about what I got up to, I received a very warm welcome.

After a while, Johnny went home to his wife and kids, and I hung out with the rest of the bunch for most of the evening. We talked about this and that until the action started at three o' clock in the morning when there was hardly any traffic about. The action plan was to see who could ride his motorcycle the fastest up and down a two mile stretch of road outside the café. This was on the Great West Road, in Middlesex which is now a part of West London.

This particular stretch of road not only had several other roads crossing it. It differed from other roads because ten yards before it went over each crossing it sloped upwards considerably, then levelled out as it went over the crossings, and then sloped downwards considerably before levelling out again and continuing on its way.

I don't know why this road was constructed that way. I do know that, because of the ramp like effect it created when you hit the crossings at speeds approaching one hundred miles an hour, you took off and flew high enough in the air to sail over vehicles that might be coming along from your right or left. To add a little bit more drama to the situation, each of these crossings had traffic lights. However, at three o clock in the morning, and with this stretch of road being part of a major trunk road, the lights usually stayed green - but not always, as you will see.

Three of the 'Better 'Ole boys', as they were called, decided to go for it - and so did I. There were four of us and the others decided to hang around as spectators manning the stopwatches. The first Better 'Ole boy clocked 98 mph on a 650cc Gold Flash, the second one clocked 99.5 mph on a 650cc Road Rocket and the third one on a standard 500cc Tiger 100 chickened out when his second set of traffic lights turned red. Then it was my turn and I clocked 101.2 mph on my highly tuned 500cc Tiger 100.

The traffic lights stayed green all the way for the one on the Gold Flash, but turned red on one occasion for the one on the Road Rocket. He had a taxi cab pass under him as he flew high up in the air. I had two red lights. A green line coach passed under me at the first one, but nothing at all was there at the second one. The upshot of this was that I became the leader of the pack. I took over from the previous one, who had been killed when he collided with a double-decker bus, just two days before I joined them.

I often wonder what the cabby said to his mates when he told them about the guy with the Road Rocket jumping it over his cab – or what the coach driver and his passengers said to their friends when I jumped my Tiger 100 over their coach in the wee small hours of the morning.

The next time we did it, two Better 'Ole boys were killed and another one was seriously injured. The Old Bill was everywhere after that, so we decided to lay low until all the fuss died down.

The Ace boys from the Ace Café on the North Circular Road, hearing that we were lying low, came to our gaff to wind us up, calling us chicken! So we went up to their gaff and sorted them out. There was one hell of a fight, with blood everywhere.

It was funny too. At one point, both sides had fought so hard that we were almost in a state of collapse and so, as if by mutual agreement, the fight came to a standstill. During the lull in the fighting, the other side had moved down to the far end of the café. Slumped over a table, with blood streaming down my face, I was taking stock of the situation and I could see that our side was going to get the worst of the fight. We needed a plan before the other side got their second wind and beat the living daylights out of us.

"What should we do?" someone whispered in my ear.

"Tell the others to gee the members of the other side up. Call them chicken and get them really mad - then when they come rushing down the aisle between the tables to finish us off, I will stick my leg out and trip them up," I whispered back.

"But some of the other side have now armed themselves with baseball bats," he whined.

Still whispering, I went on, "As the first lot go sprawling, the others, not being able to stop, will trip up and fall on top of them in a tangled heap. That's when you grab their baseball bats and let them have a taste of their own medicine."

Then spitting out a bloody broken tooth and not waiting for a reply, I snarled, "Do it NOW."

Still slumped over a table, pretending to be unconscious and looking out of the corner of my undamaged eye, I watched the changing expressions on the faces of our opponents as my mates whipped them up into a frenzy. One of my mates was making really realistic sounding chicken noises and that really wound them up. It was so funny I had to control my laughter, but I managed to remain focussed as they came charging down the aisle.

Then out shot my leg and over they went, all falling on top of each other. Those at the bottom of the pile couldn't use their baseball bats and those on top were easily disarmed - but not before we used their baseball bats on them and had broken a few heads. We then called up half a dozen cabs and carted the worst of our wounded off to hospital, and they did the same.

Three weeks later the Ace boys came down to visit us again, but this time to apologise for calling us chicken. After the fight, they eventually got it into their thick heads that we weren't chicken. They realised that the reason we weren't using the Great West Road as a racetrack was because the Old Bill was watching us like hawks and coming down on us like a ton of bricks every time they spotted us with their zero tolerance policy.

We accepted their apology and talked to each other for a very long time. We listened to them telling us all about the chicken runs and other exciting stuff that went on outside their café on the North Circular Road in London.

At this point, five Ace boys came in and told us that they had been given speeding tickets right outside our café for doing just forty two miles an hour in a forty mile an hour speed limit. They couldn't make a run for it because the Old Bill had set up a road block. This was on the very same stretch of road that we had been racing on at speeds approaching one hundred miles an hour or more, but those five Ace boys didn't know that. Neither did they know that the Old Bill was nicking anyone that looked like us, for even the slightest offence.

One of the older Ace boys said, "The Old Bill tried hitting us with stuff like this back in the early days when we first started to hang out at the Ace Café. What we did was to get them to chase us into the Ace and then, while they were looking for us, the other Ace boys would take the wheels off their squad cars and threw them into the River Brent! We were doing stuff like that, and even worse, all the time, until the Old Bill gave up and left us alone.

"Doing stuff like that without the Old Bill poking their snouts in - that's truly amazing! I don't suppose you could fix me up with a chicken run tonight?" I said, excitedly.

"Yes we can and we would be honoured to do so," he replied. A few hours later, at two-thirty in the morning, a ten ton truck blocked the North Circular Road, half a mile west of the Ace Café as if by accident. Another one did the same two miles down the road to the east. Thirty seconds later, I gunned my motorcycle down the road towards the Ace from the western end, as did the other ton up kid from the other end of the closed road.

This one came from Liverpool. He fancied himself as a hard man and had been telling everyone down the Ace that what we did in London was sissified stuff compared to what they did up there in Liverpool.

"Well matey, let's see what's so special about Liverpool," I said to myself as I was roaring off down the road to challenge him.

Seventy, eighty, ninety miles an hour - then I saw him clearly coming straight at me. Will he or won't he chicken out, I wondered, as we thundered towards each other at a closing speed of one hundred and eighty miles an hour. At first, I think he won't chicken out and I brace myself for the inevitable, but at the very last moment, he did. Boy oh boy, that was so exciting!

As for the 'Likely Liverpool lad', as we christened him, he came out with a ton of excuses as to why he chickened out. When I offered him the chance to do it again, he took off like a rocket and just kept on going all the way back to Liverpool, without saying another word.

I did many chicken runs after that with the same results. A rather macabre thing happened one night when a Birmingham ton up kid, who called himself the 'Birmingham Bomber', came down the Ace to challenge me to a chicken run. I agreed to take him on, but not until the next day at precisely three o clock in the morning when there wouldn't be any traffic about. My honour code in such matters was always to turn up on the dot, not a minute earlier and not a minute later – it all added to the tension.

Obviously, the 'Birmingham Bomber' didn't live by such a code. He arrived half an hour early at 2:30 am. Seeing I wasn't there, he assumed I wasn't going to turn up and started calling everyone 'chicken', until Ginger, one of my mates who was being egged on by the others, called his bluff and took him on. They shouldn't have done that. It was my shot and they knew full well that I would be on my way and would arrive in just a few minutes time at 3:00 am - right on the dot as planned.

Ten minutes before I set off for the Ace Café, I was talking to Johnny on the phone about this particular chicken run.

"I know you won't chicken out, but if you do - don't forget that up in Birmingham they turn off to the right if they chicken out, and not to the left like we do. Please don't take it the wrong way, but I thought I had better warn you - just in case."

I was unaware of what was going on down the Ace, and I thought no more about what Johnny said, until I was coming onto the North Circular Road and spotted a ten ton truck blocking the road. I quickly recognised that this was one of the trucks that were used to block the road when chicken runs were taking place. Hoping with all my heart that I could stop the inevitable carnage that I knew was about to happen, I squeezed through the small gap behind the truck and roared flat out down the road towards the Ace Café.

Thirty seconds later, I slapped on my brakes and skidded to an abrupt halt when I saw the dead bodies of the Birmingham boy and my mate, Ginger, laying there amongst the mangled wreckage of their motorcycles, which was scattered all over the carriageway in front of the Ace. The front wheel on one of the motorcycles was still spinning, alerting me to the fact that this horrendous accident must have happened just a few seconds before I arrived. Both boys were already dead, so they must have died instantaneously and probably felt no pain.

The Ace boys that had been watching the chicken run were still in shock after seeing the two ton up kids smash their high powered motorcycles head on into each other, right there in front of them, but none of them would look me in the eye. As I stormed up to them, I growled, "This was my chicken run which was supposed to start at 3:00 am precisely, so what's been going on?"

Shuffling their feet and looking at the ground, they said, "The Birmingham boy arrived half an hour before the run was due to start, and started calling us 'chicken', that's until your mate Ginger took him on.

"Why did he do that?" I said, testily.

"Because the Birmingham boy led us to believe that you wouldn't turn up, so we pressurised Ginger into doing it," he snivelled.

"You filthy dirty cowardly weasels!" I roared. "You haven't got the guts to do it yourselves and now you've gone and got Ginger killed and the Birmingham boy as well,"

"We didn't kill them, they killed themselves. Neither of them chickened out!"

"Listen you stupid, interfering idiots; up in Birmingham if they are going to chicken out they turn away to the right, not to the left as we would do, do you understand what I'm saying?" I said, coldly. I remained silent for few seconds to let this sink in and continued, "You stupid idiots! You should know by now that I never chicken out. Everyone knows that, even the Birmingham boy. I'm always there at the stipulated time, not a minute early and not a minute late, he knew that too. By all intents and purposes, it looks like he was starting to get cold feet and beginning to realise that he had bitten off more than he could chew. That's why he was picking on you lot to find a softer target".

I felt bad about Ginger's death and stayed away from the Ace until ten weeks later. I had been scrambling at Halstead in Essex and I was not only covered with mud as usual, but was also cold, wet and starving hungry. As I was passing by the Ace on my way home I decided to drop in and have some pie and chips.

I had just started to tuck into them when this pimply college boy called Alec sat down opposite me. He had the diabolic effrontery to say, "Give us a chip Chuck!" like as if he was a mate of mine - then immediately went to nick one right off my plate. But that was as far as he got. I raised my fork and brought it down with so much force that it went straight through his hand into the Formica table top – pinning him there.

Alec was carted off to hospital before he bled to death. The hole in the table, where the fork went through, was never repaired and the next time I visited the Ace, I saw that some joker had added his comments to it. In indelible ink, it proclaimed, 'Chuck did this - don't upset him or you could be next!' This didn't go unnoticed by the long suffering Len who served behind the counter. He was always chastising us for defiling his table tops, and scrub and scrub as he might; he never managed to remove those comments. I often saw him fiddling around with a fork after the incident, trying to work out how I did it, as did many others who were present. As for Alec, he never came down the Ace again. He was just another hanger on, basking in our glory or should I say notoriety, then telling his pals back at college that he was one of us. There were many like him, trying it on until they got a smack.

Besides doing chicken runs, there was another dicing with death activity we did for kicks - if you were crazy enough to do it! First, you put a rock record on the jukebox; then you ran out of the café, leapt on your motorcycle and rode it flat out over a pre-set course in an endeavour to arrive back before the record stopped. Our pre-set course took us out of the Ace Café, onto the old North Circular Road in an easterly direction, round the murderous iron bridge, and then back again past the Ace and then a final U-turn, which brought you back into the Ace.

Many Ace boys were killed going round the iron bridge. I say going round it, as opposed to going over it, because it has a slight continuous curve that seemed to go on for ever. If you went round it too fast, say at 98 mph or more, you would smash into the iron railing and end up like chips going through a potato chipper. On the other hand, if you went round it at less than 95 mph you wouldn't get back before the record stopped.

As this happened when the Old Bill wasn't about, all they could do was to scrape the blood and guts off the railings before the London rush hour began - they didn't want squeamish commuters getting upset! It's a rotten job, but as they say, 'someone has to do it'! Some of the bits of dead bodies landed down below and got pulverised under passing trains. That old iron bridge is a very long one, it spans the Willesden marshalling yards and also several mainline railway tracks that lay a hundred and fifty feet or so, below!

CHUCK'S STORY 7
LOVE AT FIRST SIGHT
EARLY 1960s

One boring night, down the Ace with nothing exciting going on, there were six of us sitting around a table listening to records on the jukebox. We all had our booted feet propped up on the table, with the jukebox going full blast when a very popular rock and roll star* and his entourage of bodyguards popped in for a cup of tea and something to eat - obviously on their way between gigs.

With none of us giving him no more than a second glance, he started throwing his weight about, calling us a scruffy bunch of saddle tramps - which we thought was hilarious. Not getting the adoration that he was used to, he started picking on Len, the long suffering night manager behind the counter, telling him to turn the jukebox down and hurry up with his food. When Len didn't answer, he asked, "Don't you know who I am?"

Len looked at him with his usual disinterested stare and said, "I don't care who you are, Sonny, just wait your turn like everyone else." At this point, the bodyguards muscled in on the act and started trying to grab hold of him. Now Len might be a miserable old sod - but he was our miserable old sod, so we intervened. They were so engrossed in putting the frighteners on poor old Len that they didn't see us sneak up behind them until we started clobbering them with our fists and heavy hobnailed riding boots. As soon as the rough stuff started, the pop star was nowhere to be seen, so of course, he didn't get any food!

The Ace Café was the only place open at that time of night for miles around. Many pop stars popped in from time to time on their way to and from gigs, as did people from all walks of life. I didn't take much notice - until one night, just before Christmas, when a striking nineteen-year-old girl came in and took my breath away.

She didn't just walk up to the counter, she seemed to glide - as if she was on wheels! She looked a lot like Sophia Loren, the famous Italian film star. She wasn't dolled up like most girls that passed through the Ace. She wore no makeup - she didn't need it. My mind was in a whirl and my feelings were all over the place. It was love at first sight! I felt as though I just wanted to be with her for ever and protect her from all the bad things in life.

My eyes followed her as she sat down at an empty table. My mate Kipper said, "What's the matter Chuck, you look like you've seen a ghost or something?"

"Something like that," I replied, absently, for want of having nothing better to say.

I caught the girl's eye several times while I was talking to Kipper and each time she held my gaze for a moment longer, before she looked away. Kipper, seeing I wasn't paying attention to what he was saying, got up and went off in a huff! The last time the girl looked away, I was sure that I caught a hint of a challenge in her eyes - so I went straight up to her table, sat down opposite her and said, "I know you fancy me but didn't your mother ever tell you that it's rude to stare?"

"Why, you arrogant pig!" she snarled.

"Me, arrogant!" I exclaimed.

"Yes, you are. I saw you, with your feet propped up on the table, as if you owned the place," she sneered.

"Maybe I do," I replied.

"So you're a greedy money grabbing Tory capitalist pig?"

"No I'm not, I utterly despise people like that and I wouldn't be seen dead in their company, not alone owning this stupid café," I said angrily.

"Oh!" she said, with a surprised look on her face."

"So, what's your name then?" I asked.

"Yvonne," she replied.

"Are you French or Italian or something?"

"What's that to you?" she snapped.

"You don't like men very much, do you?"

"Why should I? You're all a load of gutless losers!"

"Hah, get on the back of my motorbike and we'll see about that!." I goaded.

"Alright, but where are we going?" she queried, as she followed me outside.

"Brighton," I said, emphatically.

"What at two o' clock in the morning - and at this time of the year? It's freezing cold!" she shivered.

"Hah, now who's the gutless one?" I said, scornfully.

"I'm not gutless. I have more guts than you will ever have," she growled, getting on the back of my motorcycle.

"Put your arms around my waist and hold on tight,"

"No, I won't. I don't even know you," she spat out.

A couple of hefty power slides across the Ace car park told her that refusing to do as I asked was not a good idea, so she threw her arms round my waist and clung onto me like a limpet as we roared off down the North Circular on our way to Brighton. It wasn't until we were over half way there that she began to relax and loosen up.

Her arms were still around my waist, but to my sheer amazement I could feel her beginning to doze off, so I slowed right down from ninety miles an hour to a mere twenty. I daren't do more than that lest she rolled off and hurt herself. After a while, I teased, "Would you like me to stop, sleepy head?"

"Please don't stop," she whispered in my ear, in a tiny sleepy voice.

It was nice having Yvonne there with her arms around me and the warmth of her young body warming my back, so I said nothing as I concentrated on getting her to Brighton in one piece. When we arrived, I found an all-night café and sat her down next to a hot radiator and bought us both a full English breakfast, washed down with cups of scolding hot tea.

Watching her scoffing her food down as if she hadn't eaten for several days, I asked, "When was the last time you had anything to eat?"

"Two days ago," she confessed.

"Why didn't you get something to eat when you were down the Ace?" I prodded.

"Because I only had enough money to buy a cup of tea and I don't accept charity from anyone," she snapped.

"I'm not just anybody," I said angrily, slamming my fist down on the table.

"I'm sorry I upset you after you bought me such a lovely breakfast, but that's the way I am," she said, apologetically."

"Listen, Yvonne, I really do understand what you are saying. Same as you I've been down on my luck many times and I would rather starve to death than accept charity,"

"Really!" she said, in amazement, "I'm beginning to think that you might be my kindred spirit."

"Me too," I whispered.

"For several moments we sat busy in our thoughts until Yvonne whispered in my ear, "Chuck, down the Ace everyone refers to you as 'Chuck'. Is that your real name?"

"Yes, it is. You haven't been checking up on me, have you?" I teased.

"No, I just wanted to tell you that I don't want to go back to the Ace. I've always wanted to travel around the southeast coast, can you take me?"

"Yes, but only if you let me keep you fed and watered without complaining – after all, I don't want you dying on me," I said.

"Alright, I'll be good. I promise," she said, crossing her heart and then excitedly asked: "when can we go?"

"How about, right now?"

"Yes please!" she cried, jumping up and down and giggling like a little schoolgirl.

"Go and freshen up and then meet me outside," I said.

Five minutes later we were off, taking in Newhaven, Hastings, Folkestone, Dover and several other seaside resorts in between. By the time we arrived at Dover, it was night time and we were so tired and cold that we couldn't keep our eyes open. Neither could we stop shivering, but we couldn't find a hotel.

Riding along on the beach under the cliffs, we found a cave. It wasn't the Ritz, but it was better than sleeping on the beach. It wasn't much warmer in the cave, so we had to huddle up to together to keep warm and get some sleep.

At daybreak, we got up and after we had stretched our legs, we went to Ramsgate and Margate. After that, we went to Gravesend and took the ferry to Tilbury, and then we were back on the road to Southend.

When we arrived at Southend, Yvonne was getting even more excited because she wanted to walk along the town's famous mile long pier. All the shops and kiosks were boarded up for the winter and there was not a soul to be seen anywhere, which seemed to excite her even more.

So, hand in hand, we walked along the pier. As we walked, the December fog came down behind us, shutting us off from the rest of the world. Then, as if by magic, when we reached the end of the pier we found ourselves bathed in winter sunshine as was the surrounding sea itself. Squeezing my hand and looking out to sea, Yvonne stood up on tiptoes, kissed me full on my lips and said, "Chuck, this is so romantic."

We stood there for several minutes; chatting and admiring the view until a bitter north-easterly wind sprang up and it was time get her home. But whose home? Yvonne, I discovered, had quit her living in job and was only nineteen. I offered her money to find somewhere else to stay, but she had refused to take it. I was living in digs at Hounslow, as it suited my present lifestyle, so the only thing left was to sneak her into my room when everyone had gone to bed.

My room was at the top of a large three story house. I intended to sleep in an armchair and let Yvonne have the bed, but instead we both ended up sleeping in the bed. This was a single bed, but by spooning up together, we soon fell asleep. We meant to get up at six and be gone before anyone woke up, but because we had been so tired we didn't wake until half past eight. As we came downstairs, the landlady saw us and started screeching: "How dare you bring bits of girls in here? I won't stand for it. Get out and don't come back!"

As we went out the door, Yvonne said, "I'm so sorry you got thrown out of your digs because of me."

"That's okay, don't worry about it. Something will turn up, you will see," I said, philosophically.

"But, aren't you angry with me?".

"Angry with you, dear, never," I smiled.

"You're not going to dump me then?"

"No, I'm not going to dump you. Not unless you want me to," I teased.

"That's a relief," she whispered.

"That's settled then so let's go and find somewhere to live," I replied.

We searched all day for a suitable place to set up home, but being two days before Christmas, we had to settle for a poky one room garret for the time being. The garret's window had no glass in it so we asked if it could be fixed. The building was owned by a money grabbing little man.

"Take it or leave it. If you don't want to rent it, I will let it out to someone else," he replied bluntly.

The next morning we both woke up suffering from 'flu. I tucked Yvonne up in bed and staggered up to the shops to get 'flu medications, a bottle of rum and some soup. When I got back, I dosed us up and got under the blankets and cuddled up to her to keep us warm. Christmas day came and went, as did Boxing Day and the day after that, as we suffered. The day after that we started to feel a bit better.

Two days later, I found a really nice flat in Acton and I was just telling Yvonne the good news when the landlord knocked on our door and demanded the next week's rent. The old familiar red mist clouded my eyes as I shouted, "You dirty filthy stinking bastard! You almost killed her!" And I kicked him down the stairs.

"Is he dead?" Yvonne whispered.

"I don't think so, more's the pity. Let's scarper before the Old Bill gets here."

Ten minutes later we were sitting in our new flat drinking tea, when Yvonne said, with admiration, "Wow Chuck, you're a real goer aren't you."

"I'm afraid so love," I said.

Taking my head in her hands and looking deep into my eyes, she said "How did you get to be like that? You are so gentle and considerate with me, but when you kicked that excuse for a man down the stairs you made my blood run cold."

"I'm sorry, my love, I didn't want you to see that."

By way of explanation, I told her about what my pro-military prep school did to me and the chip on my shoulder that they put there. I also told her about my disinterest in money and worldly goods and my utter contempt for those that chase it.

After listening intently, she said, "I knew there was something about you that struck a chord in me, but I didn't know what it was until now."

"So, you're not angry with me then?" I asked.

"No, I'm not. I'm truly sorry I called you 'a greedy money grabbing Tory capitalist pig' when we first met," she said. "But you know Chuck, you're the first man I've met that's not like that!"

"You know Yvonne, you struck a chord in me too - from the very first time I saw you. It wasn't just your natural beauty, openness and poise, but also your relaxed and confident manner in a dangerous situation. You know as well as I do that the Ace cafe is a very dangerous place for a lone nineteen year old girl at two o' clock in the morning. But that didn't stop you coming in and doing what you had to do. The way your body moved as you glided up to the counter was sheer poetry in motion, and the way you treated the 'low-lifes' and their filthy comments with the utter contempt that they deserved, was nothing short of majestic," I said with admiration.

She smiled and asked, "Do you know why I was down the Ace when you met me?"

"To beat me up, may be." I teased.

"No silly, this is serious and it's a very long story, so listen carefully," she said, scathingly. Then she went on: "When I was a kid, I had a little dog called Susie who I loved dearly, but one day my Mum told me that we were too poor to keep her and so she got rid of her. We were poor because my Dad, who was a bricklayer, blew all his wages on drink until he eventually drunk himself to death. Mum was holding down six part time jobs to keep a roof over our heads, so she was hardly ever there, and as all the kids near me were boys - by the time I was thirteen I was an uncontrollable tomboy.

There were lots of rich kids with dogs who lived just over a mile away from us. I hated these kids when I saw that they made fools of their dogs and robbed them of their dignity. As far as they were concerned, their dogs were just toys to be played with and cast aside when some other toy took their fancy. My uncle Harry, who bred and trained gun dogs, taught me a lot about how dogs should be cared for, so I knew that the way these rich kids were treating their dogs was cruel. So every time I saw one of these rich kids with a dog, I punched the kid on the nose, grabbed the dog and took it home.

The first time I did this, my Mum told me to take the dog back and when I refused to do so, she called the Old Bill. Every time after that, when a dog went missing, they were round our house like a shot. In an effort to teach me a lesson, she put me into care. She wasn't very bright, and she naïvely thought that after a day or two she could get me back - but once they've got their grubby hands on you they don't let go!

One of my uncles drove a cattle truck, picking up and delivering cows, sheep and pigs from all over England, Scotland and Wales. He helped me to escape from every home they put me in. You know, Chuck, you remind me of him a lot. He was a rebel like you and he hated the British Establishment and what they stand for as much as you do. By this time, I was officially marked down as a 'thirteen year old juvenile delinquent'.

I was as passionately fond of animals as you are, even then. So, my uncle found me lots of living in jobs working with animals on farms. The pay was poor, but I loved the work and I learnt a lot. Being on the run meant that sometimes I would have to change jobs before my uncle could get to me, so he would get another cattle truck driver to pick me up and take me to another job. He was a champion bare knuckle fighter, so none of the other cattle truck drivers would dare cross him. He was paranoid about my safety and in case anyone tried to molest me, he bought me a stiletto and taught me how to use it. That's the one you saw in the secret compartment of my handbag."

"So, you were waiting for one of the cattle truck drivers to come and pick you up and take you to another job?" I asked.

"That's right. All the way up to the Scottish highlands this time," she replied.

"Yvonne you're quite a girl," I said, humbly.

Chuck and Yvonne were married at Ealing registry office in 1962

The snow started right on cue as Yvonne said those two little magic words, 'I do' during the wedding ceremony. She told me it must be a good omen for a long and happy marriage. After all, it was most unusual for it to be snowing in London at the end of March! When we got home we had a nice hot bath together and then, when we were both as warm as toast, I chuckled, "Well, Mrs Kemsley, what shall we do to celebrate our wedding?"

Ealing Town Hall & Registry Office

"Let's go up west to the cinema and see Audrey Hepburn in "Breakfast at Tiffany's," she replied. So we did, and what a terrific film it was!

We loved the song, 'Moon River' with its wonderful lyrics:

> Moon River, wider than a mile,
> I'm crossing you in style someday.
> Oh, dream maker, you heart breaker,
> wherever you're going, I'm going your way.
> Two drifters, off to see the world,
> There's such a lot of world to see.
> We're after the same rainbow's end,
> Waiting, round the bend, my huckleberry friend,
> Moon River and me.

"That's us!" Yvonne proclaimed. "We're the two drifters, off to see the world!"

It took a while, but as we began our epic and eventful journey together, I realised how apt those words were and how remarkably perceptive she was.

~~~

CHUCK'S STORY 8
LONDON & BRIXHAM
EARLY 1960s

Although we liked our life in London, we really wanted to get back to working with animals. As there were no proper animal jobs in London, we were already making plans to move elsewhere. Yvonne also wanted a greyhound, but as that wasn't possible, she settled for a cat - but not just any old cat.

The cat she eventually settled for was a Persian-Siamese cross, which she named Pinkie. I quickly realised why she settled for this one because after I trained him for her, he acted more like a dog than a cat. He growled like a dog and I almost got him to bark like one. After his training, he turned out to be a feisty little rascal

The day after Yvonne got Pinkie, we were down Oxford Street when she clutched my arm and said, "Chuck, do you see that large police sign over there? It says 'BEWARE OF PICKPOCKETS'."

"Yes I see it, but what's so special about it?" I asked.

"Well, I was wondering whether you could train Pinkie to lay doggo in my shopping bag and bite anyone who stuck their hand in there, trying to steal my purse," she said. I had trained tiny Terriers to do it for a couple of film starlets when I was in Los Angeles, so with Pinkie's dog-like character, I didn't have too much trouble training him either.

Pinkie wanted to be with us all the time and to go with us wherever we went, even when we went out on one of my motorcycles. I would never have thought he'd want to do that - but then he wasn't just any old cat. He was just like the dogs I train; when told to 'stay' he would do just that.

One day, when we went to go out on a motorcycle, I forgot to tell him to 'stay'. We were just starting to take off, when he leapt on Yvonne's back.

For want of not knowing what else to do, she put him inside her leather jacket. He was as pleased as punch about that, and even more so when he realised he could stick his head out the top of her jacket and see what was going on. We were off down the M1, and we thought it might be interesting to see what he made of that. All the way up to ninety-seven miles an hour he had his head sticking out of her jacket, and it wasn't until we were doing ninety eight miles an hour before he popped his head back in.

He wasn't scared, even when we were doing a hundred and eleven miles an hour, which was as fast as my tuned up Tiger 100 could go. He just hung in there, making his funny little growling noise, which he always did when he was having fun. He never purred in the true sense, as most cats do. Yvonne was shouting this out to me above the combined roar of the engine and the wind, so I slowed down to ninety-seven miles an hour and, low and behold, out popped his head.

We stayed at that speed for a couple of miles and then speeded up to a hundred and five. Switching between these two speeds, his head was soon popping in and out of Yvonne's jacket like a jack-in-a-box. On the way home, Yvonne said, "Let's go down the Ace and introduce him to your mates." One of my mates down the Ace was a BBC despatch rider and when we told him what Pinkie did, he told one of the BBC's reporters about him.

Doing 'The Ton', that's 100 mph on a motorcycle, was the magic speed at the time - and doing it on Britain's antiquated roads was considered to be extremely dangerous. Anything relating to that was good copy for the newspapers and TV. Pinkie was on the BBC television news the next day, along with his 'Mum and Dad', as they dubbed us. The national newspapers picked up on that for several more days. And so it was that Pinkie became known as 'Pinkie the ton up cat'.

With Pinkie becoming a bit of a celebrity, he received a lot of unwanted attention and so did Yvonne and I. Pinkie hated people pawing him and trying to make a fool out of him. Yvonne hated publicity and I didn't care much for it either. There had been three unsuccessful attempts to kidnap Pinkie and also several death threats, so when we took him out in public he stayed inside Yvonne's jacket with just his head poking out the top!

Because of Pinkie's dislike of people pawing him and trying to make a fool out of him, I trained him to bite on command. I built two trigger words into his training, one to switch him on and the other one to switch him off. Making fools out of animals and thereby robbing them of their dignity was starting to become the vogue at the start of the 1960's. We hated this evil trend and we had no scruples about training Pinkie to protect himself from it. He was always a very dignified cat and after receiving this extra bit of training, he blossomed and became even more dignified than ever.

Over the winter months we were busy making plans to get back to working with animals, but despite numerous forays to all the surrounding counties, we were getting nowhere because the proper animal jobs were further afield. So we bought a two-man tent plus all the necessary camping equipment and took off for the West Country. We rode throughout the night and landed up at Hillcrest Farm camping site, at Brixham in Devon.

Hillcrest Farm was set in an idyllic spot. It was situated at the top of a very steep hill, with spectacular panoramic views of the River Dart at the bottom of the North side of the hill, and equally spectacular views of Brixham harbour and the sea beyond at the bottom of the South side of the hill. It was a working mixed farm, with the camping site being a small sideline to that.

The campsite comprised of just twenty pitches situated in a ten-acre field, so there was plenty of space between pitches, as opposed to the over-commercialised sites where people are packed in like sardines.

There were also good washing and bathing facilities up near the farmhouse and also a farm shop. Pinkie thrived and so did we. We all enjoyed being there so much that we decided to treat it as the honeymoon that we never had.

If anyone had told us then that it would go on for nine and a half months we would have refused to believe them, but it did. We got on like a house on fire with the husband and wife who owned the farm. Yvonne often helped them out when they needed some respite from looking after the animals. Being a mixed farm there were cows, sheep, pigs, horses and a couple of sheepdogs. There was also a beautiful flock of geese.

Yvonne was too proud to accept payment for helping them, so every time that she went to pay the site rent or buy anything from the farm shop, they told her that it was on the house. I re-schooled their horses and re-trained their sheepdogs for them too. It didn't take long, just an hour a day, over six weeks. They were highly impressed and delighted with the results and paid me handsomely, on the understanding that they would be insulted if I didn't take it.

As we started to get organised, I got a part time job at a boatyard on the banks of the River Dart, at the bottom of the hill. Yvonne also got a part time job at a fisherman's café down the other side of the hill, in Brixham. The weather was glorious that year, as only in Devon it can be, and the people we worked with were really nice.

My kindly boatyard boss welcomed my engineering skills, despite my quick temper. Every time I blew a fuse, he suggested that I should take a stroll along the riverbank and not come back until I felt better. He was a wise old man who knew how therapeutic a stroll along the banks of the River Dart can be. A mile or so downriver lay the Royal Naval College at Dartmouth, where there was always a lot of exciting activity going on. Upriver, it was a lot more tranquil if you just wanted to sit and meditate.

Yvonne loved her little part time job at the fisherman's café down in Brixham. The fishermen were a jolly bunch of blokes and were very thoughtful too. They often brought her some of the famous Brixham plaice - straight out of the sea. Every time they gave it to her, the café owner told her to get off home with it and pop it in the frying pan, before it lost its flavour. She only had a little primus stove to cook on, but that didn't stop her producing dishes fit for a king!

Pinkie always seemed to know when Brixham plaice was on the menu - and he just couldn't wait for it to come out of the pan. I often smiled to myself when I thought of the sky high prices that the top London restaurants paid for it - when I knew that it could never taste half as good as when it came straight out of the sea!

Pinkie's favourite sleeping place was between the flysheet and the roof of the tent, and when there were rats about he would growl like a guard dog. He had a thing about rats, especially those great big farm rats that lived there. Every so often, in the middle of the night, he would get up and take off after them. One night, he came home with half his tail missing, but that didn't stop him. After all, as I stated earlier, 'he wasn't just any old cat'!

~~~

Brixham Harbour

CHUCK'S STORY 9
GLOUCESTERSHIRE
MID - LATE 1960s

At the beginning of November it was starting to get too cold for camping, so we moved on to Gloucestershire where we met a Mr Thomas, who owned Quedgeley Court and several other properties and pieces of land throughout the county. We told him what we were trying to achieve and he congratulated us, saying, "Put yourselves in my hands and I will help you as much as I can."

For starters, he rented us a double bedroom flat on the third floor at Quedgeley Court at a very reasonable price. He also let us have the basement, which ran all the way under the mansion, at no extra cost. Quedgeley Court, before the Ministry of Transport pulled it down to make way for a new stretch of motorway, was an old three-story mansion that had seen better days. Facing south and built into the side of a hill, half of the basement had a bright and sunny aspect to it, like as if it was the ground floor. This made it ideal for housing clients' dogs. The property also had a five-acre field adjoining it, which was ideal for training them.

Our flat was very much in need of redecoration, so we started on that right away. With the high ceilings and oak beams, we stuck to the traditional old English white walls and black beams theme. After we finished painting the walls and the ceiling in white and the beams in matt black, we started hanging some new curtains to see what they would look like.

Pinkie, who had been told off for getting in the way several times, was on his best behaviour. But seeing these great long curtains going all the way up to those high ceilings, he just couldn't contain himself any longer. He leapt on the nearest one and climbed all the way up to the top. Yvonne shouted at him and he jumped off the curtain onto the protruding end of a scaffold board. The other end of the board had a paint kettle full of black paint on it. Consequently, the paint kettle was catapulted ten feet into the air and the contents were splattered all over the freshly painted walls - and over Pinkie too. It took an extra five litres of white paint to repair his handiwork and another six months before his fur was pure white again. Every time he passed a full-length mirror he did a double take; he wasn't a very happy cat!

After we finished decorating the flat, I started schooling horses and training gun dogs again. With my foxhound background, there was no shortage of clients and I could pick and choose whose horses I schooled and whose gun dogs I trained. Yvonne took a job as a kennel maid at Gloucester greyhound track.

There were four registered greyhound trainers, with their own kennels on the premises. Each kennel housed twenty-five to thirty greyhounds. After she became matey with all the other kennel maids, she soon knew the latest form on every greyhound that raced there – which she passed on to me. You would think that having the latest form on every dog in any race, you would win a lot of money, but that wasn't the case. Time after time, dogs that should have won, didn't win - and there had to be a logical explanation. Then, one night, just before a race, Yvonne saw one of the trainers sneak off behind the kennels with the red-hot favourite and give it a drink of water.

If you are not an expert on training racing greyhounds this might seem innocent enough, but anyone who is a true expert on the subject - which Yvonne was - would tell you that this was all it takes to let the slower dog win. Over the next two months, Yvonne saw this happen on several occasions. Although giving a dog a drink of water just before a race is not injurious to a dog's health and wellbeing, there were a lot of other things, like drugs and stuff, which were. When she found out that they were all at it, she left.

Tearful and bitterly frustrated that she couldn't do anything to stop this happening, she came home and told me about it.

After she calmed down, I said, "It looks like the criminal element is behind this."

"Yes, they are. I know they are," she cried, shrugging her shoulders, emphasising the fact that she was unable to anything about it.

"I'll tell you what. Why don't you get a couple of greyhounds and go coursing with them? There's no bribery and corruption in that. It's a lot more natural than chasing a stupid electronic hare and a lot more fun too. There's not much money in it, so there's no organised crime ring messing it up."

She thought about it for a few moments and replied: "A couple of lurchers would be better for that. As long as they are greyhounds with a slight dash of collie and Labrador blood, I would be happy to do that."

"That's settled then," I concluded.

Next to greyhounds, Yvonne loved German shepherd dogs. One of her uncles used to breed them, so that wasn't surprising. So when one of our neighbours told her about an eighteen month old German shepherd dog that was being ill-treated, she was very angry. Penny was her name, and a large Irish family that lived nearby owned her. Every payday, the men of the family got drunk and beat her up. Then, halfway through the week when they run out of money, she didn't get any food.

When she was seventeen months old, she bit every male member of the family so severely that they were too afraid to enter their house. She hated all men, and attacked them on sight. However, she loved all the female members of the family, and they could do anything with her - even the little girls. So, when Yvonne rang them up and offered to take her off their hands, they were pleased to let her go.

Understandably, when I went to pick Penny up, there was no way she was going to let me into the house and certainly not let me take her away. I had to swallow my pride and ask one of the little girls to put her into our kennel van. As I got in the van, she flew at the heavy wire barricade and tried to smash it down to get at me.

When I arrived back at Quedgeley Court, I was wondering what to do next when Yvonne came up, as cool as a cucumber, and said, "Hello Penny, let's take you for a nice walk," and off they went, as if they had known each other all their lives.

When she came back, she put Penny back in the van and asked, "How on earth are you going to rehabilitate her with that whacking great big chip on her shoulder?"

"There's only one way. It might be dangerous but that's beside the point. She hasn't done anything wrong and she deserves to have a chance to enjoy life to the full," I said, still deep in thought.

She waited patiently for me to tell her what I had in mind. After about a minute, I said, "I'm going to play this by ear. Firstly, I'm going to camp out in my study and catch up with my piled up paperwork over the next two days and nights. During that time I will be either sitting or sleeping in my office chair and when I need to, I will pee in a bucket beside my chair. I'll also keep food and bottled water in my desk to keep up my strength. When I'm all set up, I want you to let Penny in and shut the door behind her, without saying anything to me or to her."

Yvonne knew enough about these dangerous types of situations to know that I might get badly hurt - if not killed, but she did exactly what I asked her to do. I knew from my own formal training and experience that deep down Penny wasn't an evil animal. She was just scared of men after what they had done to her. The first and most important part of my job was to remove that fear.

As Penny entered my study, she picked up my male scent and slunk off to the far corner of the room and lay down, just as I expected her to do. After all, this was my lair, which was a strong psychological point in my favour. Also the door was shut and there was nowhere else to go. I completely ignored her and carried on writing for five minutes. Then, as I looked up, she stood up and growled. I just carried on writing and she stopped growling and lay back down again. This went on for almost two hours. By that time, she had stopped growling and just lay there when I looked up.

Every time I looked up, I viewed her from the far corner of my eye. We, humans, have 15% more peripheral vision than dogs, so I could keep an eye on her without it being too obvious. Those of us who successfully train dangerous animals, learn how to use this powerful tool early on, as part of our formal training.

There's an old saying, 'dogs can smell fear', but it goes a lot deeper than that. They can also pick up on cool, laid back confidence and qualities of pack leadership, which will combat any fear that the formally trained trainer may have. No one is born with these subtle skills and they have to be learnt early on, as part of one's formal training.

Two hours later, I reached into my desk and pulled out the ham sandwiches that Yvonne had prepared for me. I offered Penny the last one, but she stood up and growled at me, so I ate it and made a great show of letting her know how much I enjoyed it. She hadn't eaten for two days and must have been very hungry, but she wasn't going to be won over with food. As I carried on with my paperwork, she lay down and stopped growling.

Eventually, I must have dozed off and woke up about an hour later, feeling her sniffing me all over. Obviously, curiosity had certainly got the better of her, as I knew it would. She just had to suss out this man who was so different from any other man that she had ever met before. I made out I was asleep until I considered that she had plenty of time to satisfy her curiosity. Then I whispered, "Go and lay down," which she did, with just a small inkling of respect in her body language. Still looking out of the far corner of my eye, I praised her with a whispered, "Good girl!" This came from the bottom of my heart. She knew it did and she was pleased.

I'd had a full bladder for quite a while, but I couldn't empty it until I had reached this point. Now I could relieve myself in the bucket that I had previously placed alongside my chair for this purpose. This seemed to amuse her somewhat, as she looked at me with her head cocked to one side. I smiled to myself and thought, "We're halfway there, lass. It's now, only a matter of time."

Feeling hungry again, I ate a Cornish pasty and an apple. I offered Penny some meat from the pasty. She stretched her neck out to smell it, but I could see from the look in her eye that she was still too frightened to come and get it. At least, she didn't growl at me this time!

Slow progress was made in the same manner throughout the rest of the day. At 11 pm I emptied my bladder into the bucket again. I also poured a small cupful of water in her dog dish and placed it alongside my chair on her side. After that, I pressed the recliner button on my chair and fell asleep.

I woke up at 4 am, but I didn't give Penny any indication that I had. She had drunk the small amount of water that I had left her and was lying down alongside my chair. I lay perfectly still for an hour to build on this tiny bit of the bonding process and then let my arm dangle alongside her head for a moment. She started to lick my hand, so I left it there. I would have liked to have stroked the top of her head to reassure her that she was doing ok, but I knew if I did that, I would spook her and undo all the work I had done so far. After a while, she went back and lay down in the far corner of the room to recharge her batteries, so to speak.

Throughout the day, I continued with my softly, softly approach, as I had done on the previous day. Then, just before dusk, while I was still working on my paperwork, she came over to me and started licking the back of my arm. After a minute or so, I whispered, "Go and lay down," which she did, but this time she looked at me expectantly with eyes that were no longer clouded with fear. Then, again without looking at her, I stood up and opened the door. As we passed through it, I whispered, "Come on Penny let's go."

She followed me like a shadow, down the hallway and halfway down the dimly lit winding staircase. Suddenly, I tripped on one of the stairs and tumbled over and over, all the way down to the bottom. My heart was in my mouth as one of my flailing, booted feet hit her on the head, but I didn't need to worry. When we arrived at the bottom of the staircase, she was licking me half to death!

Yvonne came out of the kitchen to find out what the commotion was about. Seeing what Penny was doing, she proclaimed, "Looks like you've now got a friend for life!"

"Yes I think I have," I replied. "So rustle up some food and water for her, while I take her out to relieve herself."

As I walked out the front door with Penny in tow, I took her up to some bushes and whispered, "There's a good gal. Go and do your jobs" And so she did. She peed and peed for ages, and what a relief it was, not just for her bladder, but also for me too, knowing that she was on the mend!

The next day, I started her rehabilitation programme with a full ten-week course of Schutzhund training, which I learnt as part of my formal training in Germany in 1949.

Schutzhund training is a form of security police dog training. Such dog training techniques work on the principle that when a dog is trained to bite on command, and only on command, it will never ever bite anyone, unless it receives that specific command. These dog-training techniques were virtually unknown in the UK at that time, and even now only a handful of people know them fully, more's the pity. They were used in Germany over several decades, not just for the training of security police dogs, but also for mandatory training of all German shepherd dogs that were kept for companionship – and no one was ever bitten accidentally throughout those decades.

After completing her rehab programme, Penny turned out to be one of the best dogs I ever had. She was so laid back and outward going that I even bred a litter of police dogs from her; that's how good she was.

The first part, of Penny's rehab was done at Quedgeley Court and the second part was done at the Salad Bowl, Leckhampton Hill on the Cheltenham Escarpment. The Salad Bowl was let to us by our good friend, Mr Thomas, and again at very reasonable rent. An old, drunken greyhound trainer had it before us and he left it in a terrible state, so we set about tidying the place up. It took us about six months and we had just finished when the local Parish Council started trying to get us evicted and closed down. The Salad Bowl was supposed to be the launch pad for our professional canine and equine services, and so we didn't take kindly to their interference.

Yvonne Penny & Chuck at the Salad Bowl

Besides the backbreaking work of cleaning up the place, we had started a thriving business buying unbroken Welsh Ponies at five guineas each from the cattle markets, just over the border. We then schooled them, and sold them as children's ponies for two hundred guineas each.

Thousands, of these wild ponies were shipped off to foreign slaughterhouses each year, so each one we bought and schooled was a pony's life saved. Moreover, there was no shortage of well-heeled families down in Cheltenham whose daughters wanted one. So the last thing we needed was some tin pot parish council interfering with our work, especially after the main Cheltenham and District Council had given us the green light to go ahead.

This particular parish council was run by old retired colonels, brigadiers and other upper class twits. Leckhampton Hill was one of the most picturesque places in the British Isles and they wanted to keep it all to themselves. They had also found a loophole in the law, and they were doing their damndest to exploit it.

Planning permission had been given for one residential caravan to be sited there permanently, many years ago. Delving into the small print of the planning permission document, the parish council's lawyers had found a clause that stated, 'If the caravan was ever taken off of the site, the planning permission would be revoked'.

They had dug up a couple of witnesses to say that one of the previous owners had removed the original caravan and replaced it, just five minutes later, with a new one. In hindsight, what that owner should have done was to put the new one on the site before he removed the original one.

Chuck & Yvonne at the Salad Bowl

Mr Thomas fought them through the courts on this issue, but he didn't have the money and power that these unscrupulous members of the British Establishment had, so he had to back off. I can't say I blame him for that, but as far as I was concerned, I was made of sterner stuff - and a dyed in the wool anti-British Establishment rebel to boot. If they wanted a fight, they were going to get one!

To enter the Salad Bowl, a council official had to come through a five-barred gate. As he was about to put his hand on the gate to open it, Penny was there with her full set of forty-two sharp teeth to stop him doing so. She had it off to a fine art. She would stay thirty yards back, behind one of the outhouses, until the official was fifteen feet away from the gate. Then she would take off like a rocket, landing up with her front feet on the top of the gate and her jaws wide open, ready to clamp down on his hand, as if to say: "Make my day!"

Council officials came and went; a different one every time - Penny must have scared them enough to give them heart attacks. They must have been running out of volunteers, because the Old Bill took over and said, "If you don't let them in, we will shoot your dog!" That really got my dander up, so I bought a high powered pump action shotgun from one of my contacts from my old gunrunning days and I was ready to blow the heads off anyone that tried to shoot any of our dogs.

By this time, the BBC television was filming all the coming and goings that were taking place. The storyline was about this penniless young husband and wife team, defending their home and livelihood against those slimy bullying reptiles that were running the parish council!

Public opinion was on our side. We were getting sacks full of fan mail every day, and so it could only be a matter of time before they would have to back down. However, Yvonne, who had tried her hardest to remain strong all the way throughout our struggle, was on the point of having a nervous breakdown. The very thought of having a fire fight against the Old Bill and getting myself killed, or spending my life away from her in prison, was too much for her to bear - so I swallowed my pride and gave up the fight.

We moved back to Quedgeley Court until Mr Thomas could find us somewhere else to live. When he came round to collect the rent, he said, "I've got my own back on those tyrants who are running the parish council. I've sold the Salad Bowl to a property developer who has got planning permission from the High Court to turn it into a licensed waste disposal plant. That's really going to get up their noses in more ways than one! Doing this will give me grim satisfaction, but I know it will give you grim satisfaction too."

I smiled and said, "Yes, it definitely will."

Slapping me on the back, he added, "You know Chuck, I admire your courage no end - but there's always much easier ways of going about things than blowing peoples' heads off with a pump action shotgun, you know!"

And then, he asked, "Why do you hate them so much?"

"It's a long story, I'll tell you someday," I said, absently.

It was while Chuck and Yvonne were living at the Salad Bowl on Leckhampton Hill that Mum went to visit them in 1966. She was accompanied by Marilyn and Christine. I don't know the purpose of that visit and I think it was probably the last time they saw each other.

Yvonne, Marilyn, Chuck, Mum & Christine - 1966

~~~

On the second day back at Quedgeley Court, we mated Penny to Mrs Coates's Rocky, who was the Canadian Police Dog Champion of the previous year. Rocky's Kennel Club name was Gruesenburg Scimitar and Penny's was Pennyroyal of Quedgeley Court. Nine weeks later, she had a litter of eight German shepherd dog puppies. When they were ten weeks old, six went to various Police Constabularies throughout England and Wales.

I kept Sheba (Miss Sheba of Keisenhelmn), the pick of the litter. I also kept one for my mate Cyril Powell, mainly because he idolised them all so much. Cyril's one was Rocky (Rocky of Keisenhelmn). This was the first litter of German shepherd dogs that we bred together. It was also the start of our Keisenhelmn line.

When the puppies were three weeks old, Yvonne heard Penny barking furiously at something. We were both in our top floor flat, so when she opened our bedroom window and looked down towards the ground, she said, "There's a really big bloke down there. I can't make out who he is from up here. He looks like a big, dark blue blob with great big shiny boots sticking out from underneath him. Whoever he is, he's looking in the basement window at Penny and her puppies - and it's upsetting her."

Leaning out of the bathroom window, I said, "It's a ruddy great big copper. I can just make out the top of his helmet."

Rushing down the stairs and out of the side door, I came up behind him and growled, "Get away from those puppies before their mother rips your throat out, you stupid prat!"

"Do you have a licence for this dog?" he asked.

"Never mind about that. What are you doing snooping around here?"

"I'm searching for stolen property. It wouldn't be the first time I've found nicked stuff in there," he replied.

"This is my basement now - and if I find you poking your nose in here without a search warrant, I'll instruct my solicitor to take legal action against you," I said coldly.

Not to be outdone, he demanded, "Is that your dog?"

At that moment, Yvonne came down and chimed in, "No, she's not his dog. She's our bitch."

"That's right, she's ours, like she said," I replied.

Scratching his nose and glaring at her, he continued, "In the eyes of the law, a dog can only have one owner and so whose dog is it?"

Yvonne firmly repeated, "She's *not* a dog she's a *bitch*."

He asked me the same question again and I replied, "No comment."

He then stated, "I am going to report you for not having a dog licence. You will be receiving a summons to that effect in due course." And with that he strutted off.

Four weeks later, we appeared at Gloucester magistrate's court for not having a dog licence. The copper stood up and gave his evidence.

"I was on patrol and as it took me past Quedgeley Court, I decided to search the basement for lost property. As I peered through the window, a dirty great big Alsatian tried to attack me and if it had not been for the heavy metal grill that was behind the window, it would have ripped my throat out."

One of the reporters tittered and the magistrate roared, "Silence in Court."

The copper continued, "It's at this point that Mr Kemsley came up behind me and said, 'Get away from those puppies before their mother rips your throat out, you stupid prat.'"

There were more titters at this from the reporters and another, "Silence in court," from the magistrate.

The copper continued, "I then asked Mr Kemsley if he had a licence for the dog. Mr Kemsley changed the subject by saying, 'Never mind that. What are you doing snooping around here?' I told him that I was looking for stolen property and that it wouldn't be the first time I had found nicked stuff in there. To which he replied, 'This is my basement now, and if I find you poking your nose in here without a search warrant, I'll instruct my solicitor to take legal action against you.' I then asked Mr Kemsley if the dog was his. Mrs Kemsley then interrupted me and said, 'She's not his, she's ours.' Mr Kemsley then stated, 'That's right, she's ours.' I then told Mr and Mrs Kemsley that, in the eyes of the law, a dog could only have one owner. Mrs Kemsley interrupted me again and said, 'She is not a dog, she's a bitch.' I put the same question to Mr Kemsley again and he said, 'No comment.'"

There were more titters from the reporters, and also jeering cries of 'stupid flatfoot' from the public gallery until the magistrate again roared, "Silence in Court."

After the tumult had died down, the magistrate gave the copper a black look and said, "It's been brought to my attention that Mr and Mrs Kemsley's bitch has produced a litter of puppies which are earmarked for various Police Constabularies throughout England and Wales."

Then, summing up, he stated, "Technically, Penny is a working dog. Therefore her owners are exempt from getting a pet dog licence. Furthermore, with your overzealous heavy-footed attitude, you could have caused untold damage to those precious puppies that are in high demand from those needy Constabularies. Case dismissed."

~~~

When Penny's puppies were old enough, I told Yvonne that we needed to get them used to the hustle and bustle of town and city life.

"But what are we going to use for transport? We can't use the Land Rover because it's in dock," she argued.

"I've got an idea. Our next door neighbour has one of those bullet shaped, open top, sports sidecars attached to a big 650cc motorcycle. If he agrees, we could use that," I replied.

So we loaded all eight of the puppies into the sidecar, but as we did, they all gravitated down to the nose of the sidecar - causing it to tip forward and dig into the ground. Yvonne laughed and said, "I thought you knew all about motorcycles."

"Yes I do, but this isn't a motorcycle, it's a sidecar," I said sheepishly.

"Same thing," she scoffed.

I was about to say something in my defence, when Cyril came up to us and asked, "Are you having a spot of bother Chuck?"

I glared at him and snapped, "Isn't it obvious!"

After Yvonne finished telling him what a twerp I was, he placed his car keys in my hand and said, "You only had to ask!"

I smiled and said, "Why don't you come with us and we will show you how puppies are socialised."

So off we went to Gloucester, and other places further afield, for an hour or two over each of the next three days. Not that they needed much of that - the little rascals were as bold as brass.

Although the motorcycle and sidecar were of no use for what I originally intended, I bought it anyway - and Penny and I had a lot of fun with it. I think she thought of it as her private chariot. Every time she thought I was going out in it, she would jump in, raring to go.

One day, on the way back from Gloucester, we were caught up in a traffic jam at the main crossroads in the city's centre. They didn't have reliable traffic lights there in those far off days. Instead there was usually a policeman, wearing long white leather gauntlets on his arms, directing the traffic. On this particular day, a young rooky cop who was definitely not up to the job, was doing it. By the aggressive way he was waving his arms about, Penny thought he was going to attack me. And so, as we passed him, she jumped out of the sidecar and bit his gauntleted arm, and held onto it.

Not knowing what else to do, I ordered her to 'Leave-it' and accelerated away. Penny, not wanting to be left behind and not wanting to let go of the rooky cop either, did what she thought was the next best thing - which was to take him with us! Fortunately, for all concerned, the gauntlet came off in her jaws as she took off after me.

The look on her face, as she jumped back into the sidecar still holding on to the gauntlet, was priceless - as if to say, "I didn't bag all of him Dad, but I did bag this bit of him!"

The first thing I did when I arrived back home was to burn the gauntlet. I would have liked to keep it as a souvenir, but if the Old Bill found it we would all be in big trouble!

When I told Yvonne about it, she burst out laughing and said, "I'm beginning to wonder what sort of mischief you and that Penny are going to get up to next. You're worse than a couple of kids."

"I know." I squeaked.

"Do you think you'll get away with it, especially after making a fool of that other one over the dog licence incident?" she asked, after catching her breath.

"Yes I do. When Penny bit him, his helmet fell down over his eyes, so he probably didn't get a chance to read my number plate." I assured her.

"Why did she do it?" she prodded.

"She did it because she hasn't finished her advanced Schutzhund training programme. She has another ten days to go before the programme is finished. By that time I will have ironed out any bugs, such as jumping out of sidecars and biting rookie coppers when they start waving their arms about. In other words, she won't bite anyone or anything until she is given the command 'Stop him' or 'Watch him'," I concluded.

Eight weeks after Penny's training programme was finished, it was time to start Sheba's preparatory training, which would eventually follow on to multi-task dog training as a gundog, sheepdog, security dog, police dog, sniffer dog and tracker dog, all rolled into one. I strongly believe, as does any true authority on the German shepherd dog, that any dog worthy of that name should be trained in as many fields as possible.

I wouldn't expect people to take this situation as far as I did, though it would be very therapeutic and so fulfilling for their German shepherd dogs if they did. However, as I had a formal training for all the above fields during my seven years of apprenticeship, plus wanting to be the first to do such a thing, I had no excuse not to.

Penny was so laid back after her rehab and Schutzhund training that, when I was with her and her puppies, she would pick them up, one by one, and place them in my lap. After a while, when their little legs got stronger, they came up to me and got up on my lap under their own steam. Before they could see properly, they would find their way to me through their noses. The scenting power of this breed never ceases to amaze me, even at that tender age.

Following strictly to the laws of Natural Rearing, which states that the lactation period of any mammal should match its gestation period, we weaned the puppies off Penny at nine weeks, as opposed to the modern fashion of wrenching puppies away from their mothers at three weeks

As Sheba's training progressed, I was worried about not having enough quality time left over to spend with Penny. I was also worried about her not having an outlet for her training and working potential. But I needn't have worried. One of Aldermaston Atomic Energy's top security patrolmen bought her from me and gave her a wonderfully long and active working life as his security police patrol dog. He had borrowed her occasionally and they were nuts about each other, so I never had any qualms about letting her go. She missed us very much at first, but she soon settled into the job, with her new master and thoroughly enjoyed it.

~~~

Shortly after that, Mr Thomas told us about fifty acres of standing timber down in the Forest of Dean that he thought we might be interested in. He had bought it some time ago, with planning permission to cut down the timber and build a bungalow on it, but didn't get around to doing it. The market value of the felled timber would cover the cost of building a bungalow and hauling the timber, with enough money left over to build kennels and stables.

I always fancied myself as a bit of a lumberjack, but after the trouble we had with the parish council over the Salad Bowl, I had lost all my confidence in having anything to do with planning permissions and

Councils, or indeed any other minions of the British Establishment. There was no way that I was going to risk putting Yvonne through that sort of trauma again.

I thanked Mr Thomas for trying so hard to help us and apologised profusely for turning down his generous offer, but he just patted me on the back and exclaimed, "You must love your wife very much, lad."

"Yes I do. She would follow me to the ends of the earth if I let her, but if I hurt her again, like last time, I wouldn't be able to live with myself," I responded.

I was a bit grumpy over the next few days. I tried not to show it but Yvonne knew me too well not to notice. I was still daydreaming about building a big log cabin in the Forest of Dean and living happily ever after! Feeling her pulling my ear and saying, "Earth to Chuck ... Earth to Chuck ... Come in Chuck!" I Mumbled, "What's that?"

"Are you deaf, or something? I was talking to you for ages and you didn't answer," she prodded.

"Sorry dear, I was miles away," I said, feebly.

"What you need is a change of scenery to take your mind off things," she said, thoughtfully.

"So what have you got in mind?" I asked.

"I've been talking to a woman who wants to start a German shepherd dog breeding kennels in Buckinghamshire. She has bought a farmhouse with several acres of land and wants us to help build and run her kennels in exchange for seven acres of land for you to start your own training kennels. Its way out in the wilds and it has a two mile cart track leading up to it, so it should be ideal for training dogs and schooling horses," she said, enthusiastically.

"Well, if, you are happy with the deal, then let's go for it!" I replied.

~~~

So off we went to Lillingstone Darrel in Buckinghamshire, along with Sheba and Mandy, another German shepherd dog bitch we had recently acquired. We started building the kennels the next day, but soon realised that the woman was not only a liar and a cheat, but was also not paying her bills and was still ordering hundreds of pounds of building materials that she had no intension of paying for.

~~~

So, we returned back to Gloucester, to see Mr Thomas. This time, Mr Thomas let us have a two bedroom town house with a tiny backyard in Cheltenham. The tiny backyard was so small that, after we had built a kennel to house Sheba and Mandy, there was no room left for them to stretch their legs so we had to take them out several times a day.

Fortunately, there was a nice big park nearby.

Cheltenham has some beautiful parks. It also has a fire brigade which, at that time, was manned mainly by part time firemen on standby. Every time they were needed, the Duty Station Officer used the old wailing wartime air raid siren to call them up. Each time the siren went off, Mandy would start howling like a wolf. When this happened, people would often stop and stare at us and say, "Look at that man with that great big beautiful wolf!" And, as we lived next door to a pub, the tales that were told about her in there were out of this world. As far as Sheba was concerned, she would look at Mandy as if she was stone staring bonkers.

Mandy was a funny old thing. She also seemed to have some sort of delayed action when I was teaching her something. When we were in Buckinghamshire, I was teaching her to bite on command as part of her training but, as far as I was concerned, I didn't think she had it in her to do it. There was a team of tough oilmen up there digging test boreholes and after we made friends with them, they acted as dummy criminals for Mandy's training. They teased and baited her, but, after trying every trick in the book, she showed not the slightest spark of aggression towards them.

Then, two weeks after we stopped her training and had given up on her, she flew at them, causing them to flee. After that, she took to it like a duck to water, making up for lost time and becoming another one of my best dogs.

The only really big problem with Mandy was that she was extremely jealous of Sheba, now that Sheba was growing up. When this happens with female German shepherd dogs, they have to be separated permanently before they seriously injure each other. This meant that I had to find somewhere where she would be happy and appreciated. Turning down ridiculously high sums of money, I finally opted to give her away to a tiny inoffensive little man who had eight small unruly children.

~~~

I was working my way down the list of potential owners, when I decided to visit this man. When I entered his house, he looked at me and Mandy and said, "I'm sorry about all the noise my kids are making. I'm trying to get them to go to bed, but they won't go. It's well past their bedtime and it's the same every night."

"Doesn't your wife help you, Mr Berry?" I asked.

"No she doesn't. She's always up the pub. She thinks I'm a wimp," he added, shrugging his shoulders.

While he was telling me this, Mandy had cocked her head to one side and started whining, just like she did before I told her to round up sheep. So I nodded my head and off she went. One moment the kids were all over the house and then, four minutes later, she had herded all eight of them up into a bunch. Mr Berry was spellbound. "I can't believe what I've just seen!

What happens next?"

"Take them upstairs to their bedrooms and put them to bed. Mandy will follow up behind and make sure that they do what they are told," I replied.

After the kids were tucked up in bed, he could hardly contain himself and, in a voice filled with awe, he asked, "How on earth did she know how to do that?"

"Well Mr Berry, her previous owner had a whole brood of kids like you and Mandy will round up anything that moves. It's in her blood," I replied.

"I just wish I could afford to buy her, but I suppose the price you are asking for her is way out of my league?" he asked, wistfully.

"Not necessarily," I answered. "It's not about money. It's more about where she will be happy and appreciated."

We talked for quite a while and I put many searching questions to him to discover if he had the potential to handle such a dog as Mandy. I was impressed by his answers to my questions. He once had a German shepherd dog until he married his current wife. She was scared of it and made him get rid of it.

"I'll tell you what. I'll give you some free lessons on how to handle her, but remember that these lessons will be very intensive and demanding. If you do ok, she can stay with you on a month's trial period, and if I like what I see at the end of that trial period, I will give her to you as a free gift."

"Oh, Mr Kemsley, what can I say, I just can't thank you enough."

He did well with the training and eventually became Mandy's new master.

Sometime later, I bumped into a man who knew him quite well.

"Hey," he said, "are you the dog trainer, who gave him that wonderful dog?"

"Yes, I am. Why do you ask?" I replied.

He grinned and said, "When we were kids, everyone picked on him because he's so inoffensive and small …." He stopped for effect and then went on, "He now walks down the street like as if he's ten feet tall, and everyone who used to bully him treats him with respect and gives him a wide berth!"

"What about his wife?" I asked.

"Oh, her! He dumped her and got a better one!"

~~~

CHUCK'S STORY 10
SUSSEX
EARLY - MID 1970s

With Mandy nicely settled in her new home, we were off yet again; this time to Palex, the UK's top international quarantine kennels and cattery, which was situated nine miles outside of Brighton.

In the early 1960s, Miss Whitock, the woman who owned the kennels, worked for Raymond Bessone, aka Mr. Teasy-Weasy, as a top hair stylist. Raymond had a salon in Mayfair, and a list of celebrity clients that made his competitors drool. Like a true maestro, Raymond would pace up and down the salon, waiting for a customer to attract his attention. He would then throw his hands in the air, exclaiming, "Madam, can you not see that I am meditating!" And his clients loved it!

As a top hair stylist in Mayfair, she soon earned enough money to realise her lifelong dream, which was to build, own and run her own international quarantine kennels and cattery. She had done a really good job at doing it too, but being the type of person that meets a challenge, conquers it and then loses interest in it, she then wanted an expert, such as Yvonne, to take it over and manage it.

In return for Yvonne's expertise, she offered us some stables and kennels plus a ten acre field for schooling and training my clients' horses and dogs. She also offered us the choice of living in her house or in a luxury caravan well away from the house. We opted for the caravan and the privacy that went along with it.

When she was taking us round the place she showed us her breeding kennels. There were ten kennels each containing a Boxer dog or bitch. She proudly explained her breeding programme and although I didn't approve of her methods, I knew Yvonne wanted this job so I just gritted my teeth. I admired Miss Whitock's ability to build and run her own international quarantine kennels and cattery, but I hoped that sometime Yvonne would tactfully put her straight about her ridiculous dog breeding programme. Yvonne never did because she knew Miss Whitock was too set in her ways, but otherwise we all got on like a house on fire.

I was very proud of Yvonne for running away from home as a young teenager to work with animals on farms and in kennels and now, here she was, managing the UK's top international quarantine kennels at the age of only twenty six.

On one occasion, Yvonne took me down the corridor of one of the kennel blocks and showed me a scenario that would haunt me for the rest of my days. She stopped at one of the kennels and drew my attention to a little terrier-type dog called Murphy, who was running round and round the top of the weld-mesh walls of his quarantine kennel run with glazed eyes and a blank expression on his face. He kept this up for as long as he could, only to eventually collapse from sheer exhaustion onto the concrete floor of his kennel run. After a short rest, he would start doing the same thing over and over. Murphy was not the only pet dog to go stir crazy! There were many more that fared no better. Quarantine kennels were designed to keep the dreaded rabies disease out of the UK. If any dog was imported into the UK, it was isolated from all warm-blooded mammals for six months. Each dog's kennel was constructed of concrete, and the walls and the ceilings of each dog's exercise run area were constructed of not just one layer of heavy duty weld-mesh panels, but two. A series of 18-inch, heavy-duty metal struts were welded in between the two layers to keep them apart, which created an 18-inch-wide cavity between the two layers, as an extra precaution.

After lunch, Yvonne took me to another kennel block where some Royal Air Force police dogs were undergoing their six-month quarantine. Each of these dogs glanced up at us as we approached them without a care in the world. Then, realizing that it wasn't feeding time, they went back to sleep - just like old trained soldiers do when confined to barracks for an uncertain length of time.

Countless working dogs like these breezed through their six-month quarantine, due to the fact that their quality of training had prepared them for any contingency – just like my own clients' working dogs would have done if they had found themselves in the same situation - which of course Yvonne knew only too well. After I had examined all the dogs, I quickly recognised that a great many of the pet dogs were extremely traumatised by the shock of being quarantined.

Yvonne said, "Chuck, this is just the tip of the iceberg, not only for pet dogs when incarcerated in quarantine kennels, but also for pet dogs in general. They're left at home with nothing to do all day, and with no proper training in place to prevent separation anxieties, fits and other mental illnesses setting in. It's these mental illnesses that cause them to do untold damage to their owners' houses and property. Misinformed pet dog owners, not having a clue as to what's going on in their dogs' troubled minds, take the stance that their dogs trashed the house out of spite, and then come out with: 'You can see by the look on its face that it did it deliberately'! But anyone with just an ounce of true dog sense can see that the looks on these dogs' faces is a mixture of bewilderment, frustration and even fear."

Seeing that I understood what she was saying, she continued, "Being on the receiving end of their misinformed owners' wrath, through no fault of their own, these dogs are punished physically or mentally by their owners. It's not unusual for dogs such as these to be re-homed and then suffer the same fate several times over, until they are eventually destroyed."

"Killed you mean," I corrected.

"Yes, killed," she said, with a lump in her throat.

"It's that bad?" I asked in amazement.

"Yes, it is. That's why you must do something to stop this happening," she cried.

"But what can I do? I'm just one man. I'm formally trained in professional training and schooling for working dogs, and I don't know anything at all about pet dogs and their owners," I parried.

"You don't have to know about pet dogs and their owners - I can fill you in about that. With my background, I probably know more about pet dogs and the cruelty that their owners unknowingly inflict on them than anyone," she cried. "Anyway, you're always saying that 'a dog is a dog!'"

Hedging for time, I muttered, "I'm too set in my ways to learn pet dog stuff, and anyway, I'm not supposed to have anything to do with pet dogs."

"Who says?"

"My mentors did when I was an apprentice," I replied.

"Why would they do that?"

"Because there would be too high a risk of degenerate pet dog blood contaminating the pure work-bred bloodlines of working dogs and sporting dogs; dogs that have been meticulously selected for their working abilities in an unbroken line throughout many centuries," I retorted.

"I know that, and I respect you for it, but the system that *was* in place to prevent this happening *has* broken down.

"Okay, for the sakes of little Murphy and his mates, let's crack on and do something for them before I change my mind. From the first day of next month I will accept a limited number of pet dogs for remedial training in my kennels, but only on an experimental basis. So get your skates on, and get some sort of scheduling organized."

The experiment lasted for three long years before I gave it up as a bad job. In the end, 231 pet dogs of all breeds were trained. The dogs received 4-6 weeks residential training - to my usual meticulously high standards of excellence; the same standards that my clients' working dogs received.

The practical obedience training exercises that I used were the same ones I used to produce the bombproof control that was necessary and essential in the preparatory training of my clients' working dogs. This happens for working dogs long before they are task-trained to hunt and destroy vermin, find and retrieve game, work livestock, or protect people and property from robbers and thieves.

Before every dog owner took their dog home after training, each one got a full demonstration of what their dog had been taught to do. In addition to this, each owner was given one-and-a-half hours of personal dog handling tuition with their dog - which emotionally is as much as dogs and their owners can contend with at this point. Owners were also offered an extra hour of personal tuition, free of charge, 10 days later - to ensure that the dog training wasn't messed up by inept dog handling.

This tuition was paid for by Yvonne out of her own savings, as was half of the training and boarding fees for owners that had genuinely fallen on hard times.

Despite everything Yvonne and I put into the pet dog training experiment, 85 per cent of the dogs were let down by their owners' complacency and lack of dog handling technique. In all these cases, a week or two after the dogs returned home, their markedly improved behaviour and emotional stability reverted back to the poor state that it was in originally. This was often because the owners did not come back for the extra hour of personal tuition. When these owners were asked why they didn't come back, they would reply: 'You were so busy - I didn't want to bother you further after all you've done for us', or: 'My dog's behaviour is so much better since you trained it that I thought there was no need for any extra revision.'

However, from the 15 per cent of owners who did come back to take the revision, it was obvious there was nothing wrong with the practical dog training exercises I had used. On the other hand, the afore mentioned 85 per cent, proved beyond all doubt that another way was needed to successfully train 100 per cent of pet dogs.

I didn't belittle Yvonne by saying, "I told you so." She was deeply saddened and bitterly disappointed by the whole affair and I didn't want to make her feel worse. And I knew deep down, for her sake, as well as for little Murphy and his mates' sakes, that I had to find a way that would work for all pet dogs and their owners, and not for just a few."

~~~

Three years later, Miss Whitock offered the quarantine kennels and cattery to Yvonne as a going concern, for a token price of thirty thousand pounds - at zero per cent interest, spread over five years. Yvonne thanked her for her very generous offer and told her that she would be just as happy managing the place, as owning it. On hearing this, Miss Whitock told Yvonne that she admired her principles and sincerely hoped that she would at least stay on as the kennels and cattery manager, making sure that whoever bought the place did not bring it down to rack and ruin – which was her biggest worry.

Miss Whitock's worries were well founded, because the new owner, Mr Doyle, was a chronic alcoholic and as such he was rude to his clients and his staff alike. Consequently, he did indeed bring the place down to rack and ruin. He also owned Finway Shipping, which specialised in shipping dolphins and other exotic animals all over the world, but this also was going downhill, for the same reasons.

To make matter worse, he had amalgamated his shipping business with the quarantine kennels and cattery business. Now Yvonne not only had to manage the quarantine business, but also nursemaid him and his shipping business as well. I helped as best I could, driving the animal transporters and getting his clients' exotic wild animals to where they had to be, as well as collecting quarantined dogs and cats from airports, seaports and London mainline stations. However, much of my time was taken up with training and schooling my own clients' dogs and horses. I could only do so much.

He was a complete liability. He had lost his licence for drink-driving and had to be driven everywhere, but despite that, he kept buying top of the range Mercedes cars and crashing them five minutes or so after they were delivered. Usually, this happened in the hours of darkness. However, as the kennels were on the main London to Brighton road, I'm truly amazed that he didn't get killed or rearrested for drink-driving. Maybe there's something in the old saying: 'God looks after drunks and fools'.

Anyway, it was probably due to the fact that he had top class defence lawyers taking care of such matters. I say this, because one day, he came up to me in the middle of a heatwave and asked, "Can you collect a quarantined Bulldog that's in distress at St. Pancras mainline station? You can take the new Ford Transit. That's the fastest one. Don't slow down or stop for anyone or anything, especially cabbies - and don't worry about getting nicked, because my lawyers will get you off."

I took him at his word and off I went like the clappers. I had several near misses and one collision along the way. This was when a cabbie pushed his luck and tried to cut me up. I rammed the off side rear wheel of the cab, thereby pushing the cab out of my way, and then drove on without stopping. At St Pancras station, I refilled the Bulldog's water dish, which was welded to the inside of his special quarantine shipping crate, and then sprayed him all over with a cold water humidifier to cool him down. I then delivered him to Palex, where Yvonne checked him out and put him in his allotted quarantine kennel, which would be his home for the next six months.

When the police asked us who was driving the new Ford Transit van on that particular day, nobody admitted responsibility so they took Mr Doyle to court. As the police inspector stood up to give his evidence, his face dropped a mile as he looked at his case files. Mr Doyle's crafty old lawyer had stolen them and replaced them with blanks! When the inspector complained to the judge about the lawyer stealing his files and replacing them with blank ones, the judge said, "Perhaps you used invisible ink by mistake. Case dismissed!"

One night, Mr Doyle messed up big time. One of his clients, the Brighton Aquarium, had imported two dolphins from another aquarium in

South California. Being drunk as usual, he mistakenly thought that one of the dolphins would arrive on Tuesday at 23:45 hours, and the other one on Wednesday at 23:50 hours.

Yvonne phoned Gatwick Airport on the Tuesday, at eight o'clock in the evening, to check on the first one's estimated time of arrival. She was informed that both dolphins were already in transit on the same aircraft and would arrive about midnight.

All our animal transporters that were large enough to carry two dolphins and their bulky life support systems were out on other jobs. So she had to rush around at the last moment to hire another transporter from a rival shipping company. All they could come up with, at such short notice, was a smaller one, which was just about large enough to carry one dolphin and its life support system. Fortunately, we had one of similar size, which was due to go out on a job the next day.

Yvonne and I were the only drivers available with dolphin expertise, so we were off post haste to Gatwick, without a minute to spare.

When we arrived, the dolphins in their shipping cradles had already been unloaded. We backed up to the dock to collect them and load them onto our transporters. We were already running late, but what really got Yvonne's goat was that there were film crews and glossy magazine reporters, dashing around and getting in our way, while half naked models or film starlets were using the dolphins as a backdrop for their posing.

Two girls were actually perched precariously on one dolphin's shipping cradle, like a pair of bookends. Not only that, but one of them was fiddling about with the valves of the dolphin's life support system.

After all the stress that Yvonne had been under during the day, she blew her top and threw the pair of them off the dock. While the dolphins were out of the water, just a small scratch from those girls' false fingernails on their dry skins, could cause them serious harm. Damaging their life support systems would certainly kill them.

The rest of the girls, seeing what happened to the other two, run off in hysterics. But Yvonne wasn't finished yet by a long chalk. She turned on the loading dock workers who were still gawking at the young, half naked starlets and told them, in no uncertain terms, to get the dolphins loaded immediately. Just as we were about to drive off, the night under manager came puffing up and told us that the main drag was temporally blocked due to a fatal traffic accident.

By now, Yvonne was almost in tears. I put my arm around her and said, "Don't worry love; we can take a shortcut through Gatwick village. Just follow me."

We were halfway through the village, when the Old Bill stopped us.

"What's in the back?" asked the first one.

"A dolphin. There's also another one in the other transporter," I replied.

"Pull the other one, it's got bells on!" the second one scoffed.

I showed them the loading manifest. "What do you think that is, Scotch mist?" I retorted.

Seeing that I was getting nowhere, I jumped out of the cab and unlocked the back door of the transporter so that they could see for themselves.

Seeing that the two coppers were about to climb into my transporter and start poking around, Yvonne came up behind them and said, in a venomous voice, "You interfere with that dolphin, you clumsy oafs, and your superiors will have your guts for garters. You're already in big trouble. You can see on the manifest that these dolphins have got to be back in the water at the stipulated time, or they will die. We are already running ten minutes late - and that's five minutes more than when you stopped us."

They rolled their eyes at each other and said, "Follow us and we will give you a police escort."

With blue lights flashing and sirens blaring, we were nine minutes ahead of schedule by the time we arrived at Brighton Aquarium. But our troubles were not yet over. There weren't enough porters there to help us carry the dolphins in their heavy cradles, up the steep flight of steps that led up to the back entrance, into the aquarium. With the help of the three porters that were there, we had got as far as lifting the cradled dolphins off the transporters and onto the beach. The porters then went off to get more help.

So, there we were, just fifty yards away from the sea, waiting impatiently for that extra muscle power to arrive. The dolphins were getting restless - they could smell the sea and hear the waves crashing onto the beach. Yvonne's face was white as a sheet and her knuckles gleamed silver in the moonlight. She gripped the top rail of one of the cradles as if her life depended on it.

"If it wasn't for these cradles, we could set them free," I growled.

"Even then, Chuck, it still wouldn't be possible. They have to have an injection to counteract the one they had when they were taken out of the water in South California," she explained.

As she said that, the extra muscle power arrived and within ninety seconds the cradled dolphins were alongside the pool with the slings of the hoist placed in readiness to lift them into it.

But alas, the dolphins' ordeal still wasn't over. The British standard size Allen keys that Mr Doyle gave us didn't fit the American standard size Allen screws that held the cradles together. So, now the only way the dolphins could be floated out of their cradles was to cut through the joints of the top section of the cradles with a hacksaw, which was not only time consuming, but extremely hazardous.

Everyone's nerves were on edge as the porters sawed through the joints, with the saw blades a mere inch away from the dolphins' dried up skins. Just one nick and they could be seriously ill and possibly die.

Eventually, with just thirty seconds to spare, the top sections of the cradles were removed and the cradled dolphins hoisted into the pool.

The vet, who was already in the pool treading water, gave them their life saving injections. The cradles were lowered to the bottom of the pool, leaving the dolphins floating motionless on top of the water.

As we waited to see if the dolphins were going to be ok after their long and troublesome journey, Yvonne was squeezing my hand so tightly that I thought my bones would break. Then, as the dolphins became animated and started to swim, she burst into tears.

"They're okay, there's no need to cry," I whispered.

"I know they're okay. I'm not crying because I'm unhappy. I'm crying because I'm so happy that they're okay!" she squeaked.

Fifteen minutes later, we were home and as soon as our heads touched the pillows, we were fast asleep.

~~~

Later on in the day, Yvonne discovered that Mr Doyle was in cahoots with the agent of those young film starlets that she had thrown off the loading dock at Gatwick Airport. This was not the first time he had pulled a stroke like that and given concessions to celebrities or would be celebrities.

On one occasion, he gave a very famous actor* a carte blanche invitation to visit his little quarantined lap dog outside of visiting hours.

The first - and last time that this particular actor came down outside of visiting hours, Yvonne said, "Come back during the official visiting hours, as stated on your quarantine document."

He raised his voice in anger, and replied, "Don't you know who I am?"

"I don't give a damn who you are," she retorted, slamming the heavy metal studded door in his face!

Over the next eleven months, one catastrophe led to another, until the week before Christmas all but one of Yvonne's quarantine staff walked out on her. Mr Doyle offered to double their wages, but it was too late for that. They could no longer put up with his rudeness and drunken mood swings.

Then, on top of that, all the cats in the cattery went down with cat flu. Despite all the havoc, she nursed every single one of them back to health, even though the vets had warned that it would be impossible!

Working all day keeping the kennels running smoothly and sitting up all night with the sick cats in the cattery, Yvonne hardly slept at all over the Christmas period. How she managed to keep it up I don't know, but she did. I did my best to take as much weight off her shoulders as I could, as did Jackie, the one who stayed on - but our efforts were puny when compared to Yvonne's. It wasn't until several days later when the cats were out of danger that she could focus on employing more staff.

Then, just as she had everything running smoothly again, Mr Doyle showed up, only to collapse in the gutter outside his office with alcohol poisoning and an overdose of drugs.

He had slunk off on a bender on Christmas Eve, without telling anyone. Yvonne rushed him off to hospital, where they pumped out his stomach and told him that he had cirrhosis of the liver and would be dead in six months if he didn't stop drinking.

He swore at Yvonne for saving his life. This wasn't the first time this had happened so she told him that if she found him in the gutter again, she would leave him there.

Six weeks later, he sold the quarantine kennels and cattery to a Poodle breeder. We both took an instant dislike to the man, who was no more than a wheeler-dealer dog food salesman, so we moved on yet again.

~~~

CHUCK'S STORY 11
BERKSHIRE
MID - LATE 1970s

This time around, Yvonne, whose services and expertise was very much in demand, opted to look after Miss Peggy Keevil's retired pack of Basset Hounds, in exchange for a country cottage with an enormous garden and outbuildings. This was deep in the glorious English countryside, in a little hamlet called Inkpen Common, on the borders of West Berkshire, Wiltshire, and Hampshire.

Miss Keevil lived in a big, old, rambling farmhouse called The Rook's Nest, where she kennelled her Basset Hounds in a large paddock behind the house. These were the famous Grimms Basset Hounds, the last surviving hunting pack of Basset Hounds in the UK. She also kennelled a Great Dane and a working sheepdog in the same paddock, together with a wild fox. She also had a few Shetland ponies and a flock of Jacob's sheep running loose in a ten-acre field adjacent to her house.

The cottage we lived in was called 'Trainettes', which was just a quarter of a mile away from The Rook's Nest.

While we were at Inkpen Common, Yvonne bought an Irish nanny goat, but sadly it died. As she was passionately fond of goats and it was the first one she ever had, she was heartbroken. Shortly after that, I was training a herding dog for an Austrian lady who bred pedigree goats high up on top of the Cotswolds in Gloucestershire. When I told her about Yvonne's sad loss, she gave me a very nice nanny goat kid on top of my fee. I brought it home three days later on Yvonne's birthday, as a surprise birthday present.

I set off at the crack of dawn on the pretext that I was going to look at a horse and as my Land Rover was in dock, I took our old Ford Thames kennel van. It was a very hot day in July and by the time I was on the way home, the radiator kept boiling over, causing me to stop every five miles or so to let the engine cool down. The heat and humidity inside the van were so high that I was anxiously wondering if I would be able to get the little goat kid home before it was boiled alive.

As soon as I was home, I rushed indoors and took Yvonne by the hand and dragged her out to the van and said, "Look inside." When she did, I said, "Happy Birthday, darling," and kissed her.

"Oh Chucky, where did you get her from, she's beautiful. She's the best birthday present I've ever had," she squealed, with tears streaming down her cheeks.

After I told her about the Austrian lady, she said, "You must have made a great impression on her."

"Well, she did tell me that I made a fantastic job of training her dog to herd goats, after every other trainer she spoke to told her that it couldn't be done," I replied.

"I could have told her that!" she exclaimed.

"Yes I know, but that doesn't count because you're my wife and she would expect you to say that," I said. "By the way, what are you going to call her?"

She remained silent for a while and then said, thoughtfully, "Gretel is an Austrian name, like in the fairy-tale Hansel and Gretel, isn't it?" I nodded my head and smiled.

"So that's what I will call her; Gretel - Gretel the Goat," she said.

Yvonne with Gretel the Goat

When Gretel had finished growing, we took her to an old gamekeeper to be covered by his billy goat, so she could give us an endless supply of milk. He told us to meet him at 11 pm when he had finished doing his rounds. When we arrived at his place, he told us to wait while he went to get his billy from a nearby field. After he disappeared into the night we waited for quite a while, then suddenly Yvonne whispered, "Listen!" As I did so, I heard a loud sort of creaking, grating noise coming out of the darkness and getting closer, until I could just about make out that the noise was coming from the old gamekeeper's billy goat.

I couldn't believe my eyes. His goat was as old as the hills and so riddled with arthritis that it could hardly walk.

"Do you think he's up to it?" I whispered.

"I can see you don't know much about goats, so you had better hold onto your hat, mister, because you aint seen nothing yet!" she whispered in my ear.

To my utter surprise, he was well up to it. A few months later Gretel had a healthy kid and, from then on, we enjoyed the sweetest, nuttiest milk anyone ever tasted. Yvonne kept several other goats while we were at Trainettes, but Gretel was always her favourite.

~~~

Sheba

My favourite dog was Sheba. As I couldn't be with her as much as she would like, I often kennelled her with one of my clients' male dogs. This was not just for company, but also to have her own favourite male dog to boss around, which always seemed to amuse her. Quite often she and her current kennelmate would hit it off so well that one day Yvonne said, "Isn't that sweet! They look just like an old devoted 'Derby and Joan' couple that have been married for years. But why does she have to be so hard on them?"

"Maybe it's because they have a job but she hasn't got one," I explained.

"Well, let's give her one!"

"Doing what?" I asked.

"She could be your personal security patrol dog."

"But I don't have a security company," I said.

"Then start one," she suggested.

"What, doing boring dog patrols?"

"No, you wouldn't have to do that. As the company boss, you could employ people to do dog patrols whilst you do the alarm calls. You would enjoy that because there would be lots of danger and excitement in it for you and you would be sending an encouraging signal to your men, saying that you wouldn't expect them to do anything that you wouldn't do yourself," she said.

"So what should I call it, if I did it?"

"Phoenix Dog Security," she stated.

"Why Phoenix?" I said, with a blank expression on my face.

"Well, as you know, the Phoenix is a mythical bird that symbolises getting good things to rise from the ashes of bad things. You are always cursing the British Establishment clowns for allowing cowboys to set themselves up as security dog patrols suppliers when they don't even know the first thing about it. I considered that by registering it as Phoenix Dog Security, it would signify what you are intending to achieve," she patiently explained.

"I can see that you have put a lot of thought into this, so yes I will do it, even if it is just to show those chinless wonders how it should be done," I said.

Phoenix Dog Security was an instant success and Sheba was my personal patrol dog until she was eleven years old, and she enjoyed every minute of it. We had many exciting adventures and hairy moments. There weren't any 'no go areas', and I lost count of how many times she saved my bacon. The greatest thing of all was the terrific bond that grew between us as we embraced those dangerous moments together, time after time. It was as if she could read my thoughts and knew what I wanted her to do without being told and sometimes, uncannily, even before the thought came into my head.

She was a very handy dog to have around. One day a publican from out in the wilds of Wiltshire rang me up and told me that his guard dog kept going berserk and biting his customers. He had already offered it to three different police constabularies, but all the police officers that had seen the dog had told him that it was too dangerous to handle. His guard dog was a big, black, longhaired German shepherd dog that he called Satan. Several of the officers had told him that, as a last ditch stand, I might take him off his hands or otherwise he would have to be destroyed.

The tiny village where the pub was situated lay in a valley and as I looked down into it, I spotted several police dog vans scattered around. I thought to myself that this publican's guard dog must have got himself a bit of a reputation and these police dog handlers are waiting to see if I will come out in one piece. When I entered the pub, the publican said, "Thanks for coming. I didn't think you would come."

"No problem, landlord, it's all in the day's work. Just put him in the back of my Land Rover and leave his lead attached to his collar," I said.

When he had done as I asked, I pointed out that there were several police dog handlers hanging around the village waiting to see if I would come out in one piece. "I want to sneak off out of the village, leaving them wondering what happened," I said.

"Hang on; I think I know a way how to do it. I will just go upstairs and check out exactly where their vans are." He was back in a couple of minutes and continued, "There's a really rough sheep track, which takes you directly to the motorway. It's too steep and rugged for their vans."

All the way up to the motorway, Satan was trying to smash his way through the cab's wire mesh barrier. I chucked my sandwiches over the top to him, to keep him off my back long enough to get to the motorway, where the icy blast from the wide-open windows held him back. After coming off the motorway at the other end, a couple of squirts from the fire extinguisher kept him off my back.

When I arrived back at kennels, I opened the kennel and run that I had allocated to him. Then, after I had placed some sausages halfway down the run to lure him into it, I opened the backdoor of my Land Rover and let him out. He went sniffing around for a few seconds before he decided to attack me. By that time, I was strategically placed to slip down one of the passageways and slam the door in his face. He showed a slight interest in the sausages, but he wouldn't enter the pen. I was just wondering what to do next, when Sheba came up behind him and gave him a few nips and herded him into his allocated kennel and run.

He made another attempt to attack me when I stepped up to shut the gate to his run, but thought better of it when Sheba growled at him as if to say: "Make my day, Sunshine!" Then, just to add insult to injury, she took the sausages away from right under his nose and placed them in my hand, just like she did when retrieving a shot pheasant.

Every four hours, when I offered him some food, he tried to attack me - and so he didn't get any. Two days went by and I was starting to get annoyed with his vicious behaviour. I decided to play it cool and call his bluff with the use of one of my dog psychology tools. This was to have Yvonne open the front door of our cottage, which was directly opposite to the gate of his run, while I sat in an armchair pretending to read a large-paged newspaper with a small spy hole cut in it. Having done this, I had her open Satan's gate. I knew it was me he had it in for, so I knew she was perfectly safe doing so.

He realised I was directly in front of him, but all he could see was a newspaper with a pair of legs sticking out from underneath it, which confused him as to whether it was me or not. As I was downwind of him he couldn't use his powerful canine sense of smell to verify what he saw, and this confused him further. Smashing the newspaper aside, he jumped up and brought his front paws down hard onto my shoulders while snarling, with his teeth drawn back from his lips and his eyes bulging out of his head, as if he was about to have an apoplectic fit.

Remaining perfectly still and observing him from out of the top of my peripheral vision, I could read him like a book. To sum him up in one word, he was a 'Fear-biter'. It would have started when, as a nervous puppy, he would hide under the furniture when strangers stared at him. As he grew bigger there wouldn't be anywhere to hide, so he would start growling at them instead. Some of them would become scared and leave him alone after that, but a few others would put out a hand to stroke him, causing him to snap. The publican, not knowing any better and thinking that he had the making of a 'perfect guard dog' would have encouraged this, thereby creating a monster.

As I remained perfectly still and observed him from out of the top of my peripheral vision, there were no triggers to feed his viciousness, so he calmed down. Not only that, he instinctively recognised by my fearless, laidback behaviour, that he might be in the presence of a pack leader that could protect him. Without moving a muscle I watched him looking at me out of the corners of his eyes as he furtively sniffed around my lair, and I knew exactly what he was going to do next, which was to cock his leg and pee up the doorpost on his way out.

Unbeknown to Satan, I had meticulously planned in advance for this precise moment. There was a large, galvanised bucket precariously balanced on a high shelf, three feet back from the doorpost. Attached to the bucket was a long piece of string, the other end of which I held in my hand in readiness for that precise moment when he would cock his leg. As the bucket hit the floor, he took off like a bat out of hell and didn't stop until he reached the end of my second block of kennels. In turn, I was out of my front door and nonchalantly leaning up against the wall in his allocated kennel space, where he felt comparatively safe.

When he came in, I fed him some liver sausage and then took him out and gave him some elementary rehab obedience training. He loved that and was so eager to please me now that I had shown him who was Boss. Within four and a half weeks he had completed his obedience training and was ready to start his task dog training. I was supplying dogs to the Army, Civilian Police and the RAF Police, but he looked more like a potential Army War Dog to me. I phoned the Sergeant Major up at the Army War Dog School, Melton Mowbray, and told him about Satan's progress and also his previous history.

Ten days later he rang me up and said, "Bring him up right away. And, while you're on the phone, have you any special instructions for us? Do you know of any quirks that we should know about?"

I explained that the only quirk I found was in the very early stages of his obedience training when he would deliberately get his front leg over his lead and tangle himself up. Then, when I went to bend over to untangle it, he would look like he was likely to bite. According to his original owner, he used to do this as a puppy. When he was nine months old he bit him several times and quite severely too. After that, he didn't put a lead on him. "I suspect that whoever takes over his training from me will need to watch his step in this area. Please bear in mind that although I can now do anything with him, he is still a very dangerous dog," I concluded.

"In that case laddie, you know the drill. Bring him to us muzzled and under sedation," he said.

The Army War Dog School at Melton Mowbray was a hotbed of gossip, and by the time I arrived, most of the young dog trainers were hanging around to get a look at this whacking great big black hairy monster.

"Satan by name and Satan by nature!" one of them quipped. They all wanted to take him on and prove to the Sergeant Major how macho they were. The fact that he arrived muzzled and heavily sedated only added grist to the mill.

Three weeks went by, and then five weeks - and I still hadn't received any news from the Sergeant Major about how Satan was getting on. Then, into the sixth week, he rang me up and said, "I'm sorry to inform you that Satan has already put four of our trainers in hospital and we still haven't got on top of that lead problem you told me about. Sadly, we have no other alternative than to put him down."

~~~

Another time Sheba saved my bacon, or should I say my reputation, was when I lost one of my clients' gundogs, which is unforgivable and extremely damaging to one's career. It was being trained to hunt, point, flush and retrieve. It was six months into its training, which the influential client had paid for in advance, when I lost it during a retrieving exercise. Something must have spooked it. As the area I was training it in was mostly covered in dense gorse and went on for miles, I had no other alternative than to wait for it to come back. The greater majority of my trainee dogs would do this -

but this one was a scatty Pointer that might not, so I went home and told Yvonne what had happened. After she had heard me out, she said, "Go back and take your 'magic' dog with you. She knows something is wrong and maybe she can help."

"I don't have a magic dog," I said, wondering what on earth she was talking about.

"That magic dog," she replied, pointing at Sheba, who was standing behind me with a puzzled look on her face, and so off we went. When I came to the spot where the Pointer had bolted, Sheba picked up its scent within a few seconds and off she went. I waited around feeling foolish for half an hour and was about to give up when she appeared, dragging the Pointer to me by the scruff of its neck. After that, until I cured the Pointer's skittishness, I took Sheba with me. It was really funny every time it thought about doing a runner and then thinking better of it because Sheba was with me.

At the end of the day, the Pointer completed its training on time. Its owner congratulated me for doing a splendid job and Sheba went on to be a legend in her time. She not only found lost dogs, but also peoples' car keys, wedding rings, jewellery and other small valuable articles and items of sentimental value, which their owners had lost in the undergrowth out in the wilderness.

One occasion that springs to mind was on a cold snowy day when Newbury Dog Rescue rang me up and asked me if Sheba would be capable of finding a Dachshund bitch that had wandered off three days previously and had not returned. She was quite frail and they feared that she might have collapsed somewhere out in the fields and was in distress. I told them that with all the dogs milling around in the area from where she had wandered off, it was extremely doubtful whether Sheba would be able to pick up her scent and track her down - but we would try.

In a field, a hundred yards away from the perimeter of the rescue centre, I found just one single footprint, which looked like it might belong to the missing Dachshund. I put Sheba's tracking harness on her, clipped the long tracking line to it and gave her our trigger word to track. Nothing happened for a minute or two and then, slowly, painstakingly, step by step, she picked up the track of whatever it belonged to. By the great effort that she had to put into her tracking, it was obvious this track was an old one but was it the right one? Sheba tracked on for almost two miles, all the way to the grass verge of the motorway and then lay down, exhausted. This was not just because she was too tired to go on, but because it was her signal indicating that the track didn't go any further!

Whose scent Sheba picked up, I thought I probably would never know. Then, three days later, the rescue centre rang me up and told me that the police had informed them that they had found a little Dachshund bitch's dead body on the motorway and buried her in the grass verge alongside the motorway. So, to verify whether or not this was the rescue centre's Dachshund, I took their secretary to the exact spot where Sheba had stopped tracking. I then dug down into the verge and there, low and behold, lay their Dachshund with her identity disc still attached to her collar.

~~~

We lived at the cottage for over five years, during which time I built up a formidable reputation as a Master Dog Trainer of gundogs, sheepdogs, guard dogs and industrial police dogs, trading as Keisenhelm Working Dog Training Kennels (KWDTK).

One day, I had brought in a batch of new dogs and tethered them temporarily to hitch rails. I was deep in thought, trying to decide where to put them, when suddenly I almost jumped out of my skin. An old, retired army colonel from down the lane had come up behind me and boomed out, "Kemsley!" in a loud voice, as if he was on the parade ground.

"Yes Colonel, what do you want? And how did you get in here without getting severely bitten?" I asked coldly, with bitter hatred showing in my eyes, which were firmly locked on to his.

"I came over from Miss Keevil's, and climbed over the back fence to tell you to train Humphrey, my wife's miniature poodle, to stop yapping," he boomed.

To say the least, I was absolutely furious with him for coming into my kennels unannounced, as if he owned the place - and also shouting at me as if he thought he was my superior. With my eyes still firmly locked on to his, I said, "So where is this poodle then?"

"Are you blind as well as stupid, man?" He said, pointing at the ground.

I snatched my eyes off his for a split second, to glance down to where he pointed, and then back up again, glaring out even more hatred and loathing as I said, "I don't do lap dogs."

As he kept on blabbering about his poodle's yapping whenever it was left on its own, a thought came into my head as to how I could bring him down a peg or two. So I pointed to a kennel and run that was too small for my clients' working dogs and said, "Put him in there and get back to me in two weeks."

"Very good Kemsley, carry on," he replied.

Thirty minutes later, Yvonne came back from Miss Keevil's and spat out, "What's that poodle doing here? He's making enough noise to waken the dead!"

I filled her in about what happened and she said, "Hah, typical British Establishment wallah with the usual bad manners. He needs to be taken down a peg or two."

"Yes, I know. I've already thought of a way how to do it," I replied.

"You're not going to teach Humphrey to bite him, are you?" she giggled.

"No, dear. I'm going to train his poodle to stop yapping, and then I'm going to play a rotten trick on him. I have two tricks up my sleeve, but at this point, I don't know which one I will hit him with," I said.

Seven days later, the Colonel rang me up to ask me how his poodle's training was going. "The actual training is going rather well, but I have hit a snag," I cautioned.

"What sort of snag?" he barked.

"Well Colonel, after carrying out extensive tests, it now appears that your poodle's yapping problem was triggered by fumes given off by solvents used in the tanning of wild animal skins, especially tigers!"

I paused to let that sink in … and then continued, "I don't suppose you brought back any stuffed wild animal trophies from India, in the days of the British Raj?"

"Yes Kemsley, as a matter of fact, I did. I will have you know that, when I was in India, I bagged more tigers than anyone in my Regiment. As a matter of fact, the wall over the fireplace in my trophy room is covered with their heads," he said, boastfully.

"Well Colonel, in that case, I am sorry to inform you that as soon as you bring your poodle back into your house, all the hard work I have put into his training will revert to nothing," I said, smiling inwardly.

"Well, I can't get rid of the brute. The Memsaab is very fond of him and she would never forgive me if I even mentioned such a thing," he roared, slamming down the receiver.

Five minutes later, he rang me back and asked in a more subdued voice, "Is there a way of counteracting these fumes?" To which I replied: "As a matter of fact there is. I have been speaking to a man who has recently invented a gadget that can counteract those fumes. The good news is that he has finished testing it and it works extremely well. But the bad news is that he has not had time to miniaturise it or design a nice looking case to put it in, so he has had to rig it up inside one of those big old fashioned biscuit tins."

"I see!" he exclaimed.

"He has welded four brackets to the back of the tin so that it can be screwed to the chimneybreast in your trophy room. Okay?

Right, what you now have to do is to draw an imaginary line down the centre of that chimneybreast and then measure two feet up from the top of the mantelpiece, because that's exactly where the tin must be placed - he was very insistent on that point." I prodded.

"Have you taken leave of your senses, Kemsley? That place is strictly reserved for the head of the very first tiger I shot," he bellowed down the phone. "Sorry about that Colonel, but that's what the man said," I replied.

"I never could understand what you boffin chaps were talking about, even during the war. But I suppose, if that's what it takes to keep the Memsaab off my back, I will send my man round to pick it up and screw it into the wall as directed," he said, grumpily.

A few weeks later, after he took his poodle home, I was down the pub staring into my beer mug, pondering over a solution to some dog or horse related behaviour problem when he came up behind me and bellowed, "Kemsley, what the devil is everyone laughing at? Every time I come in here since you trained the Memsaab's poodle to stop yapping, they're always laughing at some sort of joke?"

"I really don't know, Colonel," I replied, trying not to laugh. Practically everyone in the neighbourhood knew what the joke was, but no one ever told him.

Humphrey outlived the Colonel and his wife, or the "Memsaab" as he referred to her, by several years. One of the first things their eldest son did, when he inherited the family estate, was to open the beat up, old biscuit tin that was still screwed to the chimneybreast in his father's trophy room. He had often asked his father what was in the tin, and also why he had stopped throwing his weight about after I trained his poodle to stop yapping, but the old boy had just quickly changed the subject.

After his son opened the tin, it didn't take him long to work out how I had caused his father to lose face within the community, so he came after me, seeking revenge for 'besmirching the family name', as he put it. He had already started trying to throw his weight about in our close knit community, only to get laughed at for his pains, so he sold the family estate to a retired jockey and moved away. This aristocratic family of bullies had been throwing their weight about for centuries, so no one was sorry to see them go.

~~~

In August 1977, Miss Keevil moved to North Devon to start an animal wildlife park. She was hoping we would come with her to help her set it up and run it. Although both Yvonne and I had a fair amount of experience with lions and tigers and other big cats, we decided not to go

Chuck & Sheba

with her. After hearing that, she told us that we could continue to live at Trainettes for twelve months, with the option of buying it from her.

1977 – 1978 was not a good time for small businesses, especially ours. We had been fighting lost causes for downtrodden people and animals for years, which had drained most of our capital. Overheads were going through the roof and back taxes were crippling. It soon became obvious that we wouldn't be able to buy Trainettes or even keep the kennels open. Several of our neighbours offered to lend us substantial sums of money at zero percent interest to buy the cottage and keep my kennels open, but we were too proud to accept it.

As I was too proud to accept our neighbours' charity, Earl Craven, came up with another solution that I felt I could accept. This was to start an international security dog and handler supply service, in partnership with his Craven Estate. His family, on his American mother's side, owned a large slice of Lucas Industries, which had industrial plants all over the world. These kinfolk of his would use their enormous power and influence to ensure that each plant would have a large security dog section, providing dog patrols round the clock – and that was just the tip of the iceberg!

Although the Earl had inherited the Craven Estate when he became the 7th Earl of Craven, he couldn't put his plan into action without the approval of his trustees. Although four of his trustees had agreed that his plan was a sound one and met with their approval. Lord Searle, the other trustee, did not. He wanted the Estate to have a fish farm instead, so he vetoed the Earl's plan on the grounds that I was a bad influence on him.

The Earl and I were close friends on first name terms. This started when I was training his second personal protection dog, which was the other half of a pair that he had ordered. I hadn't met him when I trained the first one, as all business relating to training it was negotiated through Hennessy, his chief bodyguard. The Earl wasn't at all happy with this arrangement. He had heard a lot about me and my exploits and he wanted to meet me in person and in private. I duly made an appointment to come over to see him. After all, he was the one who would be picking up the tab!

When I arrived, a young man, in his early twenties came to the front door and said, "You must be Mr Kemsley. Do come in."

Recognising him from a picture I had seen in the News of the World, when he got busted for growing cannabis in one of the Craven Estate's greenhouses, I said, "You must be the 7th Earl of Craven. How do I address you?"

"Just call me Tom, please," he begged.

"Pleased to meet you, Tom," I said.

"Would you like some tea and a sandwich before we discuss my dog's progress?" he asked.

"Thank you Tom, that would be very nice," I replied.

I was expecting one of his maids to bring in the tea and sandwiches, but when he brought them in himself I started to wonder what was going on. Seeing the look of pure amazement on my face, he blurted out, "I've always wanted to do this, but never had the chance before now, what with servants waiting on me hand and foot." Then, shaking his fist, he exclaimed, "Bah! How I hate them - always getting in the way and whispering behind my back!" Gaining control of himself, he added, "Sorry about that!"

Pointing to the tea and sandwiches he had brought in, he asked, "What do you think?"

"Well, the tea is okay, but your sandwich making skills need some help," I quipped.

We drank the tea and ate the sandwiches and then we discussed his dog's training and a lot of other stuff, until we got around to the time he got busted for growing cannabis. He told me that he needed cannabis to take his mind off the hypercritical rules of the British Establishment that were doing his head in. I told him how I had suffered at their hands and that I fully understood how he must feel. He kept me talking for as long as he could. All along, I could see that he was feeling suicidal, and so I told him to call me if the going got too tough.

I came over to see him many times after that and every time I did, he seemed happier in himself. He was a great talker, and once he got started, there was no stopping him from discussing everything under the sun. We had so much in common that it seemed weird to both of us. He often spoke about his fear of the Craven Estate being broken up and sold off, but how he thought that starting an International Security Dog and Handler Supply Service with my help, would prevent this happening. The more we discussed it, the more I could see what a brilliant plan it was.

The night after Lord Searle vetoed Tom's plan, Yvonne called me to the telephone and shouted, "It's Tom. He sounds suicidal!"

I picked up the receiver and said, "What's up Tom?"

"It's that bloody Searle. It's the first time I've had a chance to use my initiative and I've been shot down in flames!" he cried.

"Just sit tight Tom, I'll be right over." I soothed.

When I arrived at his place, he was in a right old state. I poured him a large whisky and soda and settled him down for the night as best I could.

After Yvonne and I moved away from Inkpen Common, I never saw Tom again. I often thought about him and worried about him, knowing that I could no longer keep an eye on him. Of course, the fish farm was a complete failure and, as far as the Craven Estate was concerned, it was the last straw that broke the camel's back! My mate Tom, as I will always remember him, committed suicide 5 years later, at his mother's home in America. He was only 26.

CHUCK'S STORY 12
KENT
1980 - 2001

After leaving our cottage at Inkpen Common, we bought a chalet bungalow at Hoo Marina Park, in Kent. We intended to live there while we were negotiating the purchase of a boarding kennels in Goudhurst which we planned to turn into gundog training kennels. After three weeks, I could see that Yvonne was getting jittery about something and when I asked her what was wrong she said, "Do we have to go to Goudhurst?"

"Not if you don't want to," and then I added, "Why don't you want to go?"

"Everyone here is ever so friendly. They're the best neighbours I've ever had and, not only that, I have a garden!" she cried.

"You hardly ever had any nearby neighbours when we lived way out in the sticks and as for having a garden - you had acres and acres to have one," I said.

"Yes, I know, and wherever I planted something the dogs would find it and dig it up," she moaned.

"Come on Yvonne, what are you up to?" I demanded.

"Having such good neighbours and having a garden are two very good reasons why I want to stay here but that's not all. As you know, over the last three weeks an unprecedented number of pet dogs have been referred to you by law forces and humane societies in a last hope of avoiding destruction," she stated. "I call them 'Cinderella dogs' – pet dogs that are in desperate need of a chance for a happy and safe life.

"Yes, I know, but what do you expect me to do about it?"

"Well, yesterday morning you were saying that buying the boarding kennels at Goudhurst might not be such a good idea after all. On top of that, several years ago when I asked you if you would ever consider training pet dogs, you said that you would - if you ever had sufficient time, funds, and a good enough reason to do so," she explained.

"Yes, I remember catching a strange thoughtful look in your eye at the time – not to mention that enigmatic smile you sometimes have on your face when you're looking ahead to the future," I said, adding, "so what were you thinking?"

"I was thinking that I was going to have to make doubly sure that, when that time came, you would have those precious funds - even though it would take my life's savings, the total sacrifice of my career and a great deal of hardship on my part," she proclaimed.

"Wow! I don't know what to say. I'm speechless!"

"Just say you will. Please!"

"After I've told that gazumping boarding kennels owner what to do with his over-priced kennels, I will start on your 'Cinderella dogs' right away," I promised.

"Oh Chucky, thank you! Thank you so ever so much, you wonderful man! I've waited so long for this and now it's really going to happen!" she cried.

Yvonne was dead right about our new neighbours. I still owned Phoenix Dog Security Services and though most of the dogs lived with their handlers, two of the dogs lived with us – and of course, being security dogs, they were rather noisy. When we apologised to our neighbours about this, they said, "Let them bark as much as they want."

When we asked them why, they explained, "Up until three weeks ago there were gangs of villains living here. That's until your dogs scared the pants off them. Now they have all gone and they are not likely to come back while you and your dogs are here!"

This cheered us up no end. The past eighteen months had been unhappy ones in more ways than one.

Sheba

We had to have our beloved Sheba euthanized by our vet to save her from further suffering. She always seemed to be indestructible, but that was up until she turned eleven. Then, mentally she was as strong as ever, but physically everything was breaking down. Usually, when a dog reached this stage in its life, I wouldn't have hesitated in putting it out of its misery. But Sheba was always good at making out that she wasn't hurting, even when she was. But one morning, when I was following her downstairs, she tripped and fell. As she rolled over and over down the stairs, my heart was in my mouth. Then, when she reached the bottom, she picked herself up in the same manner as a highly dignified person would after tripping up in the street, as if to say, 'You didn't see that, did you?' But I did! When a working dog is trained to such a high standard as Sheba was, its sense of dignity becomes highly developed and, even more so, when in the presence of its master.

Having seen what I saw and knowing what I know, I steeled myself and took her down to our vet. As the lethal injection was prepared and right up to the time Sheba passed peacefully away, I gently stroked the top of her head as I fought desperately to hold back the tears and control my emotions. After it was over, I drove my Land Rover into the middle of a ploughed field away from prying eyes, and cried my heart out. I knew it was going to hurt, but never thought it would hurt as much as it did. Sixteen weeks went by before I could speak to Yvonne about it. She knew I was numb with grief and, though she was hurting as much as I was, she waited patiently for me to heal up enough to be able to do so.

Six months before Sheba's death, we had purchased a very special German shepherd dog bitch puppy, which we named Donner, which in German means Thunder. Both Donner's sire and dam were 'from the flocks', or in other words, they herded and tended the tough German sheep, as their ancestors had done since time immemorial. There were just two surviving strains of these genuine German sheepherding dogs left. Donner's sire was from one of those strains and her dam was from the other one.

Mrs Karen Smith, who kindly let me have Donner, lived near Guildford in Surrey. She had studied pure working German shepherd dog bloodlines in Germany, in great depth and for many years.

Two months after I had Donner, Mrs Smith rang me up out of the blue and said, "Do you remember Rolf, Donner's brother, the dog puppy I kept?"

"Wow! How could I ever forget him? He's perfect!" I replied.

"Well, he's yours!" she said.

"B ... but ... he's worth thousands and thousands of pounds," I stammered.

"Money won't help in this case. It's far too late for that. I've lost the roof over my head and you've just got to take over from where I left off!" she cried.

With Donner and Rolf, those precious, perfectly bred dogs from the flocks and, of course, my wonderful Sheba, still fit and healthy at that time, I considered myself to be the luckiest dog owner on the planet. But, though I wasn't aware of it then, there was trouble lying ahead.

Eight months later, I was coming back from London with Donner, after completing a stressful nighttime security assignment. Donner's guarding instincts were razor sharp; she had bitten a couple of thieving yobs whilst on patrol eight hours earlier. I was running late and the only thought in my head was to get us home as quickly as I could. The early London morning rush hour traffic was heavier than usual and then, to add insult to injury, a leather clad Rocker on a motorbike was tapping on the rear window of my van and making rude gestures every time I stopped at traffic lights.

The van was brand new and the rear door was locked, but that didn't stop Donner smashing the door open to get at him. It must have been the Rocker's lucky day because, at the split second Donner smashed the doors open, the traffic lights turned green. The biker, now peeing himself with fright, gunned his motorbike off into the traffic with Donner in hot pursuit. Risking life and limb, I jumped out of the van into the oncoming traffic and called her back to me, but she couldn't hear me above the noise of the traffic. I drove around looking for her for several hours without any success and then went home to face the music!

Yvonne was terribly upset, and so were the Metropolitan Police, who were first in line for two of Donner's puppies when she was old enough to have them. Half of their Dog Section was out trying to track her down with their tracker dogs during the night, but she seemed to have disappeared off the face of the earth. Despite every effort to find her, she was never found.

I didn't think my luck could ever get any worse than that, but of course it did, as I pointed out earlier. Losing Donner, on top of having to leave Trainettes two weeks later, I just couldn't help getting an uneasy feeling that, in some way or other, I was bound to lose Rolf as well, thereby letting everyone down again. I rang up Mrs Smith and told her about the situation. I asked her if she could possibly take him back, but unfortunately she was no better off than when she let me have him in the first place. After a great deal of thought, she said, "I would love to have him back but, as you see, I still don't have a permanent roof over my head and I'm relying on friends for a place to stay. But I do have a suggestion, and that is for him to be a police dog. Then, when they retire him, he can stand at stud, either at your new place or mine. It's not the perfect solution, but at least his precious bloodlines won't be completely wasted."

My heart and soul went out to Mrs Smith. In monetary terms, Rolf was worth a fortune. If she was a lesser person, she would have taken him back and sold him off to the highest bidder, but despite being stony broke, she couldn't do that. She would rather die than let him fall into the wrong hands thereby trashing all the hard work she had put in, not to mention the boring life he would have.

Fortunately I had a good friend who was a dog handler in the Wiltshire

Police. As I only had a few days to find a suitable place for Rolf, I phoned my friend right away. I told him about my situation and in reply, he said: "The new dogs have already started their courses, but we will stash him away until the next new dogs start their training in three weeks' time."

Two days later my friend rang me back and said, "The Chief Inspector has found out about Rolf, but don't worry about that because Prison Officer Roy Selby wants him. As you know, he's the dog handler who won Police Dog of the Year last year." He then went onto say: "We've only had Rolf here for a couple of days, but we've never seen a dog with so much working potential as he has. Even the Chief Inspector has commented on it, but red tape being what it is, eh?"

As for Roy, he was over the moon with Rolf, as was the Governor of the top security prison for whom he worked. Their new intake of dogs was halfway through their fifteen-week training course, but because of Rolf's working potential they put him in it anyway. The upshot was that he finished the course with ten per cent higher marks than the other dogs!

With Rolf now settled and a myriad of other loose ends tidied up, I could now concentrate on Yvonne's Cinderella dogs at long last. After a few false starts, I went on to successfully train several thousands of them in their own individual home environments. Each dog was trained with its owner. They were from all walks of life and lived in every kind of home that one could imagine - from castles and mansions to cottages, tower blocks, prefabs, and tents.

The dog-training exercises that I included in my revolutionary home visiting pet dog and owner training course were as follows:-

- 'Heel' - to walk and trot alongside his master's heels both on and off lead, without any fuss or bother.
- 'Leave-it' - to immediately stop doing anything that he's not supposed to do
- 'Sit' - to sit down, immediately and without hesitation.
- 'Sit- Stay' – to sit and stay until called.
- 'Come' - come to hand when called, immediately and under all circumstances.
- 'Down' - lay down.
- 'Down-Stay' - stay in the 'down' position for 15 minutes or more, while master is out of sight.
- 'Retrieve' – wait until the 'fetch' command before retrieving.
- 'Emergency Stop' - hit the deck on the 'sit' or 'down' command: depending on the breed of dog.

~~~

It wasn't all plain sailing. I had intended to spend just an hour on each visit, as I did with my novice gundog and sheepdog owning clients.

However, I had under-estimated the damage that had already been done over the past fifty years or so by know-all-know-nothing 'experts' who had filled the heads of pet dog owners with countless old wives tales and other erroneous claptrap.

Starting with those pet dogs that were referred to me by law forces and humane societies, the first thing I discovered was that they, in common with many pet dogs, had a major problem with their allotted role in life – that of being a mere pet. This was apparent when talking to the owners and taking down the case history of each individual dog. A great many of them had viciously resisted all previous efforts to train and rehabilitate them. Many others had just suffered in silence, which, in my opinion, was the saddest thing of all.

~~~

After home tutoring pet dog owners internationally for 18 months, the continuous jet lag and my heavy work load were killing me so I took my doctor's advice and cut down my overseas visits to just the odd one or two. I am not known to give up easily, but on my return from one particular visit to the Australian outback, I had only been home for three hours when Yvonne answered our emergency phone. After a short conversation she said, "Can you go to New Zealand? This one is in really big trouble!"

"Tell them I'm on my way," I replied. Then, as an afterthought, I added, "What's that you were watching on TV just now?"

"I was watching 'Goodbye Mr Chips' - you know, the one with the subsidiary title that says, 'To serve them all my days' - just like you do with your dogs and horses!" she teased.

Not catching her drift, I shouldered my old battered Merchant Navy kitbag and, as I kissed her I whispered, "I'll be back as soon as I can."

On the way to the airport, I asked the cabby, "Who's this 'Goodbye Mr Chips' guy on TV that everyone is talking about?"

"Gorblimey Gov, he's supposed to be a teacher at one of those posh schools. Everyone knows that!" Then, as an afterthought, he prodded, "You're not trying to wind me up are you?"

"No," I said absently. Then, suddenly realising what Yvonne had been talking about, I added, "It's just something my wife said about him this morning."

After that, whenever I was stuck with a pet dog training problem that seemed impossible to solve, Yvonne would chirp, "What do you think Mr Chips would do in such a situation?" I don't know why, but it usually worked. She was also a great admirer of Confucius the ancient Chinese philosopher. If 'Mr Chips' didn't work, then she would say, "What would Confucius say?"

One day I was chilling out in my favourite armchair after an extremely difficult day, when an RSPCA representative came on TV giving out an account of the colossal number of pet dogs that had been destroyed that month after they had bitten people or other dogs. On hearing that, I flew into a rage and ranted, "Did you hear that Yvonne? That more or less wipes out the number of pet dogs I've sorted out with the same problem since I launched my home visiting system 18 months ago! And that's without taking into account the millions worldwide that I can't get to. Do the maths, Yvonne, what we are trying to do is futile!"

"Calm down, Chucky! Just think what Mr Chips would do," she soothed.

"So what would Mr Chips do?" I retorted.

"Mr Chips would rope in a bunch of other formally trained professionals like you and found an international training college where wannabe pet dog trainers from all over the world could come and learn your revolutionary pet dog training methods, together with the underlying basics of practical dog training from retired head gamekeepers, master shepherds, and service dog training gurus, etc. Then, as fully qualified pet dog trainers, they could go back to their own countries and teach pet dog owners how to train their dogs properly, so they don't have to be destroyed," she replied.

Finding the qualified teachers that I needed to staff this projected training college was comparatively easy, but getting sufficient funds to pay for getting the college up and running was hopeless. Traditionally, funding a project such as this would have come from the British Aristocracy – but not anymore.

For quite some time several film studios had been headhunting me and offering me unbelievably huge sums of money to work for them, which I always turned down. However, as a last ditch attempt to get our college up and running, I reluctantly took a job at MGM Studios as an animal wrangler.

All went well at first, until an arrogant film director demanded that I should get a horse to do a stunt that was physically impossible. When I explained to him why the horse couldn't do the stunt he had in mind, he waddled up to me, blew cigar smoke in my face, and called me a 'lazy, limey bastard!' He had been pushing his luck for several days, but as far as my temper was concerned this was the last straw. That old familiar red mist came up before my eyes and, as quick as a flash, I walloped him!

With help from his minions, he struggled to his feet and spluttered, "Kemsley, you're fired!" Amazingly, he still had his fat cigar firmly clenched between his teeth, though it was looking a bit worse for wear. After firing up his battered cigar he added, "I will make sure that as far as the film industry in America is concerned, you won't get another job anywhere."

"That's okay, Pops," I said, "but you really should give up smoking those dreadful cigars - they're very bad for your health!"

With 'old money' and the American film industry now out of the running, we had no other alternative than to approach 'new money', but as far as new money was concerned, our training college plan was a dead duck right from the start. Our bank wasn't any help, they thought our training college plan was a hair-brained scheme. Also, as no one had ever done it before, they simply wrote it off as a white elephant. We tried several other banks and received the same negative response.

If that was the way they wanted to play it, then so be it. We didn't pursue the matter any further and continued doing what we did best; working on our own - which in this case, resulted in saving thousands of pet dogs' lives by teaching their owners to successfully train and handle their dogs, thereby enhancing their dog's lives and their own – beyond their wildest dreams.

Twenty-two years later, the bank was falling over backwards to offer us a loan to get the very same thing started. As far as I could gather, a bank official - whose dogs had been messed up at some obedience classes - was looking through her bank's archives, when she stumbled upon our business plan relating to starting such a training college.

When the bank contacted Yvonne, she venomously retorted, "By now, all those traditional, time-served head gamekeepers, master shepherds and service dog training gurus who would have staffed our international training college have passed away. Who do you think is going to staff such a college now - bank clerks?"

I suppose High Street banks must have their own grapevine, because three other banks tried the same tack, and bit the dust in the same fashion. Talk about bad timing, eh?

~~~

Providing such a personal service as I did, training pet dogs together with their owners, brought about some very poignant moments. In 1995, I was in consultation with a lady in Gillingham about her dog's wild behaviour. Five minutes into the consultation she exclaimed, "Excuse me for asking, but you seem to have a slight West Devon accent and I was wondering whether you are from those parts?"

"Not exactly, but I served my apprenticeship there with the Lamerton Hunt under Frank Gerry," I informed her.

"Heavens above, this must be my dog's lucky day!" she cried.

Seeing that I was wondering where this was going, she said, "Did they call you 'Charlie' when you were there?"

"How do you know that?" I asked, flabbergasted.

"Frank's daughter, Pamela, told me all about you - we were best mates at school!"

"Re-really?" I gulped.
"Yes, really! She was head over heels in love with you!"

~~~

I had actually been down that way several years earlier, when I'd had to bail out an old mentor of mine who was held at Bow Street Police Station for being drunk and disorderly.

He was an old Master Shepherd who suffered from claustrophobia. The old boy, who was well into his eighties, had got on the wrong train and the hustle and bustle of London was just a little too much for him.

He and I went back a long way. I was rather fond of him as it was he, along with senior huntsmen, head kennel men, head gamekeepers and men of that great ilk, who were responsible for straightening me out when I was a disoriented teenager with a massive great big chip on my shoulder. And all while they were teaching me my canine and equine crafts.

It was a long and slow journey up to London in my dilapidated old Land Rover, which like me had seen better days. As I drove, my mind flew back to when I was that mixed up teenager

When I arrived at Bow Street Police Station, I saw that my old mentor was in a right old state with his claustrophobia and was shaking like a leaf. Once I got him into the Land Rover and we had left the City and were on the open road heading for his home in Devon, he soon stopped shaking and was back to his old self again. He still lived in West Devon and he vowed that from now on, that was where he would stay. I sympathized with him and wished I was back there too. After a long, drawn out silence he asked, "So, what did you do with all that stuff we taught you?"

"I went on to successfully train thousands of dogs of all breeds and types for both work and companionship," I replied. "I also invented new dog training methods and techniques to counteract the complexities of modern living that both working dogs and pet dogs have to endure in these crazy, mixed up times."

"And did you ever lose your passion for horses?"

"No, I never did," I said.

With that he smiled and drifted off to sleep.

After seeing my old mentor friend safely home, I decided to take one last look at the old hunt kennels that I had known so well. I leaned on the old familiar five-barred gate and looked down on the kennels - like I often did in the past when I was feeling sad. Then, as I looked down into the beautiful valley where the kennels were laid out before me, the hounds, as if on cue, started 'singing'.

So deep in thought was I as I listened to the hounds making music that I failed to notice that a young lad had ridden up on a magnificent hunter with two equally magnificent ones in tow. As he dismounted he said, "That's the hounds singing, they do that when they're happy."

"Yes I know, I know," I said.

"Are you something to do with the hounds then," he asked.

"No, but I once was."

He then turned to me and said, "Oh, by the way, I'm the new kennel boy. I'm training to be a huntsman. I've been out exercising these hunters; it's all part of the job you know." We listened to the hounds for a while until he turned to look at me and said, "Are you not feeling well sir, only I thought I saw tears in your eyes."

"No lad, don't concern yourself. I'm alright. What you saw was probably just a trick of the light, it happens around these parts, you know."

With that he smiled, mounted his hunter and waved to me as he rode off to the kennels with the other two hunters in tow, just as I would have done all those years ago.

As I watched the young kennel boy with the hunters wending their way down that old country lane, I smiled wryly to myself and thought out loud: "That's right, boy, just a trick of the light - with a bunch of old memories thrown in for good measure!"

~~~

I was down in the dumps after my nostalgic trip to West Devon, but not for long. Roy Selby rang me up out of the blue and said, "Sorry Chuck, I don't know how to tell you this ... It's about Rolf."

There was a long pause and expecting the worst, I held my breath for what seemed like ages. Then he continued, "When we were on day watches at the prison everything was fine, but he wasn't so keen when we were assigned to watch the top security prisoners in the exercise yard in case they tried to escape. Having that German sheepdog blood in him, he wanted to round them all up. Of course, he wasn't allowed to, so he started to get frustrated and gave them the odd nip. So then the governor put us on permanent nights. Rolf was in his glory working nights and loved it, and so did I, but my wife wasn't too happy. She accused me of thinking more of Rolf than of her and threatened to leave me if I continued working nights.

Chuck with Rolf

So, Chuck, now you have a roof over your head again, could you possibly help me out and take him back?"

"Don't worry Roy, I'll be down to pick him up right away," I replied.

Rolf was so pleased to see me that he wagged his tail so hard and fast that, for a moment, I thought he would wag it right off! For five days he was so worried that I might disappear in a puff of smoke that he stuck to me like glue! Then, after a few more days, he was back to his old self. I was so pleased to have him back and I spent every spare moment with him.

Together, we explored every nook and cranny of the Hoo Peninsular where I lived, and also the adjoining and equally interesting Isle of Grain and Thames Estuary. Rolf's favourite walk was on top of the sea wall, which goes all the way from Hoo Marina boatyard to the Kingsnorth power station. Sometimes, when the tide was out, we scrambled down off the top of the wall onto the salt flats below, looking for sea creatures. Walking on the salt flats is very difficult and strenuous at the best of times and even dangerous in some places - at least for people. These places are like slimy quick sands and I found the easiest and safest way to move around was on my stomach with my legs spread out wide and then use my arms to claw myself along as best I could. Rolf, being a dog, and a very strong athletic one at that, was able to race around the salt flats almost like he was on dry land - which I'm sure he did to show off! He loved swimming, and with all that sea water around he was in his glory; so much so that sometimes he just wouldn't come out of the water unless I swam out and grabbed him by the scruff of his neck and towed him back to dry land.

I was quite happy to go along with this, at least for the time being, as I had a couple of serious water work tasks lined up which I wanted to train him up for. His keenness for swimming in harsh weather conditions would be vital to carrying out one of these tasks.

The first water work task I had in mind was rescuing people from the water after they had fallen in or got out of their depth. Roy had already started, but not finished training Rolf to do this as part of an EU directive, when he was a prison dog.

The second was wildfowling (retrieving wild geese from the sea and estuary under extreme rough weather conditions after they had been shot) - which he was more than eager to do, and for which he had a natural bent. I spotted this trait one day when we were walking along the top of the sea wall and stopped to watch a gaggle of wild geese fly by on their regular flight path. All the signs were apparent: the flared nostrils; the classic head and tail set, that I had seen many times before in dogs with wildfowling potential. I have often said that the more tasks a German shepherd dog is trained or schooled to do, the happier and contented he will be - Rolf was no exception to the rule. He was a star pupil and quickly became proficient in both of the above disciplines, adding them to the ones he already had. And as for refusing to come out of the water when I ordered him to do so - no problem - he was out of the water as quick as flash and ready for the next piece of action to begin.

I had a friend called Larry, who lived two miles downriver from me at Lower Stoke and who did wildfowling with a Chesapeake Bay retriever.

He was a nice enough chap, but he was forever boasting about his precious dog's prowess as a wildfowler's dog. Moreover, when I informed him that I was training Rolf up to do wildfowling, he laughed his stupid head off and said: "But he's not even a gundog breed - so how can he do that?" There's no reason to disrepute the fact that the Chesapeake Bay retriever is the granddaddy of all retrievers. If ever there is a dog that was designed for wildfowling this is it (it even has web feet). One of their notable traits, though, is that they don't suffer fools gladly.

Chesapeake Bay retriever

I wasn't going to tell Larry that, so I remained inscrutable and said nothing at that point. At 4:00 am on the first day of the next wildfowling season, I took Rolf with me and hid in a trench near the Medway Estuary shoreline and waited silently for the morning flight of geese to pass overhead. At 4:11 am, Rolf let out a low warning growl - barely audible to the human ear - alerting me to the fact that a man and his dog were approaching our hide. The sky was pitch-black as I heard the man put up his camouflaged hide. All was deathly quiet after that; you could almost hear a pin drop. That was until 4:25 am, when a bitter gale force wind sprang up, bringing heavy rain and hail stones in from the cold North Sea. At 5:05 am, with the coming of daybreak, the skies brightened slightly - just in time to see a gaggle of geese passing high overhead.

"Too high for a clean shot," I muttered to myself.

Then a shot rang out and a fair sized gander fell out of the sky. By the way it planed down and tried to gain height before it hit the water, I could tell it was wounded. I hate to see any animal suffer unnecessarily, so I was sorely tempted to send Rolf to retrieve it so I could put it out of its misery - but its bad form to take someone's bird after they shot it!

To give the man his due, he sent his dog out to retrieve the wounded bird the split second it hit the water, but then he blew it. The stormy weather had whipped the estuary up into a maelstrom and the tidal currents were at their strongest, so his dog needed to keep his mind focused on the tough job in hand. But common to most 'know-all-no-nothing-experts' that I was beginning to suspect the man to be, he just didn't know how to keep quiet when it was necessary to do so - and this was certainly one of these occasions! Right from the start, his dog's behaviour was impeccable. That's more than I can say for the man, who was running along the shoreline shouting out: "There's a good dog! There it is," causing his dog to lose concentration as it looked back over its shoulder to see what the man was blabbering about. Each time it did this, it lost sight and scent of the bird and had to swim around to relocate it all over again until it became utterly confused and finally ran off in my direction, with the man chasing after it and cursing it for being 'a cowardly cur!'

The sky was still black as thunder, and though the man's voice had sounded familiar, it wasn't until he ran past the trench where Rolf and I were concealed that I could then see that it was Larry. I should have realised it was him much earlier, but the light was poor, and Larry was supposed to be at work 20 miles away. Throughout this fiasco, Rolf hadn't taken his eyes off the wounded bird and as it was now being swept out to sea on the ebb tide, I whispered in his ear, "Hi lost!"

In response, he was off like a shot, diving into the treacherous waters of the estuary and swimming after the wounded gander as if his life depended on it. As Rolf battled with the strong currents, I noiselessly followed him along the shoreline, cursing myself under my breath for being an idiot to risk his life on such a dangerous mission. Slowly, but surely, he caught up with it and gently held the gander in his jaws. I hoped with all my heart that he had enough reserves of strength to bring such a heavy bird back to the shoreline before the pair of them were swept out to sea.

As the tide was on the ebb, and he was encumbered with such a heavy burden, I watched his progress with bated breath. This turned into pure admiration as he brought the bird back under almost impossible conditions. He gently placed it in my outstretched hands, before lying down to recuperate after his strenuous ordeal.

Larry came puffing up just in time to see Rolf gently place the bird in my hands. He blurted out, "I've lost my dog! Have you seen it by any chance?" Larry had been so wrapped up in chasing and chastising his dog that he'd failed to notice what had happened after that, so I enlightened him and brought him up to date, but not until I had quickly put the gander out of its misery as humanely as I could.

"You mean you were here when I shot the goose?" he asked hesitantly.

"I was here long before that. At 4:00 am to be precise," I replied.

"But why?" he asked, suspiciously.

"You and everyone else are supposed to be at work, so I thought today would be the best time to test out Rolf's prowess as a wildfowling dog after all the schooling I've given him," I stated.

"Oh, I see. I thought that because of all the bragging I've been doing about my dog's prowess, you had come down to catch me out," he said sheepishly.

"Well, I knew there was something that didn't ring true about the way you kept on about it, but as far as checking up on you - I just don't have the time or inclination to do that," I said brusquely.

"I'm sorry, Chuck, but when you mentioned the fact that the Chesapeake is the perfect dog for wildfowling, I was so ashamed of making such a pig's ear of the training and handling of my one, that I couldn't help myself," he bleated.

After Rolf had got his breath back, I said, "Okay, Larry, let's go and get your dog back," and to Rolf, I whispered, "Go find."

"Shouldn't we be going with him?" Larry asked.

"No. You will see why in a few minutes time," I replied.

Larry, kicking his heels and thinking I had lost my senses, suddenly perked up after a few minutes and squeaked, "Look Chuck! I still can't believe it - but here they come!" And sure enough, there was Larry's Chesapeake coming into sight, looking like a little lost lamb as Rolf herded him up from the rear.

~~~

I would like to fully acknowledge my wife Yvonne's great contribution to the thousands of her Cinderella dogs that I trained, and of course, their owners. There's certainly no way I could have done any of this without her help.

In my early years, I schooled horses and trained dogs for a living, but if anyone had told me then that for the last 35 years of my career I would be training pet dogs, I would have refused to believe them. Schooling horses and gundogs, as well as training sheepdogs and other types of working dogs in the glorious English countryside for people who had been brought up and formally trained to handle them, was nothing short of utopia. So I had no inclination or reason to do otherwise, even if I'd wanted to. My clients' horses and dogs enjoyed life - whether they were heavy draft horses, saddle horses, gundogs, sheepdogs or any other type of working animal; I cannot recollect ever seeing an unhappy or discontented one. It was truly wonderful. However, situations change with time.

In the early 1960s, when Yvonne helped me run my busy gundog and working dog training kennels, it gave me more valuable time to concentrate on training and schooling my clients' working dogs and horses. She had watched men handling many of these working dogs on the farms where she had worked as a young teenager, and had often admired their canine-human related comradeship and rapport.

As she'd witnessed these happy dignified working dogs, she'd considered that if someday ordinary pet dogs (Cinderella dogs, as she called them) and their owners could benefit from such powerfully practical and humane animal gentling knowledge and expertise, then her own happiness and life's work would be complete too. And when she dragged me down the corridor of one of the kennel blocks of Palex International Quarantine Kennels all those years ago, and showed me that poor little terrier, Murphy, displaying signs of the most chronic form of emotional instability I had ever seen, it made me see the plight of pet dogs in a different light.

I remember discussing this in great depth with the last three surviving mentors from my apprenticeship days, and they all agreed that if training pet dogs at training kennels failed, then there could be no other alternative than to train each dog with its owner on a personal home visiting basis. But we all knew that sticking my neck out as a formally trained professional was crazy, and I risked gravely damaging my reputation and career.

But when I was faced with Yvonne's sadness, and an unprecedented number of pet dogs referred to me by law forces and humane societies, I put my reluctance behind me. I missed my utopian lifestyle running my gundog and working dog training kennels, and I missed my horses too. I often thought to myself - if only someone with this level knowledge and background had stuck his neck out years ago and carried out this pet dog training task, then I wouldn't have had to do it! But I knew this was wishful thinking, so I just cracked on with what had to be done.

I'll also admit that I considered I was over qualified for this particular task initially, but then I realised I was far from it. In actual fact, it turned out to be the most difficult and most complex dog training task that I, or anyone else for that matter, had ever successfully accomplished. It took every modicum of knowledge and experience that I possessed and even then, at times, this was barely enough. It was also the biggest challenge of my whole tempestuous life, paling all other challenges I had faced into insignificance.

Although successfully training thousands of pet dogs and their owners was quite an achievement in itself, it was just a mere drop in the ocean considering there are more than six million pet dogs in Britain, and millions more worldwide, suffering a life of misery and emotional instability simply because they are not properly trained. That's why Yvonne and I fought so long and so hard to try to create an international training college, where people who wanted to become genuine pet dog trainers from all over the world could come and acquire all the necessary and essential skills. Having done that, they could go back to their own countries and teach their own people and so on. Pet dogs and their owners worldwide would then receive the proper training they so desperately needed.

Not being able to get the college up and running, I had no other alternative than to continue going it alone to train as many thousands of pet dogs with their owners as I could. This I did, with Yvonne's help, right up until her death in April 2001. I then continued on my own, until I burnt out and lost the use of my legs in 2008.

Yvonne's contribution was enormous, right up until the day before she died. Although Yvonne put a brave face on after we failed to get our proposed college, I knew deep down she was more upset than she let on. So anything that made her happy was okay with me; even more so when she became terminally ill at the young age of 55. She was 10 years younger than me, and hardly ever had a day's illness in her life. She died three years later.

Despite her intense pain and suffering, she manned her Cinderella Dogs' telephone hot line 24 hours a day. She was there for clients, new and old, right up until the day she died. Yvonne's illness was such that the only way she could sleep was in a specially customized electric recliner chair. I tried to persuade her to relax and let a receptionist man her hotline and take care of the office work, but to no avail.

As she was too frail to take care of herself properly, I cut down my pet dog and owner training visits to just two local ones each day so that I could take care of her in the best possible way. We watched TV for hours on end, and I did anything else that would take her mind of her crippling illness. It broke my heart to see her suffering getting worse and worse. Halfway through the day before she died, she cried out in a tiny voice that was barely audible, and said, "Thank you for looking after me." This between more intensive bouts of pain. Reading between the lines, I could clearly see that the relentless pain that she had suffered over the past three years had finally knocked all the fight out of her. This was the only way she had left to show her gratitude to me for nursing her through her long illness, and also for training thousands of her Cinderella Dogs. As this flashed through my mind, I felt like an iced dagger had been thrust through my heart. And so, with my voice filled with emotion and tears streaming down my cheeks, I sobbed, "Y-you don't have to thank me… I-I'm your husband… what… d-did you expect me to do? Dump you?" The last words Yvonne uttered on the day before she died were: "Write a book!"

Yvonne passed away at 5.39 on the following morning. Although she is no longer with us, her memory lingers on in my heart and also in the hearts of so many of our old dog owning pupils – who have passed on what I taught them to their sons and daughters, who in turn have passed it on to theirs. They know, as I know, that without her dedication to her Cinderella dogs, and her intervention on their behalf, none of this would ever have happened.

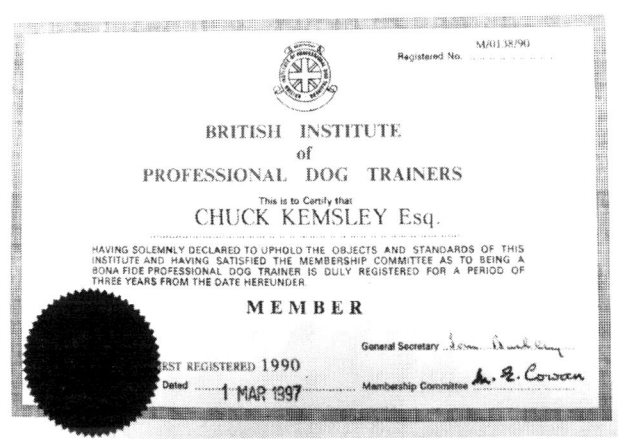

IN CONCLUSION
2001 - 2015

After Yvonne's death in April 2001, Chuck continued with his pet dog training programme until he eventually lost the use of his legs in 2008.

This was caused by CMT (Charcot-Marie-Tooth Disease), inherited from Mum's side of the family. It is a genetic condition that damages peripheral nerves and progressively worsens over the years, causing the muscles in the foot, lower leg, hand and forearm to become wasted and weak

In 2009 he became completely dependent on agency care for his security and comfort. After a lifetime of work and activity, he became very depressed. He wrote:

"My moral and inner strength were at their lowest ebb. I still hadn't come to terms with losing my dear wife and kindred spirit after almost forty years of married bliss. And then the final blow was this crippling illness that kept me cooped up indoors and prevented me from continuing my outdoorsy career that I loved more than life itself.

In November 2009, Anna McFarlane became my regular carer.

A few days before she arrived on the scene, I was secretly negotiating a deal with one of my contacts from my old gunrunning days. I wanted him to smuggle a Magnum handgun into the UK so I could blow my brains out with it - and put an end to my misery.

Needless to say, I didn't blow my brains out after Anna became my regular carer – I no longer needed to! With her help and inspiration, it wasn't long before I was almost back to my old self, with my fighting spirit as good as new. I owe Anna big time, and I won't let anyone forget it!"

~~~

In 2011, as described in Part 1 of this book, we discovered that Chuck was our long lost brother and went to visit him at his home near Rochester. We also contacted the Foundling Hospital Museum who put us in touch with one of their senior social workers, Val Malloy from Coram. (Coram is a charity committed to improving the lives of the UK's most vulnerable children and young people). The foundling hospital kept very extensive records and several weeks later, Val went to visit Chuck with a written account she had prepared for him, detailing the full circumstances of his birth and his admission to the Foundling Hospital.

Poignantly she also gave him a sheaf of letters Mum had written over the years and also a cheque for £40. (As well as the many presents she had sent for birthdays and Christmas, Mum had also sent postal orders for small sums of money, which had been put in a savings account in his name, but he was completely unaware of this.)

As Val explained in a letter:
"You may feel sad that you were never told as a child about your mother's ongoing concern for you, or about the letters she wrote. At the time, however, it was believed that children would only be confused and upset to know of a mother who had given them up and who could not give them a home, so the policy became one of saying as little as possible. With hindsight, we might feel that children would have been glad to know that someone was thinking of them. There was no easy answer, and I hope that you will not feel too burdened by knowing about the letters now."

For the first time in his life, Chuck knew the truth and it obviously affected him deeply. He wrote:
"On leaving school I was given my mother's contact details and met her several times. That's when I gave her the photo of me as a baby and when the other photos were taken. The first time I laid eyes on her I remember thinking she was so pretty – like Vera Lynn. She was always

very nice to me, treating me like royalty when I visited. She also came to see me on a number of occasions. But we were never to grow close because by my teens my heart was already hardened against her. I was treated badly at the military school and never forgave my birth parents for leaving me there. When my mother said she had kept in touch through the Foundling Hospital I didn't believe her. Now with hindsight and the proof that she never forgot me, I regret thinking badly of her. I realise that she did her best in very difficult circumstances.

When I was 34, Mum and I had cross words about something that seems unimportant now, and after that, we never laid eyes on each other again. But I'm so glad my sisters have found me now. My wife and I were never able to have children, so it means all the more to me to be rediscovering my family in my old age."

~~~

Chuck passed peacefully away in hospital on the 13th May 2015. One of his former clients, the writer and musician, Richard Cruttwell, summed up all our feelings when he wrote on Facebook:

"It was with great sadness that I learnt of the sad passing of Chuck Kemsley, last Wednesday. Chuck wasn't just a dog trainer, he was *the* dog trainer; Britain's last master dog trainer in fact. I met him back in 1986 when I enlisted his help on retraining a very unruly Alsatian which we'd acquired two days before she was due to be put down. Chuck's help bought her another 13 happy years. Never a man to bow to rules or conformity, he had punk rock attitude way before the later 70s, and over the course of his eventful life he had been an engineer at sea, a daredevil motorcycle rider, an animal trainer for Hollywood movies, and even a gun runner for the Cuban rebels, before dedicating the rest of his working life to helping unruly canines. I learnt much from Chuck, but it's only a minuscule fraction of his animal magic. I am proud to have known him, and I am proud that my dog wears his last custom made check chain. Charles 'Chuck' Kemsley, RIP."

As his eldest sister, I was given the privilege of officiating at his funeral, which was held at the Medway Crematorium.

It was a sad occasion, but also a wonderful chance to celebrate the extraordinary life of a very special person.

I was incredibly grateful for all the emails Chuck had sent me during the three short years I knew him. I learnt so much about his life and the amazing exploits and achievements of his turbulent youth.

He was a complex character with a volatile temper and a chip on his shoulder, but despite his tough exterior, he had a deep sense of justice; despising bullies and always ready to defend the underdog

Chuck was a man with a thirst for adventure and excitement, fearless, tough and invincible. He travelled the world, living a life on the edge, always seeking out danger and defying death.

He was apprenticed and formally trained as a master animal handler - and he never lost his passionate love of horses and dogs

When he was 30, he met and married his beautiful wife and soulmate, Yvonne, and together they dedicated the rest of their lives to the welfare of animals, both great and small. Together they ran a busy gundog and working dog training kennels, but Yvonne was convinced that ordinary pet dogs and their owners could also benefit from Chuck's unique expertise. Because of her encouragement, Chuck went on to become one of the world's greatest dog trainers.

It was difficult for me to summarise such an exciting life in such a short time, but other people who were present also had the opportunity to express their tributes and sincere thoughts and feelings. There was no doubt that Chuck was a very special person who left a deep impact on everybody who knew him.

Richard Cruttwell, mentioned earlier, was at the funeral and he described how they first met:

"I met Chuck through his dog training expertise when I acquired an unruly German Shepherd two days before she was due to be put down, and with his help, she became a wonderful companion, and he bought her 13 more wonderful years. I visited him a while back with my current dog when she was an exuberant puppy, and he was in bed working on his book. Tess was desperate to explore Chuck's place, and in her excitement, she didn't want to calm down. Despite his frailty and the fact that he was bed bound, he asked me to pass him the end of her lead. He worked her lead between his fingers, and said, "Watch this!" As we continued to talk, he paid her no attention but massaged the leather between his fingers, and as he did so, she inexplicably lay down and went straight to sleep. I was amazed and asked him how on earth he had done it. He smiled that Chuck Kemsley smile, and said, "It's just a knack..." Chuck had a most amazing ability to be able to understand and communicate with animals in a way that had I not seen it myself, I would not have believed. There are good men and there are great men, and Chuck was definitely the greatest man I have ever met."

After the funeral, he wrote:

"Today we said a sad farewell to a man who has been a great inspiration to me, who taught me all I know about dogs and encouraged me to write. He was a man who lived more adventures than any Hollywood bullshit actor. How many people can include gun running for the Cuban Rebels on their CVs? Not many, I'm sure. I hope that Heaven is ready for Chuck's arrival, 'cos they've got their work cut out keeping him out of mischief ;-)"

~~~

I said at the very beginning that we were faced with a dilemma. We had inadvertently uncovered a secret that my mother had kept close to her heart throughout her life. Would Mum have wanted us to investigate further? Would she have wanted us to reveal her secret to others? It was difficult to know how to proceed.

Taking everything into consideration, I think we did the right thing – and I believe Mum would have been pleased with the outcome.

Instead of the harsh condemnation and judgement she endured back then, most people today would sympathise with her predicament and admire her for the difficult choices she had to make.

Being an animal lover herself, she would have been so proud of Chuck's remarkable achievement in becoming one of the world's greatest animal trainers, and especially the fact that his unique methods were responsible for saving the lives of so many pet dogs.

As for us, Marilyn, Christine and me, we went on an incredible journey, leading to the discovery of a charming and delightful new brother - with the added bonus of his very own exciting adventure story thrown in for good measure!

It is a story that needed to be told in order to appreciate the changing attitudes and values in our modern world. I trust you found it as interesting and informative as we did when investigating those traumatic events that unfolded all those years ago. I hope, if you ever find yourself in a similar situation to us, that our experience may inspire you to overcome all the difficulties and setbacks and eventually find your missing relatives. It isn't easy but it's certainly very worthwhile.

Thanks for buying my book; I hope you enjoyed reading it as much as I enjoyed writing it! If you have a moment I would be really grateful if you could leave a review on www.amazon.co.uk or www.amazon.com

*Please feel free to contact me on: findingchuckbook@gmail.com

In memory of Chuck Kemsley
1932 - 2015

ABOUT THE AUTHOR

Sylvia Court is an award winning photographer who grew up in Kent. She attended Orpington Grammar School for Girls and then trained as a draughtswoman for British Railways, working at London's Waterloo station - way back in the golden age of steam. She married in 1965 and lived in the Cotswolds for a while, before moving to Tythecott, her dream cottage in rural North Devon where she bred Siamese cats, kept chickens and created highly acclaimed original hand-made ceramic sculptures. She is now retired and living near her two daughters and grandsons in Somerset. She has previously published 'Return to Tythecott,' which is a fictional story of the adventures of Rufus, a rescued Siamese cat. She has also written an autobiography and a biography of her late husband, David.

Printed in Great Britain
by Amazon